A
Damned
Iowa
Greyhound

A

The Civil War Letters of

Damned

William Henry Harrison Clayton

Iowa

Edited by Donald C. Elder III

Greyhound

University of Iowa Press ψ *Iowa City*

University of Iowa Press, Iowa City 52242

Copyright © 1998 by the University of Iowa Press

All rights reserved

Printed in the United States of America

Design by Richard Hendel

http://www.uiowa.edu/~uipress

Printed on acid-free paper

Library of Congress Cataloging-in-Publication Data

Clayton, William Henry Harrison.

    A damned Iowa greyhound: the Civil War letters of William
Henry Harrison Clayton / edited by Donald C. Elder III.

       p.   cm.

    Includes bibliographical references and index.

    ISBN 978-1-58729-608-6

    1. Clayton, William Henry Harrison—Correspondence.
2. United States. Army. Iowa Infantry Regiment, 19th (1862–
1865). 3. Iowa—History—Civil War, 1861–1865—Personal
narratives. 4. West (U.S.)—History—Civil War, 1861–1865—
Campaigns. 5. United States—History—Civil War, 1861–
1865—Personal narratives. 6. United States—History—Civil
War, 1861–1865—Campaigns. 7. Soldiers—Iowa—Van Buren
County—Correspondence. 8. Van Buren County (Iowa)—
Biography. I. Elder, Donald C., 1952– . II. Title.

E507.5 19th.C57 1998

973.7'477—dc21   97-32721

CONTENTS

INTRODUCTION

During the course of the American Civil War, 76,242 males from the state of Iowa gave military service to the United States government. Extraordinary circumstances made a few of them, like General Grenville M. Dodge, well known to the northern public; the vast majority, however, remained virtually anonymous during the conflict. Indeed, these individuals might have all faded into total obscurity had it not been for relatives who preserved the Civil War correspondence of a number of Iowa soldiers down through the succeeding years. These letters and diaries allow us to bring the experiences of these men, long since deceased, back to life.

This process of historical preservation has allowed me to reconstruct the story of one such Iowan. William Henry Harrison Clayton, who served in the 19th Regiment of Iowa Infantry Volunteers, faithfully corresponded with his family back in Van Buren County, Iowa, during the war; he also kept a diary during his years of service. His family passed the letters and diary down through two generations, and in 1989 his granddaughter, Dorothy Newman, donated these items to the Lincoln Shrine in Redlands, California. In 1995 I became aware of these resources, and began the task of putting his story into publishable form.

It quickly became apparent that Clayton's letters afford a unique opportunity to view the Civil War from many different perspectives. On the one hand, Clayton's experiences give proof to the old adage that a soldier's life consists of ninety-eight percent boredom and two percent sheer terror. He fought in two battles, saw action in two major siege operations, and participated in a number of skirmishes, all of

William Henry Harrison Clayton, 1864.
Courtesy of the Lincoln Memorial Shrine Collection.

which he described in his correspondence with his family. But the majority of his letters focus on the routine of army life. Fortunately, Clayton proved to be a remarkably keen observer, and his depictions of the commonplace events he experienced are quite vivid. Clayton's writings, therefore, provide an exceptionally full account of how the Civil War affected the average soldier.

Clayton's story, however, differs from that of the average soldier in the Union Army in a number of ways. First, he spent more than nine months as a prisoner of war, a condition shared by less than ten percent of all Union soldiers. While between fifteen and eighteen percent of all Union captives died in southern prison camps, he survived his incarceration. When freed, Clayton and the other members of his regiment posed for a photograph that is one of the most memorable visual images of prisoner-of-war experience to come out of the Civil War. He also wrote home about his time in captivity in Texas, and his letters about those months vividly portray the filth and misery experienced by a Civil War prisoner.

Clayton's service also showed him a great deal more of the South than the average Union soldier witnessed during the conflict. He saw duty in six Confederate states and fought in Missouri, one of the four loyal slave states in which Union and Confederate forces would do battle throughout the war. He traveled through developed areas of the South as well as the hinterland and put detailed and colorful descriptions of both in his letters. While his letters regarding the siege of Vicksburg discuss events usually covered in standard accounts of the Civil War, most of the campaigns he participated in took place in regions that do not figure prominently in such works. Clayton can therefore give readers unfamiliar glimpses of the Civil War.

Clayton's regiment sometimes found itself deployed in one location for weeks on end. On occasion, however, Clayton and his comrades had to cover great distances in a short time. Indeed, in one instance his regiment made a forced march that is truly the equal of anything that Stonewall Jackson's famed "Foot Cavalry" accomplished during the early years of the conflict. This anabasis, and other expeditions only slightly less remarkable in scope, make the story that Clayton relates distinctive in the body of personal accounts coming out of the Civil War.

Finally, Clayton can help inform the modern reader about the tenuous nature of race relations in the United States, and especially in Iowa, during the Civil War. He consistently refers to blacks by using the N-word that is so offensive to most Americans today, and while able occasionally to give black soldiers a grudging compliment, he remains to the end quite firm in his racist views. His letters serve as a reminder that many loyal Unionists, even those serving in the federal army, cared little about the status blacks would have in the restored nation. They also force the realization that Iowa, which would create an impressive record of civil rights legislation in the postwar era, counted many individuals among its population who regarded blacks as their inferiors. Clearly, Clayton compels the reader to recognize that while the Civil War struck the death knell of slavery, not every northerner reacted to the process in the same way.

For these reasons, I feel that the story of William Henry Harrison Clayton can cast new and important light on our understanding of the Civil War. To better illustrate the depth and complexity of his account, I have divided his letters into eight sections, each of which focuses on a separate and distinct aspect of his military experience. Clayton had a very good command of the English language, only rarely making mistakes in his letters; I have therefore chosen to leave his original spelling intact without using the notation of *sic*, and have added words in brackets only occasionally to clarify certain passages. Clayton seems to have based his letters in large part on the brief notations he made in his diary, so I have used it merely to corroborate the events he discusses in his letters. Wherever possible, I have provided notes to identify items in his letters that the reader would otherwise not understand; if my research did not yield a positive identification of a name or term, I made no notation of it at all. All communities referred to in the notes were located in Iowa, unless otherwise noted. With only these minor changes, this is Clayton's account as he wrote it.

In preparing this book, I have enlisted the services of a virtual regiment of individuals who were kind enough to aid me. Chuck Torre, Jack Friend, Peggy Krohn, Joyce Jensen, Al Holzmeier, Janie Chilcutt, Virgil Dean, Patricia LaPointe, James Rubis, Bobby Roberts, Mary Ann Moore, Roger Davis, Ted Snediker, Larry Rettinger, Debra Gillen, Andy Bennett, Rick Sturdevant, and Jerry Green all supplied valuable bits of information. I am deeply appreciative of their efforts on my behalf.

Certain people proved extraordinarily helpful. Dorothy Newman gave generously of her time, answering questions about her grandfather's life. Becky Hepinstall, an exceptionally gifted and talented former student of mine, critiqued my manuscript and tracked down very obscure references to people and events in her home state of Texas. Norman "Nicky" Nicholson took time out from his own research to provide me with a vast amount of historical information about Mobile, Alabama. Robert Dykstra read portions of the first draft of my manuscript, correcting a number of erroneous assertions I had made. Ronda Curtis, the person most knowledgeable about the history of Troy, Iowa (the community closest to the Clayton family farm), answered many questions. Through a chance remark she happened to make, I was able to establish that her great-grandfather was Clayton's best friend in the 19th Iowa. Mrs. Curtis also made me aware of Christine Clayton Turner, the granddaughter of Clayton's brother George, who lives on a farm once owned by Clayton's uncle. In an interview lasting a number of hours, Ms. Turner graciously shared her knowledge about the Clayton family with me. Phil Brigandi gave me a detailed account of Clayton's life after the Civil War. Ralph Arnold provided a wealth of information about Van Buren County, Iowa, as did Quentin Johnson about neighboring Davis County. Mr. and Mrs. S. Burr Brown acquainted me with the history of the 1864 guerrilla raid into Iowa. Vicki Betts proved very helpful in making me aware of sources on the prison camp in which Clayton was incarcerated. Finally, Steve Cottrell, an excellent author in his own right, shared the fruits of his research on the Civil War campaigns in and around the Ozarks with me. They all deserve special commendations for their efforts.

Historians learn quickly to use the services of research institutions, and I am no exception. I would like to thank Randy Hackenburg at the Military History Institute, the staff at the Wisconsin State Historical Society, Gordon Hendrickson and Ellen Salser at the Iowa State Historical Society in Des Moines, Don Montgomery and the staff at the Prairie Grove Battlefield State Park Museum, the staff at the Golden Library at Eastern New Mexico University, Elizabeth Hill at the National Archives, the staff at the Lee County (Iowa) Historical Society, Barbara Dawson at the Cincinnati Historical Society Library, and Emma Thomasson at the Missouri State Historical Society. Sue DeVille at the Opelousas (Louisiana) Museum and Interpretive Center not only combed the archives of her facility searching for information for me but also went out into the field to take photographs and conduct interviews as well. These individuals all did great credit to their institutions through the efficient manner in which they provided aid to me.

To lend as much authenticity to the manuscript as possible, I purchased from the K. B. Slocum Company of Austin, Texas, copies of Union Army maps made during the Civil War. The staff at K. B. Slocum proved very helpful in recommending the most appropriate maps to include. To simplify matters, when preparing the maps for publication, I removed locations that Clayton does not refer to in his letters; otherwise, these maps show the areas of battle as Union Army topographers drew them.

Special recognition must go to the staff at the Lincoln Shrine in Redlands. The curator, Don McCue, and his staff Christie Hammond, Joanne McCrary, and Kellie A. Long, all gave generously of their time in helping me prepare this book. Larry Burgess, the director of the A. K. Smiley Library, the Shrine's parent organization, demonstrated his notable abilities as a historian by offering me a number of timely suggestions. Words cannot possibly convey the sense of gratitude, respect, and admiration I hold for these dedicated individuals.

I also would like to recognize the contribution of Eastern New Mexico University to my work. A generous New Faculty Grant allowed me to travel to the Lincoln Shrine and various sites in Iowa to conduct my research, and the university administration helped fund the completion of my manuscript. In addition, my colleagues Linda Moore, Dorothy Parker, Gerry Geis, Suzanne Balch, Richard Willen, Paul Lockman, Fida Mohammad, and Rosemary Bahr all provided sound advice and support.

The University of Iowa Press deserves a great deal of the credit for this work. Holly Carver encouraged me to pursue this project from the beginning, and the staff at the press helped me present the story in a visually impressive format. The editorial staff helped shape the text with a deft hand. Any errors that remain are, of course, my own responsibility.

Finally, I must acknowledge the people who have meant the most to my work — my family. My father, Donald C. Elder, Jr., during his life encouraged my interest in the Civil War through many family trips to historic sites. My mother, Shelly Elder, helped finance my research and located in the family library an important, but quite obscure, book on Iowa during the Civil War. My in-laws, Ward and Doris Salisbury, gave me moral and logistical support while I did research for this book in the state of Iowa. The academic and athletic accomplishments of my sons, Cam and Brian, have kept me in good humor while working on this book. Cam also took a number of the photographs that grace this book, and helped prepare the maps. My greatest debt is to my wife, Janine. From a unit that she had prepared while teaching fifth grade at Lincoln Elementary in Vinton, Iowa, she provided me with a vast amount of information on Annie Wittenmyer; in addition, she has provided me with the inspiration to see this project through to the end.

A
Damned
Iowa
Greyhound

CHAPTER 1

" *We Were Mustered into the Service Yesterday* **"**

The year 1862, which started with such great promise for the Union cause in the Civil War, had taken a disastrous turn by the end of June. Major General George B. McClellan had abandoned his advance on Richmond, Virginia, up the James Peninsula, retreating to Malvern Hill instead. In his campaign, McClellan had suffered thousands of casualties and bombarded the War Department with demands for reinforcements. But the need to deploy a substantial force in the Shenandoah Valley of Virginia to counteract Confederate activity in that area had placed a significant limitation on the ability of the federal government to respond to his request. The fact that Union victories in the West earlier in the year had not come without a high cost in manpower further complicated the possibility of providing adequate troop levels in the East. These developments convinced President Abraham Lincoln that the Union army would require many additional soldiers to militarily subdue the Confederate States of America. To avoid the look of despair over the recent setbacks in the East, however, he requested that the governors of the loyal states "ask" him to call for further enrollments to exploit the successes that the Union cause had achieved. After receiving these petitions, on July 2 Lincoln issued a call for 300,000 men, volunteering for three-year enlistments, to enter into federal service.

Initially, response to Lincoln's call proved less than enthusiastic, because of the reverses suffered by the Union cause in the East. Even the prospect of a $100 enlistment bonus authorized by Congress failed to bring forth the desired number of volunteers. The disappointing

The site of the farm owned by Sammy Clayton in Van Buren County, Iowa, as it appears today. Photo by the author.

results forced the government in August 1862 to resort to a form of coercion. The Lincoln administration announced on August 4 that it would also require states to provide 300,000 militia for nine months' service and assigned each state a quota. If a state failed to meet its requirement, the federal government asserted that it would use conscription in that state to achieve the specified goal. States could avoid this odious possibility, however, by providing three-year volunteers, each of which would reduce its nine-month militia quota by four. In this manner, Lincoln hoped both to avoid using a draft and to obtain the desired number of three-year enlistments.

States responded quickly to the government's challenge. Offering financial inducements and appealing to patriotism, they all succeeded in meeting their quotas. In Iowa, for example, the federal government mandated a total of 21,140 enlistments; the state actually enrolled 24,438 three-year volunteers in 1862.

One such individual who answered the call in the summer of 1862 was twenty-two-year-old William Henry Harrison Clayton. He had been born in Pittsburgh, Pennsylvania, in 1840 and was named after the person who would win the presidential election later that year. His family moved to Cincinnati, Ohio, when he was two years old. In 1855, after thirteen years in that bustling community, Clayton's father, Amos Clayton, decided to move his family to Iowa, which had be-

Amos Clayton, n.d.
Courtesy of the Lincoln Memorial Shrine Collection.

come a state in 1846. As many Americans did, Amos, a native of
Ohio, relocated to an area where he already knew people — in this
case his sixty-nine-year-old brother, Sammy Clayton. Sammy had
bought land in Van Buren County, located in the southeastern section
of the Iowa Territory, in 1838; Amos purchased an acreage in the western portion of that county, only a few miles from his brother's farm.

Van Buren County had achieved a sizable population by the time
of the Civil War. Most of its population of 17,081 lived on farms. The
county did include two towns with more than 2,000 inhabitants:

Farmington and Keosauqua, the county seat. Other communities near the Clayton farm included Lebanon and Pittsburg.

In spite of their location, the Claytons actually did a great deal of business in Davis County, which bordered Van Buren County to the west. The land that comprised Davis County had once been part of Van Buren County, becoming a separate entity in 1844. Davis County had a population of 13,764 in 1861, and while farm residents predominated there as well, it did possess a number of towns. The closest burg to the Claytons was actually in Davis County: the community of Troy.

This town had come into existence on February 15, 1848, when Davis County officials platted land owned principally by Josiah I. Earhart. Earhart named the town after the Ohio community in which he had previously resided. Reporting a population of 101 in 1851, Troy had doubled in size by the Civil War years. It boasted four stores, a hotel, and the Troy Academy — the second-oldest institute of higher learning in Iowa. The town also supported a Methodist church and the Presbyterian church that the Claytons attended.

By the summer of 1862, Clayton's home area of Iowa had already felt the effects of the Civil War. Many males from the southeastern corner of the state had joined one of Iowa's eighteen volunteer regiments to augment the few regular U.S. Army units in the months after the firing on Fort Sumter. They participated in the northern victories at Ft. Donelson, Pea Ridge, and Shiloh. Clayton chose instead to remain in Iowa to help his father and mother run the farm. But when the state of Iowa issued its call for new recruits in August 1862, Clayton felt that his fourteen-year-old twin brothers, George Washington Clayton and John Quincy Adams Clayton, could help his parents sufficiently with the farm work to allow him to leave.

With a number of his friends, Clayton decided to go to the neighboring community of Keosauqua to enlist in a new regiment that the state of Iowa was forming in its first congressional district. Due to the rapidity with which individuals joined this unit, it received a numerical designation before any of the twenty-one other Iowa regiments that would enter federal service after Lincoln's call in 1862. Officially enrolled on August 14 into the 19th Iowa Regiment of Volunteer Infantry by Theodore Richmond (soon to be a captain in Clayton's unit), Clayton and his compatriots would journey to the Mississippi River town of Keokuk, Iowa, in Lee County, to receive training. Soon

"We Were Mustered into the Service Yesterday"

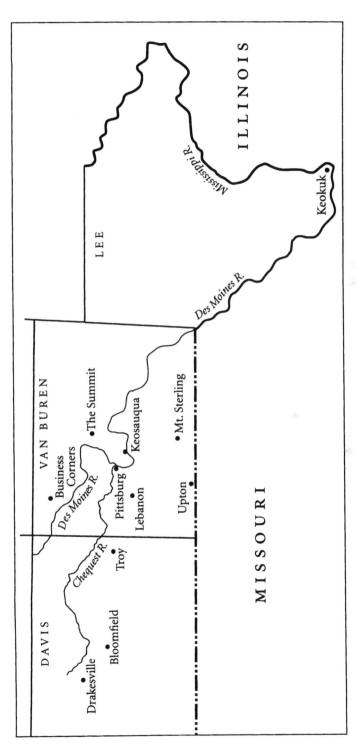

Davis, Van Buren, and Lee Counties of Iowa in 1862.

transferred to the Benton Barracks in St. Louis, Missouri, they would then await orders that would take them into active duty.

The first four letters Clayton wrote home describe this initial phase of his military experience. In them Clayton details the process by which a group of 982 civilians from six different Iowa counties coalesced into a disciplined army unit.

~

Camp Lincoln[1]
Keokuk
Aug. 22nd, 1862
Dear Father & Mother,[2]
According to promise I write you these few lines.

We left the Summit[3] as you are probably aware on Tuesday afternoon. I and three other boys staid at Judge Wrights[4] over night & got breakfast in the morning.

The boys were all very merry on the way down cheering & being cheered by everybody. We got to Keokuk about sundown and were marched to the Simpson House[5] where we remained until yesterday evening when we came here.

The camp is situated on a rolling piece of ground overlooking part of the city a considerable distance from the river. I think it is a very healthy situation. There is said to be 12 or 13 companies[6] here. The Drakeville[7] company arrived last evening & is quartered at the "Simpson" where they have the pleasure of sleeping on the floor on as soft a board as they can find.

There is 9 board shanties erected & the workmen are building more. There is also 25 or 30 tents pitched.

The buildings will accomodate 100 men each & look tolerably comfortable.

We were all examined by surgeons on Wednesday. Each one was required to undress & was examined separately. Some able-bodied looking men were rejected. 15 or 16 were turned off from our company leaving about the maximum number of 101 men. It is the largest & best looking company here.

We were mustered[8] into the service yesterday. We have not drilled any yet nor in fact done anything. Our quarters are not quite finished yet & it is not likely that we will get to going rightly until next week.

"We Were Mustered into the Service Yesterday"

Grace Clayton, n.d.
Courtesy of the Lincoln Memorial Shrine Collection.

Two of our companies have got their uniforms, we will probably get ours tomorrow. Our blankets were issued to us last evening. I like it so far very well. The fare at the Simpson house was rather indifferent especially toward the last. There was plenty of good bread & that was about all that was good. The boys left there with *groans* for "Simpson." We have issued to us here bread, potatos, salt pork, rice, sugar & coffee.

The examiner did not like the looks of AB Buckles[9] eyes. He asked him if he could see & he told him he could. He did not ask whether he could see well out of both eyes so he passed.

Since I commenced writing our quarters have been finished and we have taken possession. I think we will get along finely in our bunker.

Our company has not yet received our letter [10] in the regiment. We have formed a mess.[11] It is 8 of us boys who are acquainted: A. J. Buckles, Mooney,[12] Nincehelser,[13] George & Joseph Paxton,[14] John Stone,[15] Utt [16] the blacksmith who worked in Troy awhile, son in law of Leache's [17] & myself. All are well.

I believe that I have written all that I can think of at present.

I remain ever your affectionate son

Wm. H. H. Clayton

⤳

Camp Lincoln
Keokuk
August 31st, 1862
Dear Father & Mother:

I intended to have written to you on Friday, but it came my turn to stand guard on Friday morning. I went on at 10 o'clock & stood until 12. I thought that I would write in the afternoon but the captain [18] wanted me to write for him. I did so until 4 o'clock when I stood guard until 6, so that I could get no letter written in time to reach home Saturday. I have written part of 3 days this week for the Capt. making out rolls. One of the rolls gives the name, age, nativity, occupation, color of eyes, hair & complexion, heighth, etc.[19]

The company received their full pay & bounty [20] from the government, 40 dollars on Sunday last. I sent $35 with Abner Buckles last Monday. I thought that would be the easiest way to get it sent. I sent my clothes by Mooney on Friday. I sent all home except 1 pair of socks & my boots. I have drawn a dress coat, overcoat, pants, 2 pair drawers, 2 pair socks & 2 shirts. We have our knapsacks haversacks & canteens, cartridge boxes guns & nearly everything necessary for *going to war*. Our guns are the Enfield rifled musket [21] with raised sights, said to shoot 900 yds. It is said that they are part of the arms captured on vessels trying to run the blockade.[22] The company has been drilling this week. We had dress parade for the first time on Thursday last. Col. Crabb [23] was present. Quarters have been erected here for another regiment,[24] several companies are in occupation. One is the Bloomfield[25] company, another the Business Corner Co.[26] They have come down here & joined in with part of a co. that was in camp when we first came here.

A good many of the boys have been unable to do duty for several days. One, J. Strang[27] with some kind of fever. I have been well so far with the exception of a cold.

If I had not been on guard Friday, I think I could have got home Saturday but now I make no more calculations. I may get off but the chances are slim. The colonel is absent, gone to Davenport. He is to be back on Wednesday & some think that we will leave soon. But no one can tell anything about it.

I believe I have written all that is of importance at present so I will close.

I remain your affectionate son

Wm. H. H. Clayton

P.S. I would like for you to write or get the boys to write. They can write well enough for me to read. Direct letters to me, Co. H. 19th Regt. Iowa Vol. Keokuk Iowa.

⤳

Camp Lincoln
Keokuk Iowa
September 3rd, 1862
Dear Father & Mother:

Having a few spare moments I take advantage of them to write a few lines to you.

On dress parade last evening we received orders to march on Thursday (tomorrow). I had intended to try to get home if we had stayed until next week. It has been a very difficult matter to get home; ever since we came here married men have the preference all the time.

It is said that we go to St. Louis & probably from there to St. Joseph Missouri.

The boys from our neighborhood are all right at present. Abs. Ninchelser & John Stone were quite unwell for several days but have got about well.

I have been engaged in writing for the captain again yesterday & part of this morning. Our orderly[28] Saml. Bonney[29] is a very good writer but he cannot do it all himself. And the captain always calls upon me when he wants help. I have written more since I have been here than for a long time previous.[30]

I wanted to go to town this morning to get my likeness taken but I do not know whether I can get it taken today or not. I will get a pass and try.

The 30th regiment is nearly full lacking only one company. 3 companies came in yesterday.

Our *mess* had a couple of Troy boys to bunk with us last night: Harvey Garrett & Tanneyhill.[31] They go to Davenport to join an old regiment.[32]

Nearly everyone wishes to go east either to Virginia or Kentucky.[33] We may possibly go that way after awhile but I suppose not at present.

Give my best wishes & respect to all who enquire after me. I expect some of my friends will think that I am negligent about writing but I have not had much time and I hope they will not think hard of it.

If letters are directed here they will follow the regt. I would like very much to receive a letter from some of my friends, every evening about 8 or 9 o'clock the mail is distributed through camp and lucky is the person that gets a letter, so the rest think who get none.

Nothing more at the present but I remain ever affectionately yours,

Wm. H. H. Clayton

P.S. On dress parade companies are arranged the same as they would be when in line of battle. Company C is in the center and carries the colors. Co. H is next on the left, and as artillery is generally directed towards the colors our position will be a very important one.

~

Benton Barracks[34]
St. Louis
Sept. 7/62
Dear Father & Mother:

We left Keokuk last Thursday morning about 10 o'clock on the steamer *J. L. McGill* and arrived at St. Louis about the same time on Friday morning.

The regiment marched out soon after landing, to this place, about four miles. I was detailed to stay on the boat and see that the baggage was sent out. I rode out on one of the wagons.

"We Were Mustered into the Service Yesterday"

The boat on which we came was the same one which conveyed the Second Iowa[35] to Ft. Donelson.[36] It is a large side wheel[37] boat but it was tolerably well crowded. Our company and several others were quartered on the lower deck. At night everyone tried to get a good place to sleep. John Stone & I got upon a large coil of cable rope on the left side of the boat a little forward of the boilers. We slept very comfortably.

At nearly every town & house we passed we were greeted with the waving of hats & handkerchiefs, which compliment was returned by the boys with a will.

There was but little feeling manifested at Alexandria & Hannibal. The river is very low & our boat would sometimes drag itself over the sandbars for some distance.

These famous barracks are a great institution. The space enclosed must be nearly a mile square. The quarters are in long lines, each company is to itself. In the rear is the cooking & eating houses with tables & a furnace to cook upon. There are hydrants which furnish river water for washing & cooking. The drinking water is got out of wells. It is a very difficult matter to get out of this place. A soldier has to have a pass from his capt. signed by the col. & countersigned by the commander of the post.

The company is now divided into messes of 14 each. We get better food & more of it than when the whole company messed together. There are grocery stores & a meat store, 3 or 4 daguerrotype or ambrotype[38] establishments, a bookstore & nearly everything we could wish besides insides the enclosure.

I got my likeness taken yesterday and sent to you. It cost $1.25. I also got a 50 cent one which I sent to Aunt Jane.[39]

They take a better & cheaper picture here than in Keokuk. I do not know how long we stay here. Some think that we will leave soon, probably for Springfield Mo. There is a large number of paroled prisoners here.[40] A good many were taken at Pittsburg Landing.[41]

The boys from our neighborhood are all well & in good spirits. Write soon & let me know whether you receive the likeness or not. My respects to all friends.

I remain yours ever

Wm. H. H. Clayton

CHAPTER 2

‟ We Are in the 'Army of the Frontier' **”**

Both sides had hoped to control Missouri at the start of the Civil War. The Union saw Missouri as an avenue of invasion into the Trans-Mississippi Confederacy, while Confederate domination of the state would provide them a welcome buffer against such an assault. The Confederates had scored a significant early victory at the Battle of Wilson's Creek in August 1861, but Union forces had succeeded by the summer of 1862 in driving the main Confederate army in Missouri out of the state. The contest in Missouri then became primarily a struggle by Union detachments to curtail the activities of irregular units fighting for the Confederate cause.

Clayton and his regiment participated in this campaign in the southern part of the state from September through November 1862. The nine letters he wrote home during this period reflect the problems of a military force operating in an area of mixed loyalties. Clayton also provides a description of two battlefields upon which the opposing sides had fought major engagements. But demonstrating that he is fast becoming a veteran soldier, he spends a large amount of his time writing about what has truly been important to combatants throughout the ages — the quantity, quality, and types of food he is able to procure.

~

Camp Sigel [1]
about 5 miles from Rolla Mo.
Sept. 14th, 1862
Dear Father & Mother:

You will perceive that we have changed our position somewhat since I last wrote you. We left "Benton Barracks" last Thursday morning, early. It began to rain about the time we were formed in line, and rained on us nearly all the way to the depot about 3 miles. We were to have started at 8 o'clock but we did not get off until about 10. We were in baggage & freight cars. One or two companies rode in open cars & as it rained considerably while on the way their ride was not very pleasant. We got to Rolla 110 or 120 miles from St. Louis, about 11 o'clock at night. It was right cold after the rain, enough so to make a blanket feel comfortable.

We remained at Rolla until Saturday morning. Friday the teamsters got their teams harnessed up and broke them. Each company has a six mule team & there are 5 commissary [2] teams making 15 teams to the regiment. I went to the fortification near Rolla last Friday. It was about ¾ of a mile from our camp. It has four 32 pounders [3] mounted and commands the country around for a long distance. There are about 55 "secesh" [secessionist] prisoners there. They are kept at work some on the fort and others digging up stumps & clearing away rubbish around the camp at Rolla. Several have balls fastened to their ankles. We marched to this place yesterday morning. We have plenty of good spring water to drink. The camp is on what was once a cornfield, a piece of ground several hundred yards in width with high hills on the east and west sides. A nice *run* of water passes through the camp. The 94th Illinois is encamped above us on the run, and the 20th Wisconsin below. We are waiting the arrival of another regiment or two when we will be formed into a brigade. [4]

The country between here and St. Louis is hardly worth fighting for. All along the [Atlantic &] Pacific Railroad the soil is very poor. What dirt there is, is a red color. There is a great deal of gravel, and in fact there is *no place* in this region but what is covered with stone. The hills are a solid mass of a kind of red sandstone. There are very few farms in this part of Missouri. Wherever there is one there is plenty of peaches. We saw peach orchards as we were coming out on the

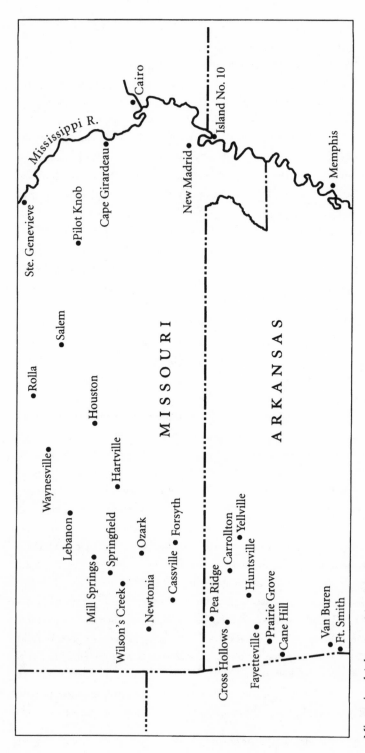

Missouri and Arkansas, 1862–1863.

railroad in which nearly all the trees were bending down with fruit. I have not seen any prairie in this state yet.

The picture at the head of this letter is a very good representation of the parade ground at Benton Barracks. It does not show the part in which we were quartered. The west end has accomodations for 3000 men.

I write this on the hillside, looking down on the camp with the paper before me on my knees, not a very good position to write easy. There will be a great many letters sent off tomorrow. The other evening a large lot of letters came for this company. I thought certainly that I would get one but I was disappointed. After we leave here there will not be much regularity in receiving mail.

The boys from our section are all well. John & George, I want you to write me, I don't care if there is not much more than a dozen lines, it will please me to receive it. I do not know how long we stay here. I think we are to go to Springfield next. It is over 100 miles from here and we will have to foot it. I believe I have written all of importance.

Give my respects to Uncle Nide & Aunt Rachel.[5] Hoping this will find you all as it leaves me, enjoying good health.

I remain affectionately your son

Wm. H. H. Clayton

P.S. I have written the directions on an envelope so that the boys can write a few lines and enclose them in it.

~

Mills Springs Mo.

Sept. 23rd, 1862

Dear Brothers:

With pleasure, I seat myself on a log, my paper on my knees before me, to write an answer to your letter. I would have written sooner but I had not time. We were in camp 5 miles from Rolla when your letter reached me. We had received orders to march about 8 o'clock in the evening, and I was helping the boys cook provisions for the next day, when the letter was brought to me. The letter was mailed on the 10th & reached me the 15th. I was very glad to get a letter from you & to hear that you were all well.

I got a letter a few days ago from Mary A. Lighthill,[6] dated Sept. 11. We reached this place yesterday and have stopped to rest for a few days, after having marched every day for the last 7 days. It rained the day before we started, so that the roads were not dusty for a day or two, but there is a great deal of travel on this road mostly U.S. teams[7] & for the last 3 or 4 days the roads have been very dusty. We were a hard looking set when we got here last evening. There is plenty of water here for all purposes. When I last wrote home we were about 5 miles from Rolla. We left the camp on the 15th under rather discouraging circumstances. The regt. was formed in line & all ready to go, when the Col. stepped out and informed us that he could not go with us. There had been something wrong about the appointing, he having been in the service before.[8] Every one seems to like him and all were [sad] to leave him behind.[9] But yesterday evening after we had pitched our tents the colonel came into camp. The boys made the old woods ring with cheers for the Col.[10] Our regiment was commanded by Major Kent[11] during the march. The Lieut. Col.[12] has not yet joined the regt. We started on the march Sept. 16th and marched about 8 miles, camped on the banks of the Little Piney. The next day started about 12 o'clock & marched 8 or 9 miles to Big Piney. Sept. 18 marched at 6 and got about 12 miles. Encamped near Waynesville, Pulaski Co. Sept. 19th marched 16 miles and camped on the banks of the Gasconade River. Sept. 20th marched about 14 miles, camped about 2 miles west of Lebanon. Company G of the 3rd Iowa Cavalry is at Lebanon. It is the Keosauqua Company. Mayne[13] was captain before the fight at Kirksville.[14] Nearly all of the boys found friends or acquaintances in the company. An accident happened after we reached camp. Several of the cavalry boys went out to camp with us. One of the boys[15] was looking at a revolver belonging to Erasmus Kent,[16] son of old John Kent. It was handled carelessly & went off, the ball going into Kent's arm & into his body coming out very near his back bone. It is only a flesh wound, no bones being broken, but if the ball had went one inch further in towards his chest it would have killed him. Albert Alexander[17] belongs to the company but is at Springfield. He and Dick Bishop of Troy got into a difficulty with some Illinois boys at the camp near Springfield. The way the story is told, there was some 6 or 8 persons belonging to an Illinois regiment who considered themselves "*bullies*." Bishop & Albert had had some words with them but left for camp. They were headed by these men and attacked. They got Bishop's pistol from him and shot at him & hit him on the end of one of his fingers, another ball went through his boot, they also shot at Albert but missed him. Albert pulled out his revolver and shot two of them killing one instantly and the other died next morning. He is now under arrest but all think that he will get off.

On Sunday Sept. 21st we marched about 20 miles, and yesterday 13 or 14. They call it about 12 miles from here to Springfield.

We have not passed through any prairies since we started. The soil is poor, very rocky and hard to cultivate. I would not live in this part of Mo. For any consideration there is plenty of fruit along the road both apples & peaches. We have our share of it, for *Uncle Sam* has been rather close in dealing out our rations, some days on this march we only had 3 crackers and a small piece of meat for a whole day. The boys grumble a good deal & confiscate a hog or calf once in awhile & chickens by the wholesale to make up the deficiency. I believe I will stop writing at the present. Direct your letters to Benton Barracks Mo. & they will follow the regt. There are 4 regts. here the 19th and 20th Iowa, 20th Wisconsin & 94th Illinois, commanding [is] Genl. Herron.[18] Write often I am glad to get letters. The boys are all well.

I stopped writing to get some dinner. I thought that I would add a little more. When the brigade is moving from place to place each regiment takes its turn to lead the advance. The other day the 94th Ill. led. They stopped to rest so often that it got those in the rear all out of patience. The next day the 20th Iowa led. They kept things tolerably lively till they got to a spring. When they stopped an hour or more & placed a guard around the spring to keep those other regiments from getting water which of course created ill feeling. Yesterday the 19th led, Companies C & H were the advanced guard. We put things through a little too fast for some and were encamped some time before the others came up. The men when on the march go 4 abreast & carry their arms at will. We carried our guns, cartridge boxes with 30 rounds,[19] canteen with water & haversack for provision. Our knapsacks were hauled. The company hired a team and each man paid 25 cts for hauling from the camp near Rolla to Springfield. A great many would have given out if we had not got them hauled. I suppose we go from here to Springfield, how soon I do not know. Postage

Major General Francis J. Herron, 1864.
Courtesy of the Central Arkansas Library System,
original owned by Greg McMahon.

stamps are worth 4 cts each here, & sutler's[20] goods have about doubled in price since leaving St. Louis.

Nothing more at present but I remain your affectionate brother

Wm. H. H. Clayton

P.S. Write soon. My pen is bad therefore excuse bad writing.

⁓

Camp near Springfield
October 6, 1862
Dear Uncle & Aunt,[21]

I seat myself for the purpose of writing a few lines to you. I had intended to write to you sooner but I knew that you would hear from me when ever I wrote home. The last letter from home was dated the 19th of last month. I wrote last from Mill Spring about 12 miles from Springfield. The next day after writing, we packed up and came to this place about 1½ miles northwest of Springfield. The location is a very good one, with one exception, that is the water is too far off. It is nearly ¾ of a mile to the spring, we carried water for awhile, but it is now hauled. It is the greatest spring I ever seen. It furnishes water for half a dozen regiments with all of the mules and horses. This place is being strongly fortified. Fort No. 1 is near our camp. There is about 850 men at work on it. About 150 of the men are "secesh," that is, men who refused to enroll themselves in the *state militia*.[22] Some of them are dressed in the everlasting butternut clothing.[23] Tell our folks that I am done wearing butternut pants, I and all of the boys are disgusted with it. The fort encloses about ten acres of ground and 5 or 6 regts can be quartered within. For the past week the whole regt. does not go at once, 17 men were detailed from our company. They work ten days and get 25 cts. per day extra. I have not been detailed yet. I would have been but the Capt. had me to do some writing for him so that I got off.

There has been a little fighting going on s. west of here. At the last account our forces held their ground and as large reinforments have been sent from here I think the rebels will be compelled to "skedaddle."[24]

The 18th & 20th Iowa regts. left last week for the *seat of war*.[25] The last named regiment came through with us to this place. The 94th Ill., 20th Wisconsin and our own regiment are encamped together. Gen.

The site of the farm owned by Amos Clayton in Van Buren County, Iowa, as it appears today. The Chequest River can be seen in the right center. Photo by the author.

Herron commands our brigade. Springfield is his headquarters. It is reported that we will stay here all winter but there is no telling. It was also said that the general has requested to have his command removed to St. Louis. It is a difficult matter to provide sustenance for the large number of troops now in the s. west [of Missouri], all of it has to be hauled in wagons from Rolla, about 120 miles. If the rebels are driven out now, there will be no use for so many soldiers here. The number in and around Springfield is estimated at 18 or 20,000 & about 10,000 left here last week going west.

From what I hear the folk about home are uneasy about us boys. I think there is no occasion for such uneasiness. We all feel perfectly safe here. I have not yet seen an armed rebel.

Newtonia where the late fighting was done is 65 or 70 miles from here. Yesterday was Sunday. George Paxton and I got outside the lines and started out to hunt grapes. The woods are full of the nicest wild grapes I ever seen. They are much larger than the grapes on Chequest[26] and very sweet. We got about 2½ miles from camp and came across a farm house. We stopped and talked with the folks and found them to be good Union people from Tennessee. The were old acquaintances of *Diesart* and Miller[27] in Troy. They gave us our dinner,

Major General Sterling Price, n.d.
Courtesy of the University of Arkansas Library, Little Rock.

a very good one. It was the first time either of us had set at a table since leaving Judge Wright's in Keosauqua. We went back this way and got them to bake up a lot of flour for us, the biscuits they made were excellent and pleased the boys very much.

I would like very much to receive a letter from you. I know you dislike writing but do write. Give my respects to all my friends. Nothing more, but I hope this will find you as it leaves me, enjoying good health.

I remain yours truly,

William H. H. Clayton

P.S. We received yesterday evening while on dress parade news of the defeat of old Price.[28] The whole regt. gave three rousing cheers and after the boys had a great jollification. The air in places was black with their caps.

In camp near Cassville, Mo.

October 16th, 1862

Dear Father & Mother,

Since last I wrote we have changed our place of residence somewhat.

We left the camp at Springfield Oct. 11th and marched about 12 miles. We passed the famous "Wilson's Creek" battleground[29] about 9 miles out. I did not stop to go over it as I would have liked to. I went over one edge of it and saw the remains of clothing, shoes, some bones and a few graves. Some of the boys who remained behind the regiment found knives, balls etc.

On Sunday Oct. 12th we marched about 17 miles and about the same distance the next day. On Election Day we reached this place. Rutledge[30] who was to have taken the vote of this regt. did not arrive. I believe some of the companies voted but ours did not.[31]

The majority of our boys are down on *Old Van Buren* [County], and talk about disowning the county on account of the manner in which we have been "bamboozled" in getting no county bounty. We do not care anything about it, but it was promised and of course it was expected that it would be paid. Other companies have received as much as $50.00 bounty to each man, from their county.[32]

Cassville is not a very large place, not much larger than Troy, but there are more stone houses, and before the war it is said to have been quite a business place. I have just come from there. The regt. is camped about ¾ of a mile from town, and I had not been there before. The 7th Mo. cavalry is camped by the town. I seen Lieut. Bonner,[33] Vol. Soliday[34] and others who were in the company got up at Upton.[35]

There is a large body of troops here, the number I do not know. Reports vary from 15 to 25,000. The 7th Mo. leaves tomorrow for Cross Hollows, about 30 miles distant. It is said that the rebels are going to make a stand there, but there is no certainty about it. I suppose we go into Arkansas when we leave here, but we will be apt to stay here for a few days longer. Our brigade teams left for Springfield yesterday for supplies, and as it is about 60 miles, they will not be back for several days. Mooney has got to be a mule driver. He drives a six mule brigade team. John Stone went back with the teams as one of the guards.

~

Friday morning Oct. 17th, 4 o'clock A.M.

I was compelled to stop writing yesterday evening for *inspection of arms* & dress parade. Awhile after dark we observed a light towards town, and the boys were out looking at it, when the *long roll*[36] sounded *to arms*. Every man who was able "harnessed up"[37] & got his gun, and we had the regiment formed up in less than no time. It was the first time that the regiment had been tried. After standing about half an hour we were dismissed.

During the night we received *marching orders*, and the cooks are preparing eatables. I think we go towards Cross Hollows. We are in the "Army of the Frontier"[38] and will be kept in this part of the country, I think.

We have received no mail since we came here, and it will be irregular from this on. I will write as often as I can, but you may not get these letters with any regularity. I got George's letter but did not like to hear of you having the ague.[39] I think I have received all the letters you have written. Walt Ferguson[40] has been unwell for sometime, something like the ague working on him. Our officers received their commissions a short time ago. They have not got any pay yet. The 20th Wisconsin is in our brigade & 1 company of the 1st Mo. artillery, six pieces of cannon, all brass, three of them rifled.[41] Abner Buckles wishes you to tell his folks that he is all right, and that he has not the time to write.

Abs. Nincehelser worked at the hospital being built at Springfield, but when we left he had to come along. The country between here and Springfield is about the same as it is from Rolla to Springfield. There is plenty of water. The last day we crossed a creek 7 times in coming 10 miles. The water was about half boot deep. The land in some places is tolerably productive. It is very rocky, in some places nothing but rock. We had the first frost the morning we left Springfield, Oct. 11. It was a heavy one. There was frost for several mornings following. Direct your letters to Springfield and they will follow the regiment.

I believe I will quit writing and make some molasses out of sugar. Give my respects to all.

I remain ever your affectionate son.

Wm. H. H. Clayton

P.S. I wrote to Uncle Nide while at Springfield. This leaves me enjoying good health, and I hope it finds you the same.

Cross Hollows, Arkansas
October 23rd, 1862
Dear Father & Mother,

I embrace the present opportunity of writing a few lines to you. Since I last wrote to you from Cassville we have done some pretty hard marching. We left Cassville Mo. on the 17th & camped 3 miles from the place. We cooked two days rations while there. We marched the next day into Arkansas & camped on the same ground that Gen. Sigel occupied when attacked at the Pea Ridge fight.[42] It was dark when we reached camp, and we did not put up our tents. There was a false alarm during the night & what sleep we got was with our guns beside us.[43] The next day, Sunday, a place was cleared off on the side hill & we pitched tents on the afternoon of the 20th. Abs. Nincehelser went on picket guard[44] &, as we expected to stay 24 hours, we had a day's rations in our haversacks. We had been on guard about two hours when orders came to march immediately. The boys at camp were just getting supper ready but they had to leave it & do without. We marched at dark & marched until 3 or 4 o'clock in the morning. We rested until daylight & started again & marched all day. Nobody had any rations prepared and a good many had nothing to eat. During the night march we passed through where the Pea Ridge battle was fought. It was dark so that I could not see it as I would have liked to have done. We got to the Elkhorn Tavern[45] about daylight. The battle was very severe around this vicinity. During the day's march we got to the Boston Mountains. We passed over part of them & camped after crossing White River. The next day we left them. They are covered with timber, some of it very good. Among the different kinds were the different kinds of oak, yellow pine, dogwood etc. We have been marching pretty hard ever since we came into Arkansas. We marched last night until midnight & started early this morning again.

"We Are in the 'Army of the Frontier'"

Last evening we changed our course. We had been going south tolerably fast. Today we have been travelling on the back track. Our brigade teams returned to Springfield from Cassville and have not yet returned. There was danger of their being cut off so we returned. Today we went on the double quick in order to catch up with them. The cavalry got after some [Confederates] about two miles from here this afternoon. Our brigade was halted and drawn up in line. Gens. Schofield[46] & Herron were on the ground. It is reported that the cavalry found a body of 4 or 5,000 on the retreat this afternoon. We are encamped at the famous Cross Hollows we have read so much about. There is Cross Roads & Cross Hollows. The Hollows is about 300 or 400 yards wide. There are a couple of houses built in it. It is said that we go back to the Elkhorn Tavern about 10 or 12 miles from here. We have not got any mail but once since leaving Springfield. The mail goes out in the morning & I have to get this letter ready by nine, this evening. If we get down in the state further the mail will be irregular. Our destination, if not defeated & compelled to retreat, will be Ft. Smith or Little Rock.

I will quit writing for the present. The boys are all well, but considerably footsore. Give my respects to all. I am enjoying very good health.

I remain ever your affectionate son,

W. H. H. Clayton

~

Cross Hollows, Ark.

Oct. 29th, 1862

Dear Father and Mother,

I once more take pen in hand to write a few lines to you, from this place having written to you when we first reached here. The day after writing it got quite cool, and on the night of the 24th it snowed on the ground. We began to think that the further south we got, the colder it was. The snow nearly all disappeared the next day and it has got to be quite warm and pleasant. There is a good many of the regt. sick in consequence, I think of our hard marching from Cassville here. There has been but one death in our company yet. It was John Strang. He died in the hospital at Rolla. We do not know much about the movements of the rebels. There is some bushwhacking [ambushing] about. Yesterday a foraging train was fired on, several miles from here, and 3 men killed.

The cavalry have taken 6 or 8 prisoners. They are in camp here and are a hard looking set.

One of our boys received a letter the other day from Keosauqua. His father wrote that there had been a bounty provided for volunteers and sent a power of attorney for him to sign. I thought I would send one and if there is anything of it you can get it. The boys from Chequest are all well except Lieut. Ferguson. He is around most of the time but looks very bad. Give my respects to all, write often.

I remain your affectionate son,

W. H. H. Clayton

~

Camp near Ozark Mo.
Nov. 13th, 1862
Dear Brother:

Your welcome letter reached camp yesterday but I did not get it until this morning & remained 24 hours. I was very glad to hear from you as I had not had a letter for a month previous. I wrote a letter to Harris Neal[47] while at Crane Creek, and if he received it, I suppose you heard that we had left Arkansas. We left Crane Creek on the 10th, having remained there 4 days. We got here after about 30 miles on the next day P.M. It rained slowly several hours, during the last days march, but only laid the dust and made it pleasant marching but just as we reached the camping place a thunder shower came up and before we got our tents up it rained very hard. But by the time we got our tent up it quit, but it did not hurt us any, we can stand almost anything now. The march from Cross Hollows to Crane Creek was the most disagreeable one we have yet had. The road was very dusty, it being 2 or 3 inches deep and we sometimes could not see more than 10 or 15 steps ahead. After marching all day we were about the dirtiest set of fellows imaginable.

There is a larger number of troops assembled here than I have seen before in one place. While on the march our brigade was by itself. Besides our brigade, Gen. Totten's[48] forces are here and some from Springfield. It is said that the brigades are to be changed. The Wisconsin boys do not like our regt. very well. They are mostly foreigners, and as a general thing they are small men and not very fast marchers. The regiments take turn about in leading while on the march, and when we led we would sometimes run right away from them. They would then curse us and call us d——d "Iowa Greyhounds."[49] We call them the "badgers,"[50] Wis. cubs etc. It is said that we & the 94th Ills. will be put together in a brigade. Our col. who has been absent ever since we left Springfield returned today. Lt. Colonel McFarlane is a very fine looking officer. He was in the Pittsburg[51] fight. Everybody likes Maj. Dan Kent. While on the march he will walk half the time and let boys who are unwell or tired ride his horse. The country from Cross Hollows to Crane Creek is a desolate looking spectacle. A great deal of property was destroyed before we went down there. On our return nearly every house was burned. The corn and forage of all kinds was used up pretty clean to feed our train. For fire wood we use rails whenever we can get them. Teams go from here several miles & haul rails off of secesh farms. Those who have protection papers[52] are exempt, and what feed is got from them is paid for. Keetsville was quite a place. It was nearly as large as Troy & 6 miles beyond Cassville. Nearly all the houses are burnt excepting 6 or 8 containing families. The secesh will not have much to live on if they return to that section of country. We will probably not stay here long. I do not know where we will go to. I think you had better direct letters to St. Louis, and they will reach me sooner if we should go east. We are now about 12 or 14 miles S.E. of Springfield. Write often.

I remain ever your affectionate brother,

W. H. H. Clayton

Camp on James River Mo.

November 21st, 1862

Dear Father & Mother,

I once more take my pen in hand, to write a few lines to you.

When I last wrote to you we were encamped about 16 miles from Springfield, southeast at Ozark. We left Ozark, I think on the 15th & marched northeast about 12 miles & encamped in an out of the way place, close to one of the nicest springs I have yet seen. It came out of a cave at the foot of a high hill. It rained the next day Sunday. Monday the 17th we started on the hardest tramp we have yet had, for the purpose of reinforcing Gen. Blunt[53] who was said to be fighting back towards Cassville.[54] We came back over the same road that we traveled going to Ozark, but under different circumstances. It had rained before we started, and it rained on us from dark until we stopped, about half past 8 p.m. We stopped in a field and built fires. It continued to rain all night, sometimes tolerably fast. The roads were so bad that our wagons did not get up with us until 8 or 9 o'clock next morning. We made some coffee, & started again about noon on the 18th. It rained on us nearly all day, making the road very muddy. We reached this place about two hours before dark, and after making a charge on the wheat and straw stacks, we sat down and waited for our wagon to come up with our tents & provision. It soon began to rain but the wagon did not make its appearance. The teamsters of some of the wagons that got through informed us that Buckles' mules had given out and he had stopped about 4 miles back. We sat around until after dark when the captain got the use of the Lt. Colonel's tent if we would put it up. I and the others soon raised it and having plenty of straw we slept nicely. The other boys scattered around among other companies and got lodging. Two other company teams failed to come up and a good many staid out all night, it raining a good part of the time. It quit raining the next day and the sun came out enabling us to dry our overcoats and blankets.

We are camped on a clover field, part of a fine large farm on the bank of James River, a good sized stream about 15 miles from Springfield. About the nicest thing I have seen yet took place the evening we came here. The 94th Illinois regt. came in, in good order, and our Col.[55] who is commanding the brigade complimented them for it. They stacked arms and gave him three cheers. They were ordered to break ranks, and every one of them started as fast as they could run for the wheat stacks. They soon returned every fellow loaded with sheaves of wheat. As soon as we reach a camp and stack arms we make for a fence and make the rails fly. They make the best wood we can find. Rails between here and Cross Hollows are getting to be tolerably scarce.

No person but an eye witness can imagine what destruction an army the size of ours can make. The cavalry men lay down fences to take short cuts or to get feed for their horses. There is now 4 or 5 regts. of cavalry with us, and their horses and mules belonging to the

"We Are in the 'Army of the Frontier'"

Major General James G. Blunt, 1864.
Courtesy of the Central Arkansas Library System.

wagons, clean the country for a long distance around of forage, so that we can not stay long in a place. We live very well while in camp. While we were further southwest, the boys jayhawked[56] every thing they wanted. In this part of the country we trade coffee for delicacies. We have sold over $4.00 worth of coffee within the last two weeks. We get 35 cts. per pound cash.

We are now awaiting further orders. I have no idea what course we go next. Before we returned we were going northeast and I thought that we were probably going to St. Louis. We ought to go someplace and rest awhile. I think it is three months today since we were mustered in. Since leaving Rolla we have marched 500 miles. There is now only 45 men reported for duty. When we first started in there was 98. There is not much the matter with those "present, unfit for duty," the worst cases being sent to Springfield. All of the boys from our neighborhood are well excepting "Nincy" as the boys call Nincehelser. He is getting along first rate and will be all right before long.

We have been moving so much of late the mail did not reach us regularly. Yesterday a large mail came in but I received nothing. I would like for you to send 2 or 3 stamps every once in awhile when writing to me. There are no stamps to be bought in camp. Stamped envelopes sell at 5 cts apiece.

Write whenever you can conveniently. I am always glad to receive letters. I have very poor ink to write with and you must excuse bad writing.

You may direct letters to St. Louis at present. I do not know what course we go from here, but direct these and the letter will come to the regt. wherever it is.

Give my respects to all.

Nothing more at the present, but I remain your affectionate son.
Wm. H. H. Clayton

~

Camp Curtis,[57] Missouri
November 29th, 1862
Dear Parents:
I once more take of my pen to write a few lines to you.

I last wrote from James River on the 21st. We marched from there on the 22nd and came here. It was a short march of only about five miles. Company H was part of the *rear guard* that day, there being one company from each of the three infantry regts., 20th Wisconsin, 19th Iowa, and 94th Illinois. The column commenced moving about 7 o'clock A.M. but we had to wait until everything had started before we commenced moving. We did not get off until after 2 o'clock P.M. There is two brigades here now and the cavalry and the train[58] belonging stretches out a good ways. The forward regiments were camped here before we got started from the other camp.

"We Are in the 'Army of the Frontier'"

We have had right nice weather since the rain I spoke of in my last. Some nights it freezes right hard, making it muddy in camp. We have fires in our tents and we sleep tolerably warm. We have not got blankets enough yet, having but one each, [so] two lay together laying on our overcoats and have two blankets over us. Requisition has been made for more blankets and we will be apt to receive them before we leave here. One reason of our stay here is to get our winter clothing.

While in camp we have plenty to eat, in fact almost too much. All that ails me is that I have too good an appetite and eat too much. It is so with all the boys who are well. While on a march we do not get meals whenever we want them and men exercising without sufficient food get hungry and then when they get camped and stop awhile they are eating all the time. I believe it makes a good many sick to go half starved awhile and then lay around camp without exercise, and eat as much as we do. It would amuse you folks at home to see us about meal time. If a person does not watch and *pitch in* he will come out *minus*.

The cook gives the word "Dinner's ready" and each one grabs his haversack and pitches out of the tent to get his share. The cook then gives each one his share of bread, 3 cakes or whatever it may be. Someone then divides the sugar, giving each one a tablespoonful each meal. By this time a person thinks of meat, if it is boiled he will get plenty, but if it is fried and he does not come in about first he will often go without. So it is with almost everything. First come, first served. After each one gets his share of everything on his plate he sits down on the ground on his knapsack and proceeds to dispose of it. We have all got used to this style of eating, and it would go awkward with many of us to eat at a table. Our rations consist of flour crackers[59] and fresh beef every other day. Salt pork, familiarly known by us as "sow belly," beans, rice, coffee, and sugar. The boys have for awhile past traded coffee for cornmeal and as we have two good dutch ovens we have good corn-bread. We have soda and the cooks make tolerably good biscuits. There is 16 in our mess and we have some jolly times in our tent during the evenings. We can talk and tear around as much as we want to until after 8 P.M. or "taps."[60] After that time there must be silence in the camp. A night or two ago a corporal in the tent joining ours got to talking in Irish style with an Irishman in another tent. They made quite a noise and the colonel sent the officer of the guard and some men after him. Since that there has been better times for sleeping.

Last Sunday I and three others got a pass to go to Wilson Creek battleground, which is about two miles from here. Yesterday the regiment with the exception of the guards and some who did not feel like going, went out with our guns. We stacked our guns after arriving there, and went over the ground. The trees and saplings showed the scars of cannon & musket balls. A good many small balls were found on the ground. I have one I got there. In some places there are perfect rows of horse bones, laying I suppose as they were killed, while in line of battle. I also saw the sink hole into which it is said a great many bodies were thrown and covered up with stones and dead horses.[61]

It is only 12 miles from here to Springfield. I am unable to say how long we stay here. Nothing is known of our future movements. I suppose if us boys had remained in the Business Corner company we would now be at Helena. We have seen some hard marching while the 30th regt. was laying at Keokuk.[62]

The boys from Chequest are all well. Some who were complaining awhile back are now able to dispose of their full share of rations.

Standing guard is the hardest part of soldiering. It is not very pleasant to stand guard while the rain is pouring down, nor of a night when it is freezing right hard. I have not stood guard much since we left Keokuk. I act as clerk for the captain and am relieved from guard duty. I wish you to send a stamp or two every time you write. There is none to be had here, and stamped envelopes sell at 5 cts apiece. Money is getting rather scarce in camp. It is hard to tell when the paymaster will make his appearance. I do not expect him until after the first of January. Write as often as you can. The last letter from George I received on the 13th, dated the 2nd.

Give my best respects to Mr. & Mrs. Neal and family. Hoping this will find you all as it leaves me, enjoying good health I remain your affectionate son.

Tell Uncle Nide that I would like to receive a letter from him. I will write to him soon again.

William H. H. Clayton

CHAPTER 3

"*It Was a Perfect Slaughter Pen***"**

After suffering setbacks at Wilson's Creek and Lexington in 1861, Union forces in Missouri had rebounded by early 1862, driving the organized Confederate armies out of the state. The victory by General Curtis at Pea Ridge, Arkansas, which lay just south of the Missouri border, in March of that year solidified Union control of the state. For nine months only irregular Confederate units operated in Missouri. But the Confederates still had hopes of reversing the blue tide in that theater of operations and in December 1862 initiated a series of attempts to regain what they had lost.

The first effort came from a newly formed Confederate army under the command of Major General Thomas Carmichael Hindman. Noting the distance between a Union force under the command of General Blunt at Cane Hill, Arkansas, and its source of reinforcements in the area around Springfield, Missouri, Hindman developed a plan to crush the advanced column. He could then direct his forces against the rest of the federal army in southern Missouri. Accordingly, in the first few days of December 1862 Hindman moved his army to engage the unsupported Union troops in northern Arkansas.

Detecting the Confederate advance, Blunt sent an urgent telegram to Springfield, asking for reinforcements. General Herron, camped near the Wilson's Creek battlefield, responded with alacrity, immediately putting the two divisions under his command into motion. Through prodigious marches, he moved his command the 110 miles to Fayetteville in only three days. There he allowed his troops a few hours' sleep in the early morning hours of December 7 before they would undertake the final part of their journey.

As the federal force bedded down in Fayetteville, Hindman learned of their arrival. Previously unaware that any Union troops had set out to reinforce Blunt, the Confederate leader felt compelled to alter his original plan. Erroneously believing that Herron commanded fewer troops than Blunt, Hindman decided to attack the relief column first. Keeping his camp fires conspicuously burning, and ordering a small detachment of cavalry to demonstrate in front of Blunt's position at first light to keep the Union force in place, at 4:00 A.M. on December 7 Hindman moved his army north toward Fayetteville, completely undetected by Blunt.

Hindman's soldiers were not the only ones on the move that morning, however. Eager to link up with Blunt, Herron had put his weary troops into motion at virtually the same time that Hindman had ordered his men to move. Advanced cavalry units of the two sides would make first contact at daybreak; the main forces would collide a few hours later near a meeting house called the Prairie Grove Church. This engagement, known as the Battle of Prairie Grove, would serve as William Henry Harrison Clayton's baptism of fire.

Although the Confederates lost the battle, other southern generals refused to let the dream of possessing Missouri die. Brigadier General John Sappington Marmaduke, who had fought under Hindman at Prairie Grove, led two separate expeditions into Missouri in early 1863 to weaken the Union cause there. While the 19th Iowa would not directly engage Marmaduke's forces, Clayton's regiment would move throughout southern Missouri in response to the Confederate thrusts.

The thirteen letters Clayton wrote during this period of the conflict show two very different sides of the Civil War. He gives the reader a gripping account of what combat was like during the war in his letters about Prairie Grove, the type of action that most people associate with the Civil War. But Clayton also shows what the war meant for a nation at war with itself — guerrilla conflict. While Clayton details his anger toward the secessionists for their treatment of loyal Unionists, he discusses as well the toll that the Northerners took on civilian property as they advanced further south. All in all, these letters show that for Clayton there was no longer hope of a peaceful reconciliation between the two sides.

~

Battle Field Illinois Creek [1] Ark

Dec. 8th 1862

Dear Father & Mother:

Knowing that you will be anxious to hear whether I got through the battle safely I hasten to inform you that I was not injured much. A spent ball [2] struck me on the right side under the arm; it did not go through my overcoat but bruised my side a little. Our captain [3] was taken prisoner but released the next day on parole. Our Lieut. Colonel was killed. [4] 8 of our company were killed on the field, one has since died. 12 or 13 were wounded. Nincehelser got through without a scratch, also Lt. Ferguson. Benton Liming [5] was killed on the field. He was the only one from Chequest Valley. It was a perfect slaughter pen into which we were led. The 20th Wisconsin charged up the hill and took a Battery. [6] The 19th Iowa went up double quick [7] to the left of them. They began to fall back before we got fairly up the hill. Our regt. pressed on firing to a fence going across an orchard. We halted there and fired into the brush when the Col. ordered us to cease firing. Just as we ceased 5 regts. raised up out of the brush and with a yell commenced firing on us. We were ordered to retreat. The rebels came very near surrounding us, they fired into us from all sides but one. How I ever got out safely as I did I cannot tell. The bullets blew around like hail. Large numbers of the rebels were killed. [8] I think our regiment suffered more than any other. [9] The morning after the fight we could raise only 220 men. The number of rebels it is difficult to state. I think if Gen. Blunt had not come up, we would not have got along so well. [10]

I will not write any more at present.

I remain your affectionate son,

Wm. H. H. Clayton

P.S. The battle was fought on Sunday the 7th and the ball was opened by the rebels.

~

Camp Prairie Grove, Arkansas

December 12th, 1862

Dear Father & Mother:

I embrace the present opportunity to write to you again since the battle. I hurriedly scratched a few lines with a pencil on the morning after camping here and sent it to Fayetteville with one of our boys who was going back to that place.

I last wrote before Camp Curtis Mo. about 12 miles this side of Springfield on the 29th of November. At that time we did not know which way we would go when we started from there. We received orders to march and on the 3rd of this month we started to reinforce Gen. Blunt who has been out in this section all along. We reached Crane Creek after dark and built fires and laid around until about 4 o'clock the next morning when we started again and went on to Cassville about 30 miles, arriving there after dark. Started before daylight on the 5th and passed again over the Pea Ridge battle ground & camped 3 miles this side, marching about 25 miles. On the 6th passed Cross Hollows, came on about 8 miles and got supper. Started after dark and came on to Fayetteville about 28 miles from where we started in the morning. Between Cross Hollows and Fayetteville we passed through the finest country I have yet seen. The houses along the road were principally frame, with outhouses and other conveniences handy. Fayetteville is the nicest country town I ever saw. It is situated on a large rising piece of ground, a kind of mound, with a low piece of ground all around and hills in the distance. The houses are generally frame, nicely painted, the yards enclosed with railing fences or board fences nicely whitewashed. Some of the private residences are beautiful. Some have Porticoes in front with nice Fluted Columns. Everything looks nice and tasty. The inhabitants are principally secesh.

On the morning of the 7th we left Fayetteville before daylight. We came out about 6 or 7 miles[11] and met portions of the 1st Arkansas[12] & 7th Mo. Cavalry, a good many of them without their hats, their horses wet all over with sweat. We had heard some firing ahead, and they said that they had been attacked unexpectedly. I have since heard how it happened. The 1st Iowa, 7th Mo., 1st Arkansas, and other Cavalry were sent on in advance of the Infantry. The 1st Iowa suc-

"It Was a Perfect Slaughter Pen"

The point at the base of the ridge at Prairie Grove from which the 19th Iowa began its assault, as it appears today. Photo by Cam Elder.

ceeded in getting through and joining Gen. Blunt's forces. The balance started about midnight and got on ahead a considerable distance. They stopped awhile after midnight to feed their horses in a lane, tying the horses to the fence on each side. Some had the bridles off, some were making coffee in tin cups and no one was thinking that the enemy was close for they let the advanced guard go by unmolested. The first thing they were aware of was the firing of the secesh upon them. Everyone did as well as he could under the circumstances to get out of the way. A good many were taken prisoners.

After meeting the cavalry we were ordered forward on the double-quick. Nearly every one had sore feet from the effects of the hard march, but we all forgot our feet and pushed forward. After going nearly a mile we were drawn up in line of battle on a piece of rising ground. We remained here probably an hour or more when we were ordered forward again. We had gone but a short distance when we heard the cannon of the rebels firing on our advance. We went on at the double-quick and after going a mile or more we came to a creek called Illinois Creek. We crossed it and laid out along the bank, while the skirmishers[13] went out.

After they had been out awhile the rebels commenced shelling the

The site of the Confederate position at Prairie Grove assaulted by the 19th Iowa, as it appears today. Photo by Cam Elder.

position we held. Pieces of shell fell close by us but no one was injured. As soon as the rebels commenced firing our batteries replied. Our batteries continued to fire for nearly an hour, silencing their batteries.

The 20th Wisconsin, 19th Iowa, & 94th Illinois were ordered forward in line of battle, the 20th on the right, the 19th in the center, and the 94th on the left.

The 20th was in the advance & charged on a rebel battery on top of a hill. They succeeded in taking the battery and advanced on the rebels beyond. We were to the left of the Wisconsin regt. and the firing getting too hot for the 20th they began to fall back.[14] We were ordered up the hill at the double-quick and after getting up were ordered forward across an orchard[15] to the fence close to the brush. The 19th pressed on to that fence and fired several volleys into the brush which was filled with rebels lying down. All at once the Lt. Col. ordered us to cease firing, but all did not hear at first and firing was kept up for several minutes. At length we ceased firing and the rebels all at once rose out of their hiding place and began to fire at us. We were ordered to *retreat* which each one did as best he could. The balls fell like hail on all sides of me, one as I wrote struck me on the right side. But it

"It Was a Perfect Slaughter Pen"

was a spent ball and did not go through my overcoat. It made a blue spot though.

There were several regiments concealed where we advanced on them, some say 3 some 5.[16] When the foremost fired they laid down and the one behind fired. We were also exposed to cross fire. The 20th Wisconsin fell back and all the rebel fire from the right side was directed on us. They also tried to get around us on the left side and if we had remained in the orchard but a few minutes longer we would all have been killed, wounded or taken prisoners. Our captain was taken prisoner but released the next day on parole. He was not injured much. He was lame with Rheumatism before the fight and was lame in his knee. In getting over a fence he was run over and hurt some. He remained by the fence until the firing slacked a little when he started off, but a lot of rebels came around the barn and took him. He seen General Hindman,[17] General Marmaduke[18] and another one.[19] They treated him very well while they had him in their possession. After we fell back Gen. Totten's command[20] moved forward and engaged the enemy. I believe we would have been defeated had not Blunt attacked them about this time. The report of musketry was terrific. About dark the firing ceased and we built fires and passed the night as well as we could expecting to go into it again in the morning. We were ordered out again early in the morning and took our positions. The rebels had sent a flag of truce in the morning and after negotiations had ended they had cleared out leaving their dead on the field. We were informed that the victory was ours and after giving three cheers we went over the place where we had fought the day before. We had 8 of our Co. left dead on the field, one died before morning making it 9. 14 were wounded of our company, they were taken off during the night in ambulances. Lt. Col. McFarlane, the Sergeant-Major[21] and 2 Lts.[22] were killed. 3 Captains[23] & 2 Lieuts.[24] were wounded. 47 were killed in all in the 19th regt. and 147 wounded making in all killed & wounded 194. Our regt. used them up pretty hard while we were in the orchard.[25] I counted 42 dead rebels in one pen & 10 or 11 in another place. They had hauled off their wounded during the night and gathered the most of their dead in piles. Their loss altogether was immense.[26] They had all the force they could raise in this part of Arkansas from Little Rock, Van Buren & other places, in all about 25,000 men.[27] There was about 3,000 men in our Divi-

The site of the Borden Orchard at Prairie Grove, as it appears today.
Photo by Cam Elder.

sion in the fight. I cannot tell how many Blunt had.[28] Our Artillery
made great havoc in their ranks, and had it not been for it we would
have been defeated. From those who have given themselves up we
learn that it was the intention of the rebels to fight their way to Springfield Mo. and from there on to St. Louis I suppose.

They say that there is nothing to eat south of the Arkansas River
and they wanted to get up north where there was something. Some
think that they will now go to Mississippi. They had no idea that there
was as many of us as there was before the fight. They supposed that a
small force was coming with a large train to the aid of Blunt. They got
between us and Blunt and thought to take us and our train and then
they could take Gen. Blunt at their leisure. As it was we came to reinforce Blunt and just saved each other. If we had not got here as we
did Blunt would have been taken and had not Blunt came up and
helped us it would have been much harder with us.

The 19th is badly used up but I think our company suffered about
as much as any in killed.[29]

We have present here now 36 enlisted men. There is only a little
over 300 men in the regiment. Our 1st Sergeant Samuel Bonney was
killed in the fight.

"It Was a Perfect Slaughter Pen"

I have been doing most of the writing, making reports and so on since the fight. I have not been very well for a day or two past but feel better today.

Give my best respects to all the friends of our neighborhood.

Nothing more but remain your affectionate son,

Wm. H. H. Clayton

Write often. Direct to Springfield Mo.

～

Camp near Fayetteville, Arkansas

January 4, 1863

Dear Brother:

I received your welcome letter of the 14th Dec. on the 28th. I was very glad to hear from you all again and also to receive the stamps inclosed therein. There is no stamps for sale anywhere in these "diggins" and I concluded that I would have to quit writing on that account.

Your letter found me tolerably well at Prairie Grove, which place we left on the 2nd of January and came on White River about 3 miles from Fayetteville and 13 miles from the battleground.

While at Prairie Grove the command was ordered to have 6 days rations packed up and be ready to start on the 27th Dec. towards the Arkansas River. All who were not able to stand rapid marching were to remain in camp and take care of things. I had been having the diarrhoea for a week or more so that I did not feel able to march and I did not go.[30] The boys returned on the 31st having been as far as Van Buren on the river. Gen. Blunt had taken the town before Herron arrived.[31] They took four steamboats and burnt them. They also took a number of wagons, horses, mules, cattle, commissary stores etc. I wish that I had been able to have gone. The roads were the roughest, so the boys say, that has been traveled over yet, the Boston Mts. having to be crossed. Gen. Blunt had command of the expedition, Gen. Herron being second in command. The battle at Prairie Grove was not so disastrous to the rebels as their loss by the recent expedition. Gen. Blunt seems to have the confidence of the men in our whole army and I believe if he and Herron were let alone that rebellion would suffer somewhat from their hands. But I hear that Gen. Schofield (who has returned and took command) was much displeased with the actions of the above generals and has had them arrested. Gen. Schofield had command on our former trip into Arkansas as far as Cross Hollows. He was tolerably successful in having the men run down by hard marching but accomplished nothing else. Everyone here was surprised when we saw it stated in the papers at the time, that "the Army of the Frontier had successfully accomplished its mission." Schofield no doubt envies the praise which Blunt & Herron have gained by their operations here and thinks he will do something to injure them.[32]

There is a general feeling of sadness at the ill success of Burnside's movement in Virginia.[33] We look upon that as the main point and the defeat of our forces there lengthens our stay in the army. I received a letter from George Smith[34] a short time ago dated 8th Dec. He was in the hospital at Hampton VA. His wound was healing slowly. I also received a letter from Lizzie Cooper[35] yesterday dated Dec. 21st. They were all well excepting Aunt Agness.

The weather here seems singular to one who has been accustomed to cold weather at this time of year. I have not seen ice yet that would exceed ½ inch in thickness. Since the battle there has been but two frosts. Wheat that was spilled on the ground there after we camped there, had sprouted and was 2 inches high when we left. A great many go without coats it is so warm. We came here on the 2nd and expected to leave the next day, but we did not and thought we would go today but we are still here, probably we will go tomorrow, where I cannot say. The boys did not think it worth while to pitch the tent and lay it on the ground to sleep in it. One blanket apiece is enough here. You wanted to know whether my boots were worn out. The soles had worn through by the time we reached Cross Hollows the first time about 25 Oct. I could not get them mended right away so I drawed another pair. They will last awhile longer and I will get the old ones half soled as I have them with me yet. The uppers are good. I write this in a hurry. It is now after *taps* and I will soon have to close.

Our captain is not yet exchanged but is expecting to be every day.[36] Lieut. Kent[37] & Sergeant Baker[38] of our company start tomorrow for home on a recruiting expedition. I cut a sassafras stick from the fence now, to which our regt. advanced in the fight. It was placed in a box which Baker had to take home along with one that Lieut. Ferguson sent. The box was too short to take in one the right length for a walking stick. It may reach home and it may not. I suppose the box will be inspected at St. Louis. The company is now in the command of Lt. Ferguson. I have been very busy for the past two days in making our muster rolls. The regiment has to be mustered every two months. I finish tonight. Abs. Nincehelser and A. J. Buckles are well. John Stone has been at Springfield in hospital since we left Camp Curtis on the 3rd of Dec.

I have not received the papers nor Harris Neal's letter. I am sorry that they did not come.

Nothing more at present. Give my best respects to all friends.

I remain ever your affectionate brother,

Wm. H. H. Clayton

Write often as you can

Jan 5th   Last night an order was received stating that there would be a review of the troops here today at 10 o'clock. The review has taken place and we have just returned to camp. Gen. Herron's division only was present. The troops were drawn up in a long line and Gens. Herron & Schofield & staffs rode by. The generals then placed themselves in a conspicuous place and the different regts. passed by. I hear today that Schofield has not had Herron and Blunt arrested. This leaves me enjoying good health & I hope it will find you all the same.

Yours,

W. H. H. C.

P.S. I wrote to you on 9th Dec. and again a short time after. I hope the letters were received.

Camp at Forsyth MO

January 31st 1863

Dear Brothers:

I received your welcome letter dated 18th of this month on the 28th. I was very glad to hear from you all. I also received one on the 23rd written Dec. 30th. I was glad to get the stamps contained in each. But if we had continued to travel over an *out of the way* part of the country like we have been since we left Fayetteville, stamps would be of little use. We received no mail from the 2nd of January until after we arrived here. And no mail was sent off. I last wrote from near

Fayetteville. We left Prairie Grove on the 2nd of Jan. and marched through Fayetteville camping about 3 or 4 miles east of town on the head waters of White River.

On the 7th we again took up the line of march in an easterly direction. On our first day's march we passed some very nice farms, well improved, but on the second day we got into a rough country. We arrived at Huntsville in the evening. We expected to stay at that place some time but were disappointed for we received orders and started on the 10th still coming east. We did not know what the cause of our sudden movement was at first, but we soon heard that we were sent out to *head* Marmaduke if he should try to retreat in that direction from Springfield.[39]

We continued on until the 12th when we arrived at the town of Carrolton. The weather up to that time had been excellent, warm & more like spring than winter but on the 14th it commenced raining and turned to snow in the evening. In the morning the snow was about 4 in. deep. It thawed very little for a day or two but we had plenty of *rails* and we kept a good fire in our tent and got along finely. On the 17th we left Carrolton for this place. I forgot to mention the discovery of a lot of mail matter that had been captured & robbed by the secesh and taken to Carrolton. The letters were all cut to pieces so that it was impossible to find one whole one. Some of the letters were from Iowa and some from Illinois.

The snow nearly all went off the day we started and the roads were very bad. We traveled 7 miles the first day, the next day 21 miles, the last 15 without seeing a house. The road all the way was on top of a ridge which was covered with pines. We bivouacked in the pines that night. Soon after dark it commenced sleeting & continued to do so nearly all night. As we had no tents up you can imagine that it was not a very pleasant place to sleep.

The next day, the 19th, we arrived opposite Forsyth. Here we had White River to cross. It is about ⅔ as wide as the Des Moines[40] and not fordable. They commenced to cross the train soon after arriving. The ferry runs the same as the one at Pittsburgh[41] only it was not half as well got up. The old *flat* was very shallow and there was no side railing. It is a wonder that a number were not drowned for it was a *ticklish* concern. We kept waiting for our turn to come. At last orders came one evening to be ready to cross at 10 that night. It was raining

"It Was a Perfect Slaughter Pen"

Brigadier General John S. Marmaduke, n.d.
Courtesy of the University of Arkansas Library, Little Rock.

hard when the order came and it continued to do so all night and until the afternoon of the next day. Our commanding officer Captain Bruce[42] went to see about it and got the order countermanded so that we got to remain in camp until the next day afternoon and by that time it had quit raining. The regt. however did not get to cross until after dark.

This was on the 26th just one week from the time we arrived in camp over the river. There was two or three regts. crossed after ours.

I was not very well when we left Carrolton but marched nearly all of the first two days, but the third day I rode in a wagon all day, and while in camp over the river I had to take medicine for this fever.[43] I did not get so but what I could go around although I got very weak when our regt. crossed the river. I crossed in an ambulance and staid in the court house at Forsyth over night. I had no appetite to eat anything for nearly a week and of course I lost a good deal of my strength. My appetite now is pretty good and I am getting stronger every day. I expect we will move from here next week. We were ordered to be ready yesterday morning but the order was countermanded. It is said that we go toward Springfield. Rumors have been numerous in camp for some time that we will go to Rolla and I suppose from there to St. Louis. I know not whether it is so or not. One thing is certain, we will have to go some place where forage is more plenty.

Our regiment is in rather a bad fix for officers. Maj. Kent was left sick at Huntsville as also was Lt. Ferguson of our company. Capt. Bruce of Co. A has had charge of the regiment since leaving Huntsville. Col. Crabb is commander of the post at Springfield.[44] Co. H was without a commissioned officer until the 28th when Capt. Richmond, who had been exchanged, returned to the company. Walt Ferguson was very sick when we left him.

A. J. Buckles is well and as fat as he can be. A. Nincehelser is *allright*. M. E. Mooney has returned to the company. He had been driving a brigade team but got sick and unable to drive. He is getting better now and if we could stay awhile somewhere would soon get well. Jo & George Paxson are well & enjoy themselves finely. There is 45 men of Co. H present, 10 are absent on detached service, the most of them teamsters, & 28 absent sick. In all there is 83 men in the company. We had 97 men when we started.

I believe I have written all that I can think of at present so I will close by sending my respects to Uncle Nide, Aunt Rachel, Uncle "Sammy," Mr. & Mrs. Neal and family & to you all.

I remain your affectionate brother,

Wm. H. H. Clayton

P.S. Write often. I am always glad to receive letters from you.

~

Camp near Forsyth MO

February 14th, 1863

Dear Father & Mother:

I once more take up my pen to write a few lines to you.

I last wrote to you from this camp and nothing of importance has transpired since I last wrote.

I was not very well at the time but have been improving in health ever since.

The last letter from the boys was dated Dec. 28th. Abner Buckles received a letter from home a day or so ago stating that the last letter from me was dated Dec. 12th. I have written 3 or 4 times since that.

While coming from Fayetteville to this place by the way of Huntsville and Carrolton, Arkansas, we neither received nor sent any mail for about 3 weeks.

I received a letter from cousin Mary Lighthill dated January 25th. They were all well excepting Aunt Agness.

The last mail brought a couple of papers from you. They were Dec. 11th & 18th. The *Dollar Times*[45] was familiar and put me in mind of "old times."

I had not seen one since leaving St. Louis. The long looked for individual, the *paymaster*, has at last made his appearance. Our regiment was paid yesterday & day before. We were only paid up to the last of October. We received one month's pay in advance when we were paid in Keokuk that paid me up to the 13th of September. From that time until the last of Oct. my wages amounted to $20.36 which I received. The officers of the regt. had never received any pay until yesterday.

Lieut. Ferguson has handed in his resignation on account of disability. It has not yet been accepted but undoubtedly will be. He is now with the company having joined us a couple of weeks ago. He leaves tomorrow for Springfield where he will wait until he hears from headquarters at St. Louis. He may be compelled to stay there some time.

I have sent $15.00 by him. He could get a large amount of money to take home for the boys but he refuses to take it as he will have to stop at Springfield for awhile and does not care about being troubled with it. It will not be safe to send money in letters as it is known that the paymaster has been around, and would not wonder if the mails would be robbed.

We had quite a snow here about the first of the month. The snow was about 8 inches deep. It was right cold for a couple of days after but in a week it was all gone. Today it is very warm & pleasant. We have a first rate camping place here. It is on a side hill, and the surface is rocky so that it does not get muddy. We expect to leave here soon probably on Monday. I do not know which direction we go. We are compelled to go somewhere for forage. Our teams have had to go on 2 and 3 day trips for forage for sometime past. Some think that we will go down White River. They have been engaged in making a ferry boat ever since we crossed the river. What it is for I do not know. I hope we will not have to recross this river again and go into Arkansas.

Maj. Dan Kent has been promoted to Lt. Col. and Capt. Bruce of Co. A to major.

From reports in the papers I suppose that there is considerable opposition manifested towards the administration and the war. They also say that a good many of the officers in the army have resigned on account of the proclamation.[46] I have not heard of any in this division of the army.

I hope the people of the North will do nothing to bring on a collision between the two parties.[47] I am sure that if some of the leaders would take a trip through south west Missouri and northern Arkansas and see the destruction of property that an army causes in its passage through the country, they would return home with the desire that such would never be the fate of the section of the country in which they lived.

If an army even the size of our small division was to camp near Buckles for two weeks there would not be anything left in Chequest Valley. The fences would all be used for fuel. All of the corn, wheat, etc. would be taken for forage and everything would be destroyed whether of use to the army or not. I have seen strawpiles larger than any we ever had at home, all carried off in an hours time for beds. When we stop to camp all of the houses around are visited by soldiers and every thing in sight of the eatable kind is *confiscated*. The boys have had no money to buy tobacco, but they have kept a pretty good

"It Was a Perfect Slaughter Pen"

supply on hand of the raw material which they twist up and use both for smoking & chewing.

The boys who are here from Chequest Valley are enjoying good health.

I guess that the recruiting officers who are at home will hardly raise many recruits from what they write. I would advise no one who has a notion to enlist to come to this, that is if we have to be run over the rough country like we have been.

I believe I will bring my letter to a close. Give my best respects to Uncle Sammy, Uncle Nide & Aunt Rachel and to all enquiring friends. Write often.

I remain your affectionate son,

Wm. H. H. Clayton

~

Forsyth MO.

February 22nd, 1863

Dear Parents:

I again take up my pen to write you a few lines.

I last wrote on the 14th from our camp a short distance below town.

The rest of our division left here on the 17th leaving the 19th & 2 companies of the 1st Iowa cavalry at this place. They are building 2 flat boats similar to the ferry boats on the Des Moines. I don't know what they are intended for unless it be to cross troops at some point below. We are staying here until the boats are finished, probably longer. One of them was launched a day or so ago. They are about sixty ft. long and 16 ft. wide. The division is camped about 40 miles N.E. of us and 20 or 30 from Springfield. There are none of the citizens to be found, nothing but soldiers & a few "Butternuts"[48] from the country are to be seen.

Where the former residents have gone or when they went, no one appears to know. Curtis remained here a short time last spring before he started to Helena. The court house, a square brick building two stories high, has three large holes in one side made by his cannon before he entered the place.[49] There is two tolerably nice stone houses here, or rather there was for since we came here we have fixed things to suit ourselves. All of the shelves have been taken to board up windows and for bunks, firewood, etc. Co. "H" occupies one which in out-ward appearance very much resembles Earharts store in Troy.[50]

When we moved here some of the companies preferred tents to going into houses and about half of the regt. is in tents, the balance in houses. There is but few houses standing and they are generally old ricketty concerns half torn down.

Teams have to go 3 and 4 day trips for forage. Some of our teams have just come in. One from our company brought in quite a lot of smoked meat so that we will have a more plentiful supply of "short-ening" for our biscuit. We soldiers have great times. I am sure that if some of the good cooks in your vicinity were to see us at times they would laugh at our attempts to get up big dinners. I have never yet suffered from hunger, nor have we ever been compelled to eat mule-meat as some of the boys have heard we did in their letters from home.

Once in a while when the roads are bad and it is impossible for supply trains to come up in time, we have been saving up for a few days, but that is more apt to do us good than harm. We have no reason to complain of provisions or clothing.

Today we had a turkey for dinner. We had no way of roasting it so we had a good dinner of *turkey pie*. The other day a peddlar came along from Springfield with a load of butter and sausage. It was after the division left so that we had a good chance to get a supply. He sold butter at 40 cts. per pound & sausage at 15 cts. per pound. He had a "nigger" boy driving for him and after he commenced selling out his butter at one end of the wagon that nigger thought he would sell sau-sage at the other for 10 cts. He would fill a tin plate heaping full, or if 20 cts. worth he would put it [the same amount] all on the plate. Our boys found out how he worked it and bought an indefinite number of 10 cts. worths. We got enough to do our mess of 16 two or three days at about 5 cts. per lb., cheap enough. Soldiers get pretty sharp and are always on the lookout for No. 1.

Well I believe I have scribbled enough at present and will stop "*pretty sudden*" as the fellow said. The boys from Chequest are all able for their rations at present.

Hoping these few lines may find you all as it leaves me, enjoying good health.

I remain ever your affectionate son,

Wm. H. H. Clayton

John & George, I want you to write as often as you can. I am always anxious to hear from *home*.

Forsyth MO.

March 15th, 1863

I have had 2 1 ct. stamps for a long time and can't get another so I sent them in this letter to pay postage on a paper or two.

Dear Father & Mother:

I have just received John's letter of Mar. 2nd and was *very* glad to hear from you all. It had been so long since I got a letter that I thought you had forgotten to write. I am glad to hear that you are all well. I forgot to say that I had received the papers you sent. Our mess made up $2.00 and sent for the "Missouri Democrat."[51] The first paper came last week.

This is a very *dry* place as far as news or excitement is concerned but we had a little sensation yesterday to arouse us from our lethargy. Our forage train was out and we were looking for it in yesterday. A messenger came in about noon and reported the train attacked about 20 miles from here. A force was immediately started to reinforce them. But the reinforcements had not got more than 5 or 6 miles out when they met the advance of our men coming in. The two parties were in line of battle for some time, and the "Feds" [Federals] kept advancing and the rebels fell back. Our boys gave them a volley or two and they skedaddled. There was about 400 rebels. With the train there was about 50 of the 19th and 75 cavalry. There was no one hurt on our side and it was not ascertained whether any of the rebels were or not. Blood was found on the ground they occupied so that something must have been hurt. The provision train from Springfield is coming in. It is 4 or 5 days behind time, but we had enough to keep us "chawing." We sometimes get the hardest crackers ever made, so hard that it is almost impossible to break them. But we make them "git." I am fond of the crackers when they are the right kind. We get half flour and half crackers. Plenty of sugar, a ration being about two table-spoons full a day. We do not use half the coffee we draw. We sell it at 40 cts. per pound. We get it ready for use, that is, it is browned.

"Uncle Sam" furnishes plenty for us to eat and if we were some place that we could buy vegetables etc. we would live finely.

The weather for the past week has been excellent. The ground is dry and in good order for plowing, but we see none of that kind of work going on. A detachment of men have been engaged for a week or two in getting out timber for a stockade around the court house. The balance of the regiment are kept for guard duty. There has been no drilling. Some of us have easy times doing nothing. The mail that came in today had got wet and a number of us boys had a *devil* of a time getting our stamps loose. Mine came out all right after a good soaking. Nearly all the stamps we get come from Iowa.

I suppose the boys enjoyed themselves finely at the parties. I would like very much to see the old place but cannot tell when I will see it. I enjoy myself well and would rather be here than at home while the present state of things lasts. I want the boys to write often. I am always glad to get a letter. Give my respects to all my friends. Nothing more at present.

I remain your affectionate son,
Wm. H. H. Clayton

~

Forsyth MO.
March 26th, 1863
Dear Uncle & Aunt:

I take up my pen this evening for the purpose of writing a few lines to you. I have been thinking of writing for some time past, but not having anything of importance to communicate I neglected doing so.

You will see by the heading of my letter that we are still in the same old place, where we have been for the past two months. We have been holding the "*post*" here during the time mentioned, but once or twice have thought of "driving it in the ground" and leaving but have not done so as yet. In one of my letters home a short time ago I mentioned that our forage train was attacked by the rebels and although three times as many in number as our men, they retreated after our men gave them one volley.

The commander at Springfield hearing that there was a force marching upon this place sent down a reinforcement of about 200 men of the 13th Kansas infantry & 4 field pieces. They remained here a few days and then returned to Springfield, forage being so scarce in this part of the world that it is impossible to keep a battery here. Things quieted down until a few days ago, when a couple of suspicious looking fellows came around examining things and were caught in trying to get through the pickets after dark. They immediately were put under guard, and one of our *Union* butternuts[52] with them. During the night this fellow by playing secesh got out of them, that they were *spies* and were to get $300 apiece for coming here to find out our numbers and position and report them to the rebel commander at Yellville on the morning of the 24th and then it was their intention to attack us with 5000 men and some artillery. Nearly the whole regiment was set to work erecting breastworks.[53] A number of log houses were torn down and the logs piled up and a long line of breastworks was put up in short order. We worked at them yesterday and the day before. Today the usual quiet reigns in camp, there being only a few men at work putting on the *finishing touch.*

I apprehend no attack here at the present time anyhow for we have reinforcements within a day or two's march, and they will never attack us unless they have five or six times as many as we have.

A large number of Union refugees are here or have passed through here going north. Last Sunday 20 Union men came in. They are recruits for an Arkansas regiment being made up at Fayetteville, one of them an old man 57 years of age had been shot through the left shoulder by the bushwhackers a short time before they came away. The most of them had been lying out in mountains for a good while to escape being taken to the [Confederate] army. Several of them were *conscripts*[54] and were with Hindman at Prairie Grove. Hindman's army was completely demoralized at that fight. One of these men said that all in the regiment he belongs to deserted, except 3 men.[55] They also say that Hindman had 32 regiments in that engagement. We fought them in that long-to-be-remembered fight from 10 o'clock A.M. until 4 P.M. with only 6 regiments. Blunt then came in with 3 or 4 more regiments and we cleaned them out.

We have witnessed some painful things here. Members of families have passed through going north. They generally have cattle yoked to their old ricketty wagons, and often they are driven by women or very small boys, the father being either in some of the Missouri regiments, killed by the bushwhackers, or conscripted into the rebel army. To see women trudging along through the mud, poorly clad, and driving ox teams or as I saw in one instance when five women came from Arkansas all walking, two or three of them carrying infants in their arms and several children beside about "knee high to a duck" (they were hardly old enough to walk). Some of the women carried a few articles such as tin buckets etc. and the balance of their property was packed on an old grey horse. The "secesh" had taken everything from these women because their husbands had enlisted in the Union Arkansas regiment. Such sights make the blood boil and to make a person come to the conclusion that there is no punishment severe enough for those scoundrels who have brought about the present state of affairs by their taking up arms against the best government that this world has ever seen. There is another thing that "kinder gits" [kind of gets] us, that is the action of a set of men in the North who are blind to their own interests and are endeavoring to *kick up a fuss* in even our own state of Iowa.[56] Would to God that some of the leading copperheads[57] were compelled to come down to this region and if they had to live here six months I think it would cure them and they would be content to go home and stay there and let the government take its own course in putting down the rebellion. One consolation is that they find little sympathy in the army and I assure you that some of them would be roughly used if they were where the soldiers could get hold of them.

The 19th adopted a series of resolutions a short time ago assuring the people of Iowa and all others that we give the government our undivided support. We enlisted for the purpose of aiding in putting down this infernal rebellion and we intend to do so. I have heard a number of the regiment express their views in regard to these northern *traitors* for they are nothing else and always there is ten times the hatred towards the northern traitors there is to those who are in arms against us.

We have two new recruits in our company who came from Texas.[58] They came in and desired to enlist and were taken in our company.

Today 5 more came in and have enlisted in another company. Part of them have been in the rebel service. The rebels are conscripting in

"It Was a Perfect Slaughter Pen"

Arkansas, and numbers will doubtless be compelled to go who would rather be on our side.

We have had excellent weather for 3 weeks past. Part of the time it was nearly warm enough for summertime, the ground was dry and in good order for plowing but there is none of that kind of work going on in this vicinity. The grass is coming along nicely, and the woods are beginning to put on their coat of green.

Peach trees are out in blossom. There has been a few cold mornings lately but I think not cold enough to kill the peaches.

The past winter has been very favorable as far as cold weather is concerned, to us soldiers. I have not seen the ground froze more than 2 or 3 inches during the winter. I believe I have scribbled enough for one time and will bring my letter to a close.

Uncle Nide, I know your dislike of writing but I want you to write me a letter if it is ever so short. If Uncle Sammy Clayton is at your house tell him to write also. I send my best respects to him. Tell the folks at home that I am all right. "Nincy" and Ab. Buckles are well.

Hoping this will find you as it leaves me, in the enjoyment of good health.

I remain ever your affectionate nephew,

Wm. H. H. Clayton

P.S. I suppose that Lt. Ferguson has reached home before this time. Tell him that Lt. Sommerville[59] has been and is yet very sick. Disease typhoid fever. He was taken to a private residence about 3 miles up the river a week or two ago. Also that our devil Bill Hartson has come to the company.[60] All quiet on White River at the present.

Forsyth, MO

April 5th, 1863

Dear Brothers:

I again seat myself to write a few lines.

I received George's letter yesterday, also one from Harris Neal, both mailed March 26th.

I was glad to see the improvement in the writing and the *length* of your letter, for I assure you it is much more pleasant to peruse a long letter than one which occupies but a minute time. When you write I

Captain George Sommerville, 1864.
Courtesy of the Lincoln Memorial Shrine Collection.

George Washington Clayton (left) and John Quincy Adams Clayton, 1862.
Courtesy of the Lincoln Memorial Shrine Collection.

would like for both of you to try your hand and fill up a *big* sheet, no matter what with, anything from home is interesting to me. I received a paper you sent, a short time ago.

I think I have received all the letters you have written. I was a little disappointed in not getting any stamps in my last letter from you but if there was none to be had, of course I could not expect you to send any. All that the boys get come from home. There is none for sale anywhere in this region. The demand is so great that it is impossible to keep them on hand in Springfield.

I was glad to hear that Lt. Ferguson had arrived home safely. I wrote a letter to him as soon as I heard that he had left Springfield for home. I had not heard from Brinsons for a long while. I believe I will write to Dan soon and get John's address.

I had a letter from cousin Mary Lighthill on March 9th. She stated that Jennie[61] would write to you soon and I suppose has done so in this time. She said that George Smith had got home but did not say whether he was discharged or not, but I expect he is. It is *no foolish* job to get a *discharge*. If a fellow gets right sick in hospital at Springfield they try to keep him there until he dies. So I am informed by boys who have been there a good while. They say that surgeons get $10.00 a head for all that die, I suppose to cover the expenses of burial, and therefore the more that die the better it is for them. 7 of our boys were discharged last month, some of them had been in hospital for 3, 4, and some 6 months, and some who were wounded at Prairie Grove were also discharged.

John Stone returned to the company from Springfield a day or two ago. He looks as well as I ever seen him at home.

Everything is quiet at this place. The 1st Division, Army of the Frontier, has moved down to Arkansas, it is at Carrolton at present. Our forage train came in today, having been out on a five days trip. The train from Carrolton joined ours somewhere down there and foraged together. They had some artillery along. They ran into a band of 400 rebels & scattered them, taking a number of prisoners.

A supply train passed through here today going to the 1st Division. I got into a conversation with one of the drivers, and found him to be Hannible Robinson, one of William Robinsons sons.[62] He left home last fall and went to Kansas. He there commenced driving a team for "Uncle Sam" and has been so engaged for the last 5 months. He says that Jake Moyer[63] enlisted in the 10th Kansas regiment and was discharged. He has since been driving a government team and is now with the 1st Division. John[64] is in the 12th Kansas infantry. Pete[65] belongs to an artillery company stationed at *Fort Scott*.[66]

The drums are now beating for roll-call (8 P.M.) and I will have to stop awhile.

"It Was a Perfect Slaughter Pen"

Well roll-call is over. I went downstairs and the first name called was "*Sergeant* Clayton." I did not know anyone in the company with such a given name and did not, at first, know who was meant but after the orderly had called it several times and no one answering it I came to the conclusion it must be me, 3rd Sergeant Russell[67] was discharged last week and I take his place. My appointment was altogether unexpected to me.

Today a citizen came in who had been shot in the shoulder. He and another person were fired on by bushwhackers, one was killed and this one wounded. It happened only 6 or 7 miles from here up the river. The wounded man escaped to the river which he swam and came right in.

Since I have been writing a cavalry scout passed by. They are going to try to take in the gang who did this act. If they don't find them they will destroy all their property. And if any of them is caught they will never see daylight again.

A number of families came in with our train today. The secesh have driven all the Union men out and they are getting their families away as fast as they can. Some of these men are the *true grit*. There is 4 young men, who stay here, belong to two different families. The secesh killed their fathers and they have sworn revenge. They go out with the forage trains showing the places to get forage. They are a perfect terror to the "Rebs" down there and have no doubt made many a one bite the dust.

It is getting late and I will quit my scribbling. My writing table is *tottery* and you must excuse all writing from the army anyhow.

Give my best respects to all my friends. Hoping this will find you all as it leaves me, enjoying good health.

I remain ever your affectionate brother,

Wm. H. H. Clayton

~

Salem, Dent Co., MO

May 3rd, 1863

Dear Brothers:

With pleasure I take my pen, to again write you a few lines. I have received two letters from you since I wrote last. One was a short one and contained 2 stamps. The last was written April 12th and also contained 2 stamps. I received it while near Ozark, on this trip.

We have had a long march and for a *beginning* it has been rather hard on us. We left Forsyth on the 22nd of April.[68] All of our baggage was ordered off, several days before we left, we kept 5 days rations. Our train went to Springfield and on the 22nd we started for that place. We marched 20 miles the first day, arrived at Ozark about noon on the second day, here orders came for us to take another road, the one going east. Our train had left Springfield a day or two before and we were to go on and overtake it. We stopped about 3 miles from Ozark and staid over night. Started early next morning. A heavy rain came up, and made the roads quite muddy. Marched on until noon when we stopped a couple hours to rest. We have heard that our regimental and supply train was 6 or 8 miles ahead of us, we started on and kept going until about 10 o'clock at night when we got up with the train. The last 5 or 6 miles was up a small creek. The rain had swelled the streams and this creek was a good deal of trouble to us. We crossed it about 20 times in going 5 miles. Sometimes it was over boot-top deep but the boys did not mind it and just waded through. Started next morning April 25th. Just as we moved off it commenced raining and rained nearly all morning. The roads were very muddy but we made about 12 miles and camped. We pitched tents the first time since we left.

Started again the next morning. Our regiment was ahead of the 9th Wisconsin[69] and our teams were ahead of theirs. The first 5 or 6 miles were almost impassable. Every team to its own way through the brush and over hillsides for it was impossible to keep the road, afternoon we got into a different sort of country and the roads improved very much. We reached Hartsville[70] about dark. Just as we got there it commenced raining and it poured down for awhile. Co. "H" took refuge in a blacksmith shop, we spread our blankets and were soon sound asleep. Next morning the creek that we had to cross was almost swimming high to horses. We put up our tents and thought that we would get to rest that day. "Old Wier"[71] had a detail made to fix a way to cross and the creek having fallen a foot or more we were ordered to march. We crossed two good sized streams on foot logs. The teams forded, the water running into the wagon beds. The 9th Wisconsin was stuck in the mud beyond Hartsville and the 19th was by itself. Hartsville is the place that Marmaduke attacked last winter after he was driven from Springfield.[72] The court-house has a number of cannon-ball holes through it. Next morning the 28th we started again and made about 12 or 14 miles. This evening the 9th came up. They started on ahead the next morning and the 19th was ordered to wait for the supply train, which was still behind. We waited until afternoon and started, the train being still behind. Marched 16 miles by night, camping on Big Piney. The roads were very good this day or we would not have been able to make it. The army regulations say that troops shall not be marched over 15 miles a day unless circumstances require it. But we are not controlled much in that respect by regulations. We generally go as fast and far as we possibly can go.

April 30th Started this morning passing through Houston, Texas Co. This is not much of a place. A portion of the 3rd Iowa cavalry were here all winter.

Camped in the evening about 8 miles from Houston. Passed through some rough country here, a good deal of pine growing in this section.

May 1st Marched about 17 miles today. It rained on us for the last 4 miles, wetting us thoroughly. Arrived at this place yesterday. It is quite a place and about 25 miles from Rolla. I expect that we will probably go there.

This is about the longest march we have had yet that is to go right along. We have come 150 miles and been on the way for 12 days past.

We passed some good farms between Ozark and Hartsville. I noticed a good deal of corn was planted. Fall grain looks fine in this part of the world.

I do not know what our destination is at present, but I think that we will stay in Missouri. Take it all together this has been a hard trip on us, marching so hard in the start it used our feet up. I had to ride one day on account of sore feet.

We have not been paid off, yet the paymaster was at Forsyth several days before we left. He spent 3 or 4 days in paying 5 or 6 companies of cavalry and we had to come off without the "spondulicks."[73] I think we will be paid soon, we will get four months pay and maybe 6 months.[74]

Well I must close. The boys are all well. Hoping that you will write often.

I remain your affectionate brother,

William H. H. Clayton

P.S. The boys are laying around in the tent joking and laughing and I would have to join once in a while so that I could hardly get my ideas together long enough to write a sentence. You must therefore excuse all mistakes.

I will write soon again.

⟿

Camp of the 19th Iowa near Salem, MO

Sunday, May 10th, 1863

Dear Father & Mother:

With pleasure I take my pen for the purpose of writing you a few lines. I wrote to the boys a few days ago and gave them an account of our march to this place. I also wrote Uncle Sammy a day or two ago, I got a letter from him which was very gladly received.

We are getting along finely since we came here. We got 4 months pay on the 3rd of this month. Ab. Buckles and two others from our company got furloughs and are at home, I expect before this time. I sent $40 home with Abner, keeping $12. Enough to do me until next pay day.

The boys have been living highly since pay-day. The sutlers are doing a big business and can hardly keep a stock on hand. They sell at exorbitant prices, but the boys don't care for expenses. They have been kept away out in the southern part of Missouri almost out of hearing of civilization and are going to make up some of their lost time.

Yesterday we drawed quite a lot of good potatoes, also dried apples & peaches and some nice white fish. Tomorrow we get cabbage, pickles, and some other articles. We have never drawn any of the above named articles from the quartermaster dept.[75] before. We get butter occasionally from the citizens and can buy canned honey from the sutler. We have plenty of everything to eat except meat. We sometimes get out of meat but if there is none to be had at the commissaries, we do as we did a day or two ago. 5 or 6 got after a good hog that would weigh over 2 hundred and run it down (we are not allowed to shoot

"It Was a Perfect Slaughter Pen"

them), skinned it and we have had plenty of meat and plenty of grease for biscuit.

Once in awhile Mooney makes us some "salt rising" bread. He can makes as good bread as I ever eat.

We were much elated at the good news from Hooker's army for a day or two but do not like to hear of his falling back across the Rappahannock.[76] It may be for the best but looks too much like a defeat. We still have confidence in him and think that he has given them a blow that they will not recover from soon. We have yesterday's paper and it appears that Grant has commenced in the neighborhood of Vicksburg.[77]

I hope that something will be done this summer to shorten the days of the rebellion.

We will be apt to stay here for some time, our teams are run down and it will take a good while to get them in order. This country does not afford much forage. Baled hay and large quantities of grain in sacks are brought from Rolla. It is only about 25 miles to Rolla and we can get the news, that is published in St. Louis one day, on the next day.

We had some very cool weather a day or two ago. There was quite a frost the other morning. It has got quite warm today.

We can get stamps here so that you need not send any more until we get where they are not to be had. I have not had much of importance to write so I will quit.

You will be apt to see "Buck"[78] and get all the particulars from him.

I want the boys to write as often as they can conveniently. The last letter was dated April 12th. I got a Dollar Times a day or two ago.

Give my best respects to Uncle Nide and Aunt Rachel and to all friends.

Hoping that these lines may find you all as it leaves me, in good health.

I remain ever your affectionate son.

Wm. H. H. Clayton

~

Camp of the 19th Iowa Inft.

Near Salem, Dent Co., MO

May 13th, 1863

Dear Brothers:

With pleasure I take Pen to write a few lines in answer to your welcome letter of May 3rd, which was mailed on the 7th and received yesterday.

I was very glad to hear that you were all well at home and getting along so finely with the work.

Having written once since we came to this place, I have nothing of much importance to write today.

There has been no movements of troops in this vicinity since we came here. The train of the 2nd Division, Army of the Frontier, passed through here a few days ago on its way to Pilot Knob. Part of the division is there having gone there when Marmaduke made his late raid.[79] The balance of the division, the 20th Iowa infantry and 26th Indiana, are at St. Louis and will go to that place on the [Saint Louis &] Iron Mountain railroad.

All of our teams started to Rolla this morning. It is the intention to get good mules in place of those that are *used up* and to get everything again in complete order.

I think we will remain here a week or two and perhaps longer. I suppose that you have seen A. J. Buckles and heard from him more particulars than I can write. I sent $40 home with him. I want to get a *gum blanket*[80] and don't know how, unless he will buy one at St. Louis on his return to the regiment. I wish father would see him and if Buckles will go to the trouble let him have 5 dollars to purchase one with. I think one can be bought in St. Louis for $2.50 or $3.00. But it may cost more. Lt. Sommerville thought for a time that he would have to [go to] St. Louis but he has altered his notion. 18 or 20 of us gave him money to get us blankets but as he did not go we got our money back again. They are light to carry and keep a person dry if he is in the rain all day. I want one about 6 feet by 4 ft. with brass eyelets around the edges to fasten it with.

If Mother has a pair or two of socks that she can send to me they will be very acceptable. The socks we draw are poor things and are hardly worth drawing.

"It Was a Perfect Slaughter Pen"

I suppose that there is a very large emigration to California from what you and others write.[81]

Nearly all of the boys know old Crans Allen[82] and think that the county is doing well to get rid of him. We have a great dislike of men of his stamp.

We have had very pleasant weather since we came here until yesterday evening. It commenced raining and rained all night. I was and am yet on duty as sergeant of the patrol guard. It was so wet and disagreeable that I took the guard off until this morning.

We are very anxious to get the news today, we could get no paper yesterday. The rumor is current that our flag floats over the Rebel capitol. We hardly know whether to credit it or not. I hope it is so but it is almost too good news to be true.[83]

I answered Uncle Sammy's letter a day or two ago. I also wrote to cousin Lizzie Cooper. I have had no letter from any of them for some time.

Well, I must quit writing for the present. Hoping that this will find you all as it leaves me, enjoying the best of health. I remain

Your affectionate brother,

William H. H. Clayton

~

Camp of the 19th Iowa Inft.

Salem, MO

May 30th, 1863

Dear Brothers:

I received your letter of May 22nd (mailed on the 25th) today and was really glad to hear from you again.

I had written several times and had almost got out of patience, waiting for an answer.

The mail comes in every evening and goes out every morning. I have been watching for a letter every evening since the time that a letter would be due after Buckles got home.

I got a letter from Lizzie Cooper on the 18th. She wrote that all were well, excepting Aunt Agness. They have no hopes of her recovery.

George Smith's wound prevents his working at his trade, and he had started down the river on a coal-boat going as cook.

I will not send any money home this time. We may not get paid so promptly the next time, and if I should happen to get a furlough I will want a little to pay traveling expenses, but I make no calculations on going much before fall or winter.

Nothing much has transpired to mar the monotony of camp life since I last wrote, and have not got much of importance to communicate, except that we were paid two months pay on the 23rd. We are now paid up to May 1st. I received $29.45, one month and a few days pay as a private, the balance as a sergeant. The pay of sergeant is $17.00 per month, $4.00 more than a private.

I came off duty today at noon, as sergeant of picket guard.

The 19th furnishes guard for 3 posts. All that I had to do was visit the different posts once during the day, the balance of the time I remained in camp.

We get daily St. Louis newspapers every morning. The news from Vicksburg so far appears favorable, but I am fearful of something happening yet that will prevent our forces taking the place. It is so strongly fortified that it will require time to reduce it, and the rebels will be apt to send an army, and attack our forces in the rear. I hope that it will be taken. Its fall would greatly discourage the Rebels and encourage us.

We have had very pleasant weather, rather warm during the day but very cool at night.

It has been showery for a few days past. It is raining while I write. Quite a number of ladies from Iowa have visited the regt. since we came here. They are generally the wives of officers. Lt. Col. Kent and Capt. Richmond have both had the pleasure of seeing their wives at this place. They departed a few days ago, after remaining a week or more. A person can make no calculations in regard to anything that he wants to do, while in the army. Therefore I have made no calculations on getting a furlough. The capt. says that he will promise no more until the time comes for them to go, so that we are not yet certain who goes when Buckles & the others return. I know that I will not go the next time.

Give my respects to all friends. My love to all.

I remain your affectionate brother,

W. H. H. Clayton

"It Was a Perfect Slaughter Pen"

CHAPTER 4

❝ *Vicksburg Is Ours* ❞

In November 1862, Major General Ulysses S. Grant, Commander of the Department of the Tennessee, had embarked on a campaign to capture Vicksburg, Mississippi, the northernmost post still held by the Confederates on the Mississippi River. After a number of failures, Grant finally found a viable strategy in the spring of 1863. Marching his force down the west bank of the river to a point south of Vicksburg, he then had his troops ferried across to the Mississippi shore. In a brilliant campaign, Grant defeated Confederate forces in detail, then laid siege to the city. Needing more troops both to keep the defenders of Vicksburg penned up and to prevent them from receiving reinforcements, Grant convinced the War Department to send Union regiments from a number of separate commands to support him.

One such regiment was the 19th Iowa. Clayton and his compatriots helped slowly tighten the noose around Vicksburg and celebrated the surrender of the city on July 4, 1863. His regiment then participated in an excursion deeper in Mississippi before being transferred to a camp just north of New Orleans.

In the twelve letters Clayton wrote during this period, he shows quite different extremes of the wartime experience of a Union soldier. While in the trenches at Vicksburg, Clayton faced the ever-present danger of sniper fire and Confederate artillery barrages. Moving against the Confederate garrison at Yazoo City likewise put Clayton in a situation fraught with danger. But life at Port Hudson or Carrollton seems almost like a paid vacation for the twenty-three-year-old Iowan. Whether under fire or enjoying the charms of New Orleans,

Clayton demonstrates in his letters that he has lost none of his ability to provide accurate and interesting descriptions of his adventures.

∾

St. Louis
June 5th, 1863
Dear Father & Mother:
You will be apt to be a little surprised at seeing the heading of my letter.

We have just arrived and the regiment is now on the wharf ready to go on a boat. The 94th Illinois is also here and will leave with us. The 20th Wisconsin has gone. This is all of the infantry belonging to the 3rd Division. The artillery and cavalry remained where they were. I have just seen Buckles. We met him and Lt. Kent[1] and the other boys here.

We left Salem on the 3rd having received orders the night before, about 9 or 10 o'clock. The 1st Division is still at Salem, consisting of the 9th Wisconsin and the 10th & 11th Kansas.

I am unable to say what our destination is, probably Vicksburg. Some think that we may stop this side at some place left vacant by troops who have gone forward. We will know in 4 or 5 days more.

We left Rolla about 5 o'clock last night and got here between 2 and 3 this morning. Buckles got a gum blanket for me, gave $2.75 for it. Some of the boys paid $5.00 for one like it, at Rolla. He also handed me the little package. Socks I think. I have not had time to open it yet. I am glad to get them for we can draw none worth having.

I will write as soon as I can again.

This leaves me in good health and hope will find you all the same.

I remain your affectionate son,
Wm. H. H. Clayton

∾

On board steamer *H. Choteau*
June 8th, 1863
Dear Father & Mother:
I thought that I would write a few lines today, and have them ready for mailing at Memphis. I wrote a few lines while at St. Louis inform-ing you that we was coming down the river. We left St. Louis last

Friday evening in company with the 94th Illinois on the steamer *Minnehaha*. The river between St. Louis and Cairo is tolerably low and the boats laid by during the night time.

On Saturday morning arrived at St. Genevieve just as two steamers pushed off loaded with troops. We learned here that 5 or 6 regiments had gone on. Took on Battery "B" 1st MO artillery, 6 brass guns. In the evening arrived at Cape Girardeau. Laid a few miles below town all night.

On Sunday morning started after daylight. Had to go slow on account of low water. Got to Cairo about 9 o'clock A.M. Things looked considerably warlike here, piles of heavy cannon lying on the wharf and U.S. transports and gun-boats anchored in the stream. We remained there until after dark last night on the waters of the Ohio, the difference in the color of the water is plainly visible. The deck-hands were busy all day taking on coal. The *Minnehaha* got ready and left a good while before dark.

A regiment or two of troops came in on the railroad and camped above town. They were part of Burnsides army, 7,000 or 8,000 were expected there yesterday.[2]

We left about 10 o'clock last night and were below Columbus [Kentucky] this morning at daylight. We passed Island No. 10 this morning. Quite a number of troops were on the island. It is right in a bend of the river, and its situation and appearance were well described by newspaper correspondents during the long contest between our forces and the Rebels here.[3] The island has steep banks and is of the same height as the land on the Kentucky side.[4] On the other side the land is low sand bar for some distance. It looks as though the river once all ran on the Missouri side, and that it had filled up and the river broke across on the Kentucky side, cutting off the island.

We have been making good headway all morning and will be apt to get to Memphis this evening. Corn in some places along the river looks fine and covers the ground. Wheat is ready for cutting all along the river, between St. Genevieve and the cape a good deal had been cut, and the shocks were standing thickly over the ground.

The boat shakes so that I can hardly write and don't know whether you can read it or not. I have nothing more of interest to write at this time and will close.

I am well, and hope that this will find you all the same. All of the boys are well.

Your affectionate son,

W. H. H. Clayton

P.S. When you write, direct to 19th Iowa Vol. Infantry via St. Louis, MO. Direct in that way at present. The letter *would* come without the name of any particular place being mentioned. When letters get to St. Louis they are sent to the 19th, wherever it may be.

~

Young's Point, Louisiana

June 12th, 1863

Dear Father & Mother:

We have at last got in sight of the Gibralter of the West.[5] We arrived here yesterday morning, that is we got to the mouth of the Yazoo River at that time. There was 12 or 14 boats in the fleet that came down with all loaded with troops. We all went up the Yazoo about 12 miles, to Sherman's Landing.[6]

We remained there an hour or two & then 5 or 6 of the boats returned, and came to this place, about 2 or 3 miles below the mouth of the Yazoo.

Vicksburg is in sight, across a big bend in the river. We can see the earthworks above the town. It is about 5 miles distant.

Our mortar[7] boats lay about 2 miles below here, and fire across the bend into the town. They fired a good deal last evening. After dark we could watch the shells in their flight to the Rebel strong hold.

We heard heavy firing back of town last evening and early this morning. The reports of musketry could be distinctly heard. We don't know how it resulted.

There is a force on this side of the river some 10 or 12 miles back. They had a fight a short distance above here last Sunday. There was but [a few] of our men on this side, and they were badly cut up by the enemy who greatly outnumbered them.[8] Had they been so inclined they could have taken everything here, but they was afraid that they would find the gun-boats if they came too close. There is 6 or 8 regiments here now. We were ordered to have two days rations in our haversacks this morning. It is uncertain where we move from here.

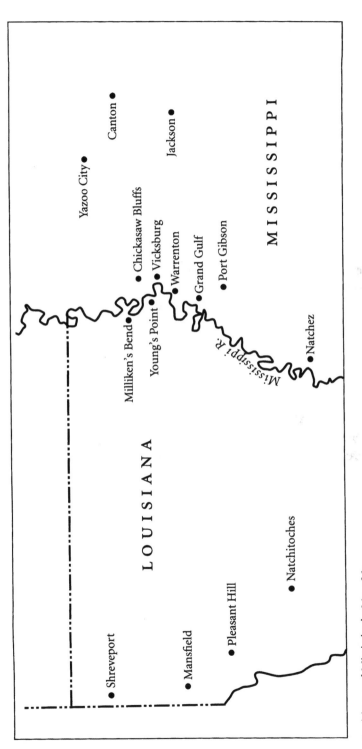

Louisiana and Mississippi, 1863–1865.

We may go down across the bend & cross to Warrenton and get in the rear of Vicksburg on our left.

While I write the boom of cannon is heard, at intervals.

Several boats had been fired into on their way down, but we came without interuption. We are laying now on a large plantation. Every thing is destroyed. The levee runs along between us and the river. It is 10 or 12 ft. high.

The famous canal to get around below Vicksburg starts across about a mile below here.[9] I have not seen it yet.

The water here is bad and there will be apt to be considerable sickness here before long. All the boys you are acquainted with are well. Abs. Nincehelser, Ab. Buckles, John Stone, and George & Joe Paxton are here. We saw several boys from the neighborhood of Troy at Helena, they belonged to 3rd Iowa Cav. Ras. Tadlock, and Grinstead's son and others. Dan Bell [was] taken prisoner by the Rebs some time ago.[10] He was taken by them to Little Rock and had not got back when we passed there. The situation here is about the same as it has been for some time past. Our forces are closely investing it and we have them in a tight place.

I saw two confederates this morning who had left Vicksburg last night. They swam the river and came to our picket post this morning. They say that they got tired of staying there and determined to escape. They say that provisions are getting tolerably scarce there. The bread is a mixture of cornmeal and peas. They also say the large bombs from the mortar boats have not killed many persons yet but that they tear things up like ever thing where they light. I know that if one would light near any body it would be apt to hurt him. Last night we could see the shell from the time it left the mortar until it fell in the town and then would see it burst.

Our boats are not near unloaded yet. The greater part of the artillery is off. Well I must soon quit writing. It is reported that no letters are allowed to leave, but I will try to get this off. We may get to someplace where we cannot send letters at all.

Give my respects to all. Write often.

Your affectionate son,

W. H. H. Clayton

~

Camp of 19th Iowa Infantry
In the rear of Vicksburg
June 18th, 1863
Dear Father & Mother:

Having a few spare moments, I thought that I would improve them by writing and give you an account of our movements since leaving Young's Point, LA. at which point I last wrote.

We left there on the 12th, marching across the bend, and reached the river 3 or 4 miles below Vicksburg and in full view of the town.

We have 5 or 6 steamboats below Vicksburg that are used for carrying troops, supplies, etc. across to Warrenton. Some of these run the blockade and are pretty well used up. The *Forest Queen* is a nice sidewheel boat, the others are stern-wheelers. The ram *Switzerland* was there and is as good as ever. When running the blockade a ball passed into one of her boilers and let the steam out in a hurry but did no other damage.[11] Several gunboats are stationed there to watch the river. The *Tuscumbia* [12] is a large boat and looks like a large turtle with its back out of water.

We crossed to Warrenton 6 or 8 miles below Vicksburg, on the *Silver Wave*. Her guards [13] had been nearly all torn off some how and was a hard looking boat.

At Warrenton we remained over night. Here I saw 3 large guns that were captured by our forces at Grand Gulf.[14] They are having them brought up and will soon have them planted opposite some of the Rebel forts here. The Rebels had a pretty strong earthwork at Warrenton & places fixed with railroad iron and logs to protect the men. All is destroyed now.

We first used our shelter tents at Warrenton. They do well enough to keep off the sun but will not turn much rain. Each tent is composed of two pieces about 3 yards square and is for two men each of whom carries his piece and one pole each about 4 ft. long, when the two pieces composing it are put together. When we pitch tents we button the two pieces together, fix the "sticks" in the center and stake down two ends. The sides are open and permit the air to circulate freely! [15]

On the 13th we marched 3 or 4 miles towards our lines and camped that night. On the 14th we took our present position, to the left of the center. We are camped *under* a hill side, to shelter us from the Rebel shells which come over occasionally. It is not a mile straight across to the Rebel line. We, that is Co. "H" and 5 other companies of the 19th were on picket yesterday & last night.

We acted more as skirmishers than anything else. We were strung along behind logs and stumps and kept popping away whenever we would see a shadow of a Rebel, our guns with the sights raised to 300 yards would strike their outer works every time, some of their pickets were not more than 150 yards from us, but they had holes in the ground so that we would not see them and could only tell where they were by the smoke when they discharged their guns. The discharge of small arms is almost constant along the line, but they don't do much damage on either side. A fellow has to keep his head pretty low though, for some ball would whistle by, very close. Occasionally the heavy artillery takes a turn and makes things "git."

I and one of our boys yesterday, saw 5 or 6 "Rebs" on their works some distance off, and thought that we would see how close we could shoot to them. We raised [the gun sights] to 800 yards.[16] He shot and we could notice that one got out of that place in a hurry. I then shot at them standing all together in an embrasure[17] of a fort, the dust flew up close by them. It was not more than 2 minutes before *boom* went a gun and a shell came crashing over us. They fired three times but hit no one.

Our forces along this part of the line have advanced sevral hundred yards, and will be apt to go farther, not however without digging in on the right and center. Our boys are close under their guns, so close that they cannot fire them. Some of the 15th Iowa boys have been down to see their friends. They said that they had worked in the trenches not more than 20 yds. from their forts.

I expect the people of the North are getting impatient because Grant does not take Vicksburg, but if they were here for themselves they would not wonder at the delay. It is certainly the roughest country I ever seen. The hills are not so very high, but the whole country is nothing but a succession of hills and hollows about like some places on the Buckles farm.

The Rebels have forts thrown up about 200 or 300 yds. apart all along their line, with heavy guns mounted and forts in the rear of these, making the place almost impregnable. I do not believe that another place in the country could be found that is so naturally fortified. They had forts outside of our present lines that they evacuated, that would have been hard to take. The hills in places rise abruptly, and look almost as though they had been drawn up purposefully for a fort. The boys who have been here since the siege began appear to be in good spirits. They say that it will be almost [impossible] for Johnston[18] to get in with reinforcements. The timber has been cut down for miles and we have a large force on Big Black[19] watching him. I don't see what Pemberton[20] is holding out so long for. It looks almost impossible for reinforcements to reach him. I suppose he will hold out until his provisions give out, and that may be sometime longer. Deserters say that they are living on quarter rations. The weather here is right warm. The magnolia trees are in full bloom. There is lots of them in the woods. I saw some green figs a day or two ago. Peaches are nearly full size. The blackberries are ripe in this part of the world. Corn is out in tassel in places. I have not seen much around here but I suppose there is plenty of it growing further back.

I was a good deal surprised to see the cane here grow where it does. I always thought that grew in swamps or in the low grounds, but here it grows on the hills. Where we are camped it is thick, some of it 25 or 30 feet long.[21]

The boys are all well at present. I had an idea that the change would make us sick, but it has not made much of a difference in the sick list yet. John Stone is one of our company cooks. The cooks do nothing but get our "grub" ready for eating, have no other duty to perform. Mooney is cooking for the col. and captain. He is a very good hand at the business. There is a little insect that bothers us a great deal. They are called "jiggers," "chickers," or something like it.[22] They are little red things not bigger than a pin point. They stick like a tick and raise little places like muskuits[23] bites. As I expected the furlough business has *played out*, I suppose no more will be granted until after Vicksburg is taken.

Give my respects to all friends.

I remain your affectionate son,

W. H. H. Clayton

~

Camp of the 19th Iowa

In the rear of Vicksburg

June 28, 1863

Dear Brothers:

I received John's letter of the 7th a few days ago and was glad to hear from you again.

I have nothing of interest to write, but thought that I would send a few lines to let you know that I am well and getting along finely.

We have been here two weeks. Nothing of especial importance has transpired along our part of the line.

We have mounted several siege guns[24] since we came here. They fire on the Rebels occasionally and make them hunt their holes. The Rebels fired at us considerably for a few days after our arrival here but since then have not fired much, only when our guns opened upon them, and for some days past they fired none at all.

Yesterday however they opened on our battery from a mortar that they had planted under a hill so that our guns could not reach them. Our camp is in range of their shells and some that came over the battery made us lay "kinder" close. The pieces flew around considerably but luckily no one was hurt.

There has been no firing on either side today. It is said that our gun boats got range of the mortar that disturbed us and silenced it. I hope it is so for it is not pleasant to hear shells buzzing around. The blamed things are apt to burst and the pieces go every direction. We have been on picket 4 times since we came here. The last two times we were up or awake all night. One night it rained the whole night slowly. I tell you, I would not have taken a good deal for my gum blanket that night. We laid within a few hundred yards of a brigade of Rebels, so we have learned since from prisoners. There was nearly two companies of us, we were there to prevent a movement on our guns. The 94th Ill. and 20th Wis. have taken 20 or 30 prisoners since we came here by charging upon their (the Rebels) rifle pits. But such work don't pay. The last *sortie*[25] of this kind was by a company of the 94th. They took 8 men, and had one mortally wounded, he died an hour or two [later], and another wounded so that it will render him unfit for service. The Rebels could have the rifle-pit defended by eight more men, right away, for it was not held by our men. Thus by the operation we lost two men and the Rebels got rid of feeding 8. I think the more men we can keep in there, the sooner will it surrender. There is no telling anything about how long it will hold out. Some prisoners & deserters say that they have not got much provision and others that they have enough to last 2 or 3 months. There has been no mail received here for several days. It is reported in camp that letters from here do not go further than Memphis. I think if such was the case we would not be allowed to send them from camp.[26] I would like very much to hear how the Rebel raid into Pennsylvania terminated.[27] We [have] no news later than June 17th. It takes a letter at least 10 days to come from Iowa here. We are in as bad a position to get news as we were when at Forsyth away down in Missouri. It is 10 or 12 miles around our line[28] and we know no more what is going on at the other end of the line than you do. Sometimes it is reported that they have had a big fight on the right or in the center, and they have heard that we have had a battle here when there was nothing of the kind. We would like to get the St. Louis daily papers so that we could get news from Vicksburg!

The weather is very warm especially so in the sun. We lay around in the shade the most of the time when not on duty. The boys stand the change much better than I expected, but of course the sick list is larger than it was at Salem. Co. "H" has 47 men for duty, and 7 or 8 sick. The water here is not very good. We get it by digging 10 ft. It goes rather hard after being used to good spring water. The Chequest boys stand it "Bully" all being able for their rations.

There has been an oven erected here, and all our flour is baked and issued in loaves by the quartermaster. I like it much better than the biscuits our cooks make. I never did like hot or warm bread, but have had to get used to it, and sometimes glad to get anything in the bread line. We get half our bread rations in hard crackers.

Col. Kent was honored today by a visit from Mrs. Wittemeyer,[29] U.S. Sanitary Commission[30] agent, from Iowa. I suppose she is on a tour of inspection. Gen. Herron was also here today.

Well I must quit writing for the present. I want you to write whenever you can.

I remain your affectionate brother,

W. H. H. Clayton

VICKSBURG IS OURS

Vicksburg, Miss.

July 5th, 1863

Dear Father & Mother:

It is with great pleasure that I pen the following lines. Yesterday, the "*glorious* Fourth of July" was made doubly so, by the *surrender*, and *occupation* of this, the strongest rebel position in their Confederacy.

It was an event that we, and I suppose the whole Northern people, have been patiently waiting for, for months past, and what is better than all it fell without the necessity of storming the works and thus losing numbers of valuable lives.

We have *starved* them out, they held out until they could do so no longer, and they were compelled to come to terms.

I saw from the Keosaqua papers that there was to be celebrations on the Fourth at a number of places in the county, one being at Lebanon. I would have given anything almost if I could by some means, have been conveyed from here, there and given the joyful news. What a celebration there would have [been] had you only known the situation here. I imagine that copperheads would have looked down their noses and wish themselves hid from the gaze [of] exultant loyal people. My sincere wish now is, that Lee and his army may get the *devil* from Hooker [31] or someone else. I think that the Rebs would be about *played out*.

Hostilities ceased here on the 3rd before noon, they had hoisted a flag of truce. Negotiations were pending until the morning of the Fourth, when they surrendered.

I have not yet learned the terms. The prisoners are still in places they occupied yesterday morning. On the 3rd when firing ceased, our boys laid down their guns and went over to their rifle pits and forts and had quite a chat with them. It looked singular to see men, who but a few minutes previously were shooting at each other, mingle together and shake hands, and be as friendly, apparently, as brothers, but such is among the incidents of war.

Our batteries had been well supplied with ammunition and it was the intention to celebrate the Fourth on a *grand* scale, by shelling the town's 7 fortifications, but owing to the surrender only the National salute was fired, with blank cartridges.

We received orders, and at 9½ o'clock Ormes' brigade started for the inside of the fortifications. It was very hot and dusty and the march was very fatiguing. It is but a short distance from here to our old camp, but by the wagon road it is 2 or 3 miles. We are a mile or two from the town but as we are inside the works, considered that we are in Vicksburg, and began my letter accordingly. We received orders before we started in to *not cheer* or make any demonstration upon coming in. The Rebs were surprised at our conduct, and were as friendly as could be expected under the circumstances. Some of them are fine looking fellows, and some are very reasonable and admit that they are defending a bad cause. I have talked with a number that say they will fight no more if they can possibly help it. I was talking to one awhile ago close by an earthwork where our regimental flag was waving to the breeze. He said it looked better to him yet, than any other flag.[32] I have looked in vain for the Rebel flag (the stars & bars) but have not seen it *yet*. I have seen their battery flags flying at the different forts. That of Georgia is a red flag with two black stripes diagonally across it, another flag was white with a large spot in the center. I asked a fellow this morning what kind of flag they had, but he could not tell me, he said they had several kinds but could describe none.

If we had charged these works there would have been great loss of life, for they have an abundance of ammunition and the works command each other so that if one should be taken there is two or three others ready to open upon it. They say that we never could have taken the place if they had plenty of provision, but I think it would have been taken anyhow.

They acknowledge that we did as much work in a nights time building forts and digging rifle-pits as they could do in a week. They say that we are western troops or the place never would have been taken. They seem to think that eastern troops do not possess the valor of western troops. After we entered the works the gunboats above steamed down and each fired the National salute as she rounded to. A number of boats came down during the day, screaming and blowing around as though glad to once more pass the spot so long barricaded.

Numbers of the prisoners say that they have had but one biscuit a day, and a piece of meat about the size of a persons finger, twice a day

The Iowa State Monument on the Vicksburg Battlefield, dedicated on November 23, 1906, as it appears today. Photo by Danny Strickland.

for two weeks past. The meat gave out toward the last, and I have it from a number of them that they actually eat mule-meat. They say that if the place had not been surrendered when it was they would not have stood it much longer, but laid down their arms and refused to fight longer. We have made a *big* haul, from 20 to 30,000 prisoners, the same number stands of arms and *lots* of field artillery & heavy

Dugouts excavated by Union soldiers for protection during the siege of Vicksburg. Courtesy of the Old Courthouse Museum, Vicksburg.

guns,[33] and any quantity of ammunition for them. It has been the most glorious event of the war. I would not have missed being here for a good deal. Herron's command occupies the right of their defenses or the left of our army, being below town. I received a letter from Lizzie Cooper yesterday. All were well excepting Aunt Agness who was no better. She said that there was considerable excitement there in regard to the Rebel invasion, but that preparations were being made to give them a warm reception if they should make their appearance there. The boys are all well and are pleased to be present at the fall of Vicksburg.

Give my respects to all my friends.

Your affectionate son,

W. H. H. Clayton

P.S. As I write the poor devils are running around trading tobacco for bread or anything to eat. There is so many that it takes a long time to issue provisions to them. Our boys have given them all that we could spare. They have drawn tobacco since they came here & have plenty.

The 19th had but one man wounded during our three weeks stay here.[34] We have been lucky, were as much exposed as the other regiments that had some killed and wounded but we passed through without loss.

~

Camp of the 19th Iowa Inf.
Vicksburg, Miss.
July 10th, 1863
Dear Father & Mother:
I again write you a few lines from this place, having written to you on the 5th and give an account of our entrance to this place. I received George's letter of June 22nd on the 5th after my letter was sent off. I was glad to hear from you all again, and to learn that you were getting along so well with the work.

The troops here have been busily engaged since we came in here, at filling up our rifle-pits and other works used by us — the heavy guns we had mounted will be brought inside and placed in position.

The more the Rebel works here are viewed the stronger they appear and they have done but little work to make them so, for the foundation is naturally very strong. When we get heavy artillery mounted in place of the field artillery they had, and do other things that the "Yankees" can do the place will be absolutely impregnable against any attacking party. The only way to take such a place is to surround it and starve out the garrison.

The Rebs here say that we are not Yankees, but call us North Western men. They say that the real Yankees would never have taken this place. They seem to look upon the eastern troops with contempt and say that they can't fight. It is provoking and at the same time amusing to hear them talk, and it is surprising how ignorant some of them are. I have heard some say that the Yankees were a dwarfish race of people, inferior to both the Southern and Western people, another one appeared to think that they were all foreigners who came over and make their living by swindling & cheating, — "Why" — says he — "they would canvas blocks of wood, and send them down here and sell them for *canvassed hams*, and wooden nutmegs by the quantity. It was enough to make us fight & hate them." He also thought that these

Yankees were so plenty [in the] east, that they controlled the elections and had everything their own way.

I find that the reports in regard to the South given in our papers telling how the people were *deluded* and led into it by the leading men were true, many of them have told me that they did not fight with a good will. The reports about exorbitant prices is also true. I saw a watch bought for $4.00 Greenback.[35] It was a good looking watch, but had the crystal broken out. The fellow who owned it was offered $22.00 by one of his comrades in Confederate money. They pay 3 to 4 times as much for shoes, boots & clothing as we do.

The prisoners are all here yet. The greater part of them have been *paroled* or as they call it *pay*-rolled.

The taking of this place is the most important event of the war, and what makes it the more so is that the surrender and occupation took place on the glorious 4th of July.

Hereafter the 4th will be celebrated not only as the anniversary of the Declaration of Independence, but as the day on which Gen. Pemberton surrendered at Vicksburg, Miss.[36] His whole army of 32,000 men, 60,000 stand of small arms, and over 250 pieces of artillery, falling into the hands of the U. States forces under Gen. Grant. We have good news from Helena. It appears that Price & Co. got recently whipped there.[37] I got a letter from George Smith yesterday, the first for a long time. He is well. He wrote that they had exciting times in Pittsburgh in regard to the Rebel invasion. Aunt Agness continued to get worse, they have given up all hopes of her recovery.

The weather here has been very hot and dry. Last night, however we had a good rain. It is rumored in camp that we will move soon, some say to Port Hudson.[38] I don't know whether there is any reliance to be put in it or not. Our regiment have got possession of a set of instruments for a brass band. They belonged to a Georgia regiment.

I was through town last Sunday. I saw nearly all of the water batteries.[39] They are got up in good style and have heavy guns in them. A great many of the houses in town show the effects of the bombardment. I did not notice any blown to pieces. But pieces of shell and balls have passed through many.

All of the Chequest Valley boys are well. Our *squad*[40] has been fortunate, the majority of us have had but little sickness.

There is a good deal of sickness here, but few cases however, very serious.

I must close for the present. Give my respects to all friends.

I remain as ever your affectionate son,

Wm. H. H. Clayton

~

Camp of 19th Iowa Infantry

Yazoo City, Miss.

July 15, 1863

Dear Father and Mother:

I have the pleasure of writing to you from this, another *Rebel* city.

We entered the place night before last, the "Rebs" having *skedaddled* upon our approach.

When we received marching orders on the 11th it was the general supposition that we were bound for Port Hudson. We marched on board the steamer *Tecumseh* and remained, waiting for orders to start. In the afternoon, however, a vessel came up and brought the news of the *surrender* of Port Hudson.[41]

We now thought that our expedition was at an end, but we remained on board all night, and were ordered here. The expedition is composed of Herron's division, the old Army of the Frontier. On 6 or 7 transports and 3 gun-boats — the *DeKalb* is the only regular gun-boat, the other two being marine boats used to keep the river clear from guerrillas, they carry several cannon each — the *DeKalb* carried 13 guns.[42]

On the 12th we left Vicksburg and came up the Yazoo River, stopping over night some distance above Haine's Bluff.

Got under way at 3½ o'clock on the morning of the 13th. Passed slowly up the river which is very narrow. In places it looks more like a canal than a river and it is so narrow in places that two boats could not pass each other without running against the timber on either side. The banks are nearly *straight up and down* and the river is very deep. There has been a good deal of rain up this way and the river is up. The Mississippi at Vicksburg had risen several feet and was in good boating order. Along in the afternoon we arrived within a few miles of the town and the transports then stopped. The *DeKalb* passed up and fired a few rounds at the batteries. The Rebs replied but did no damage.[43] Awhile before night the 94th Ill. and the 19th were ordered ashore, the Rebels endeavored to burn a bridge across a swamp but our boys were *too* quick for them — drove them away and saved it.

The 94th passed on and after awhile reached town but found no opposition. The 19th had been stationed along the road on picket, and received orders after midnight to go up to town — about 3 miles. Yazoo City is quite a place — a large number of business houses and some splendid residences. There is bluffs back of the town that the Rebels had fortified and some heavy guns in position but as the infantry flanked them and was coming up in the rear they were obliged to leave. There were but few prisoners taken. A number came to our pickets and gave themselves up, about a hundred or so. We have been living well here — plenty of vegetables and *fruit*—such as peaches, apples, nectarines, a fruit resembling a peach, watermelons, etc. There is some excellent plantations on the river, planted principally in *corn*, which looks well as a general thing. Flour is a scarce item here among the inhabitants — a barrel is worth $160. The people are all secesh of the strongest kind but many of them think it useless to fight much longer. Buckles, Nincehelser, Stone, Mooney are here and in good health. I am well and hope this will find you all the same.

I remain your affectionate son,

Wm. H. H. Clayton

P.S. As the boat was leaving Vicksburg we received a mail. I got a letter from Cousin Mary Lighthill dated June 30th. She said that they had received no letter from you since Christmas — they were all well.

This paper on which I write was "captured" at this place.

〜

Vicksburg, Miss.

July 22nd, 1863

Dear Brothers:

In haste I pen these few lines in answer to your welcome letter of the 7th. I was glad to hear from you all again.

I last wrote to you from Yazoo City, 110 miles by water & 60 by land from this place.

We left there yesterday morning arriving here after dark last night.

We left the boat about noon today and are at present in our old camp where those who were unwell remained while we were gone. It is reported in camp that we go back on the boat yet this evening — destination uncertain — some say — down the river — I am sure that I do not know anything about it — this military business is a curious thing. The soldier never knows when he will be called on to go — nor where he will go to.

While at *Yazoo* we started out on a five day expedition toward Canton — we were gone 4 days — marching out 23 miles to Black River and back. We passed through the richest country we have ever seen yet. The plantations are numerous — the houses are all well built. Every plantation has its cotton gin & press attached.

The plantations are generally planted with corn — although we saw several large fields of cotton. Some of the corn is very good — in other places the soil is so worn out that corn will not do much. The soil all along the route, until Black River bottom was reached, is yellow clay with sand mixed. There is apparently no end to sweet potato patches. We got a large lot of cotton from the surrounding country, several hundred mules, and two boat loads of "contrabands," [44] besides other things too numerous to mention.

We lived finely while there — having plenty of peaches, apples, roasting ears, etc. The stock of preserved fruits & jellies and other good things belonging to some of the *Southern chivalry* [45] also contributed much to our comfort in the eating line.

The inhabitants seemed to have plenty of such stuff, but their breadstuff was not so plenty. Some of them have not had any flour for a year or more. It was worth $1.00 a pound up there. They have had no coffee at all for a long time. Well I will quit for the present and write more the next time when I am not in a hurry. Write often. Chequest boys all well.

Give my best respects to all.

I remain ever your affectionate brother,

W. H. H. Clayton

P.S. I will send a couple of papers — one *Rebel* and the other *Yankee* — published in Yazoo City.

Port Hudson, Louisiana

July 27th, 1863

Dear Brothers:

Seated on the ground, in my little *shelter* tent, I proceed to write a few lines to you.

I wrote last at Vicksburg on the 22nd after our return from the *Yazoo* — informing you that we were again under marching orders.

Accordingly on the 24th we again marched to the river — this time taking our transportation and everything with us.

The 19th got aboard the steamer *Sunny South* and steamed down to Warrenton 6 or 7 miles below. We here awaited the arrival of the balance of the fleet so that we all could start out in the morning in regular order. There is 13 boats altogether, and when under way, keep 50 to 100 yds. distance between each of the boats.

Early on the 25th the fleet started, we saw nothing worthy of notice, except occasionally one of the gunboats which patrol the river to keep its banks rid of guerrillas.

After noon awhile we passed Natchez, we could not see much of the upper town. We did not stop but continued on to this place arriving here before daylight.

We are, at present, encamped below the place on the river bank. We are awaiting orders. Gen. Herron went down below yesterday and upon his return, which will probably be today or tomorrow, we expect to again embark and go down, probably to *New Orleans*.

Our final destination is not known, but there is, as usual, all sorts of rumors. One is that we are going to Mobile, another, that we go to Galveston, Texas. There is no very large force of the enemy in this vicinity at the present so that our service is not needed here.

One thing about this movement looks curious to me, that is, all of the sick who were able to travel were brought along. It may be all right, but I always thought that the sooner our sick were sent *north* the better it was for them.

The health of our company & regiment continues better than it could be expected, considering the change of climate, water, etc. Captain Richmond has been sick for 2 or 3 weeks, he is not bedfast, but does not appear to mend much. Four of the company were left at

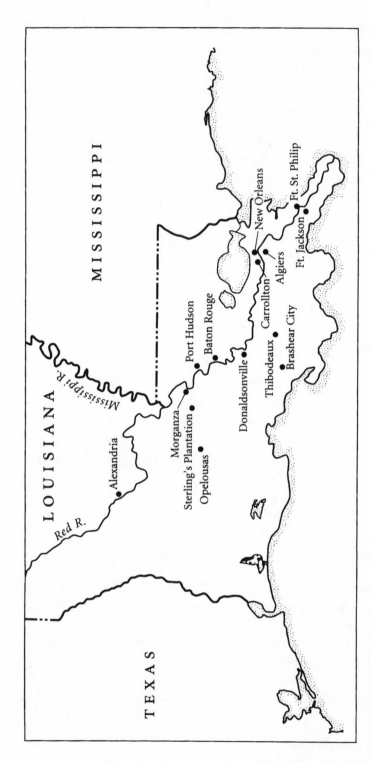

Louisiana, 1863–1864.

Vicksburg, among them George Paxton. He has been sick for some time. The 38th Iowa started down the river when we did. They were 800 or 900 strong, they had been doing garrison duty the most of the time previous and have had no marching or other hard service to perform. The regiment cannot now muster 100 men for duty, the balance being sick with fever, ague, diarrhoea, etc.[46]

For myself, I can say that I have had better health than I had in Missouri and so far have stood it well, but if I had my *choice* I would prefer a *cooler* climate. Well, I sometimes think that this thing will soon run itself out, and that we each can go wherever we please. I hope the time will soon come. The chivalry around Yazoo City seemed to be much discouraged by the fall of Vicksburg and all seemed anxious for the war to cease.

Be good boys and write as often as you can.

I will write frequently as I can let you know of my whereabouts. Give my best respects to Uncle Nide and Aunt Rachel and to Cousin Ellen[47] if still there.

I remain ever your affectionate brother,

W. H. H. Clayton

P.S. We have a guard around our camps, so that we can't visit the fortifications of this place which I would like to do. They are very formidable along the river, but it is not as rough and hilly as Vicksburg.

Buckles, Nincehelser, & Stone are well, at least they are able to take care of their rations, and that is a tolerably *good sign*.

~

Camp of the 19th Iowa Infty.

Port Hudson, La.

August 4th, 1863

Dear Father & Mother:

Having a favorable opportunity I concluded to write a few lines this evening and let you know that I am well.

I wrote to the boys on the 27th of last month, soon after our arrival at this place. At the same time I sent two papers, printed at Yazoo City. I hope you received them. They were poorly printed but nevertheless I thought that it would be something of a curiosity to you all.

When I last wrote we were expecting orders daily to proceed on our journey somewhere — but did not know where that place would be. Gen. Herron & staff had gone to Orleans and we supposed that we would learn something in regard to our destination upon his return.

He was gone for 3 or 4 days and when he did return we were as much in the dark as ever, for no one knew anything about it.

We were camped on the river bank during his absence and had several rains during that time so the camps had got quite filthy.

After his return we were ordered to move on higher ground. We did so willingly and now have a nice place. The ground is tolerably well shaded and is easily kept clean. There appears to be more magnolia trees here than any other kind — one, not more than 5 or 6 yards from my tent is 2½ or 3 feet in diameter and high in proportion.

The boats are still lying where we left them, a portion of the artillery and other things, still remaining aboard.

Soldiering here is somewhat different to what it was in Missouri — here we have boats at our command to take us wherever we wish to go (but somehow we cannot get them to take a northerly direction and keep it). While in Missouri if we had a journey of a hundred miles to perform there was no way to do so but to "foot" it through.

It is too hot in this climate to march long at a time — but few men could go 5 miles a day if they had to carry knapsacks.

There is a large pond or lake about ½ mile from camp that is full of alligators and fish of various kinds. I saw two alligators there a day or two ago, the first that I have yet seen, they were about 10 ft. long. I was inside the works at this place last Sunday. They are well got up, being more substantial than those at Vicksburg. But the natural position, though good for defense, is nothing like that at Vicksburg.

There is a lot of zouaves [48] at this place. I have seen numbers of the men but have not seen the regiment on parade or drill which I would like to do. It is the 165th New York regiment. Their uniform is the regular oriental of Turkish style of dress. For pants they wear a red flannel *petticoat*! which comes down half way between the knee and ankle and is sewed up at the bottom leaving two places for the feet to go through. It is then drawed together at each leg. A blue jacket with a large red sash around the waist & a turban or fez completes the uniform. For illustration see *Harpers Weekly*.[49] I have seen pictures that exactly resemble them.

Give my respects to all.

I remain your affectionate son,

W. H. H. Clayton

P.S. Captain Richmond has resigned and gone home. Every man in the company was sorry to have him leave us. But his health was bad and he could not get leave of absence to recruit up, so at last he concluded to resign. One of the boys, Joseph Lannum, grandson of old Johnny Spencers,[50] accompanied him home.

Co. "H" has about 50 men present about 35 of whom are fit for duty. I and the orderly are the only two sergeants who have been on duty for some time.

Buckles, Stone & Nincehelser are well. Tom Humphrey[51] has been unwell for some time but is getting better. Jo. Paxton is well. George was left sick at Vicksburg.

~

Camp of the 19th Iowa Infty.

Near Carrollton, Louisiana

Sunday, August 23rd, 1863

Dear Parents:

Having some spare moments I have concluded to improve them by writing a few lines to you. I would have written sooner but was waiting *for something to turn up* in order to have something to *write about.*

I wrote to Uncle Nide on the 11th from Port Hudson, having received a letter from W. C. Ferguson. I answered it on the 17th. I suppose you will hear from me by those letters.

I received a letter from Cousin Lizzie Cooper a day or so ago — date August 6th. By it I learned that the sufferings of Aunt Agness had come to an end, by her death on the 22nd of July last. She has had a long illness and to hear of her death, was not unexpected by me.

Well, since I last wrote to you we have travelled *some more* and at present are enjoying ourselves in the *nicest* camp that we have ever had. The whole ground is shaded the entire day by the wide-spreading branches of numerous live-oak trees. From every limb and branch, clusters of the moss, peculiar to this part of the country, hangs down giving the camp a curious appearance, especially after night when nothing but the moss is to be seen. The camp is kept clean & it is as nice a place to stay as anybody need want. But it is uncertain how long we remain here; we are under marching orders and are liable to be ordered off at any time — maybe not for a week.

Carrollton is the name of the place where we landed, our camp being about 1½ miles below town — another little town is only a short distance below here and then it is town nearly all the way to New Orleans — about 5 or 6 miles.

There was a grand review of the troops at this place yesterday, by Maj. Gen. Banks.[52] There was about 25 regiments out — all western boys who took part in the siege of Vicksburg. The review passed off right pleasantly and I think creditably to all concerned.

We did not put on so much *style* as eastern troops do, but when anything is to be *done*, the *western* boys are the ones to do it.

After review I and three others of Co. "H" procured a pass and visited the Crescent City.[53] We went down on the cars[54] and arrived there about 10 o'clock A.M. Taking the street cars, which run almost everywhere through the city, we soon had gone the entire length & breadth of the city.

The *Levee* was about the first place visited. Here we saw any quantity of ships, steamships and all other kinds of sailing vessels. Several men-of-war vessels were anchored in the river, and 6 or 8 of the common Mississippi steamers were lying at the wharf. The Levee is very large, but there was not much stir on it, this infernal war having paralyzed the once extensive trade of this great city. Among other places of interest visited was the statue of Henry Clay and Jackson Square. In the center of the Square is an equestrian figure representing Jackson on his spirited war horse. It is a very natural figure and is worth seeing. The pedestal on which it stands is 12 or 15 feet high and on each side has inscribed those memorable words of Jackson — *The Union, it must be preserved.*[55] What an eyesore these words must have been to the seceding scoundrels who at one time had control of the city.[56] They had not however the hardihood to deface the inscription, as the devils did at Memphis, Tennessee.[57]

We ran about town until evening seeing what was to be seen. When we left the streets were all lighted up with *gas*. There is some nice buildings in the place, but it can't near come up with St. Louis or Cincinnati in that respect.

The country around here is level for miles & if it were not for the levee the river would have to raise but little to overflow it all. It is well drained however — that is ditches are dug to take off the water but where it goes I do not know. Last week we had showers every day, but it did not rain enough to make the ground much wet. It was cool and pleasant a few days ago — there being good breezes from Lake Ponchartrain. Today it is *hot* and the shade is quite acceptable.

Notwithstanding the ground is much lower here than at Port Hudson, the health of the troops appears to be improving, the sick being principally those who got sick at the latter place. Col. Kent's health has not been very good for some time — he started home a few days ago on a short leave of absence. Many however think that he will never come back.

We received two months pay a few days ago — we are paid up to June 30th.

The boys live high here. We can get almost anything to eat that we want & at reasonable prices. We have not had as good living, as we have now, since leaving home. The bread is first quality and a 5 ct. loaf, with other articles, makes a meal for two men. I will give you our bill of fare for dinner today — good bread, baked pork & beans, boiled beef, boiled *sea-crabs*, sour-kraut! pickled beets, butter jelly and tea with plenty of *confiscated* loaf sugar to sweeten with, or if we had chosen we could have had ice water, ice being plenty at 4 cts. a pound. Now if that isn't good living for soldiers, I would like to know what is. We can get all the pies & cakes we want from peddlars who are numerous.

Well, I must soon close for want of room. I, and all the Chequest boys are well. Buckles is on detached service, driving team at headquarters. Give my respects to all.

I remain as ever your affectionate son,
William H. H. Clayton

New Orleans

September 1st, 1863

Dear Brothers:

Your welcome letter of August 13th was received a few days ago, and I was truly glad to hear from you again. I hope that you will continue writing as often as you have heretofore, for I assure you that I am always glad to hear from home. We have been receiving mail more frequently of late than before coming here.

We are still in our old camp from which I have written several times before, since we came here. Having as I said written from here so often, I have nothing of importance to communicate at present.

The weather for a week past has been tolerably pleasant our camp being shaded at all times of the day. We are not exposed to the burning *sun* the rays of which sometimes come down without mercy. Several mornings of this week it was almost uncomfortably cool to do without a coat.

In my last letter I stated that we had received marching orders, these have been renewed, we are ready to march on 12 hours notice in "light marching trim" — that is, without knapsacks, tents or other heavy camp equipage. These are all to be left here and a man from each company to take care of them. Paint is being furnished and everything has to be *marked*.

The papers for sometime have had Gen. Herron's division at Mobile. It was the first division of western troops to come this far south, and it was the general opinion of nearly all that our destination was Mobile, but we have been stopping here now for a couple of weeks, and the balance of the 13th Army Corps[58] has arrived from above and is encamped here at present.

It is doubtful about our going to Mobile, the knowing ones say that we go to *Texas*. I am inclined to believe so from what I have heard from different sources. I believe that I would rather go there than to Mobile. But we can't tell where we go, for certain until we get started, and get to the place, and stop.

I used to think that I might probably get a furlough sometime this *fall*, but none has been issued to well persons here and as the army is about to move none will be given until the coming campaign is over. I have been saving money enough to take me home but I guess that I need make no calculations on getting there until the war is over, or the term of service expires. Several of the company who have been sick and got able to stand travelling have received furloughs from 30 to 60 days in length of time. I think Geo. Paxton will get one in a few days. He has been quite sick for 60 days and should go home. There was another grand review last Saturday of the 13th Army Corps. The ground which is level and about a mile square had been previously cleaned off — all the weeds cut down — so that a good view of the review was to be had. Each regiment was out in its best trim.

50 regiments of infantry passed by Gen. Banks in review besides a long train of artillery, some of the pieces being drawn by 12 horses, & 4 battalions of cavalry, all forming what is called the 13th Army Corps commanded at present by Maj. Gen. Washburn.[59]

When we leave here — having to leave our knapsacks we will have no way to carry paper or envelopes and I may not be able to write as frequently as I have been.

Give my respects to Uncle Sammy Clayton, Uncle Nide and Aunt Rachel and to J. W. Jones[60] if he is still *thereabouts*, and to all my friends in general. Hoping this finds you all as it leaves me, enjoying good health.

I remain ever your affectionate brother,

Wm. H. H. Clayton

P.S. The picture on this sheet represents the statue of Henry Clay in New Orleans. It is a tolerably true picture in outline but the *features* of the great statesman are not correctly given.

CHAPTER 5

"We Held Them at Bay for Two Hours"

After receiving the surrender of the Confederate garrison at Port Hudson, General Banks envisioned using his troops in an operation against Mobile, Alabama. President Lincoln had other plans for this force, however, ordering Banks to make his objective Texas instead. Lincoln had two motives in desiring this offensive. First, he hoped to counter what he perceived to be a violation of the Monroe Doctrine committed by Emperor Napoleon III of France. Lincoln had taken objection to the French ruler's efforts to place a puppet ruler on the throne of Mexico during the Civil War, but protests by the Department of State had proven fruitless. Lincoln thought that putting a Union force near the Mexican border might make Napoleon more amenable to the American point of view. And second, Lincoln wished to secure the entire state of Louisiana for the Union, thus expediting his opportunity to begin the process of reconstructing the nation. If Banks moved on Texas up the Red River through Louisiana, Lincoln reasoned, his Union army would drive the Confederates out of their last stronghold in Louisiana along the way. In addition, from a military standpoint, moving a Union force into the Red River area would prevent the Confederates from moving troops to the Louisiana bank of the Mississippi River to impede traffic on that waterway. For these reasons, then, Banks would have to put his Mobile campaign on hold.

The government had not specifically ordered an advance into Texas via the Red River, however, giving Banks instead the discretion to choose his own strategy for bringing a force into that state. Aware that the level of the Red River in the fall was not sufficient for the draft of many Union navy vessels, Banks immediately embraced the freedom awarded him to adopt another plan. He chose instead to mount an amphibious assault directly on the Texas coast; the particular stretch of coastline he selected would allow him to then move his invading force along a railroad line against Houston.

Unfortunately for Banks, on September 8, 1863, one fort on the Texas coast, defended by only a fifty-man garrison, repulsed his assault fleet, capturing two of the vessels. This engagement, known as the Battle of Sabine Pass, forced Banks to adopt the strategy for invading Texas originally suggested by the War Department.

Banks had in fact already taken a step in that direction. On September 5, 1863, he had ordered the deployment of a division at Morganza, Louisiana, located near the junction of the Red and Mississippi Rivers. Banks had sent this force there to curtail the activity of Confederate troops in that area who were harrassing traffic on the Mississippi River. The Second Division of the XIII Corps received this assignment, and by September 9 that unit had arrived at its destination.

On September 12, the commander of these troops, Major General Francis Herron, moved a mixed force of infantry and cavalry to Norwood's Plantation, a tract of land in Point Coupee Parish about eight miles from Morganza. From this position, the Union advanced force could monitor the approaches to Morganza from the vicinity of Opelousas, thus guarding the division against a Confederate attack from the interior of Louisiana.

It soon became apparent that this detachment, numbering around five hundred, could not be quickly reinforced in the event of a Confederate assault because of the poor quality of the road to Morganza. Adding to the danger, the vegetation in the area provided natural cover for any force to move against the Union troops without fear of detection, thus making it likely that an attack would come without warning. Acting on his own initiative, the commander of the federal force moved his troops from Norwood's Plantation to a more defensible position at Sterling's Plantation, approximately one mile to the east. This still left the Union force vulnerable to a surprise attack, however, and the commander tried to make General Herron aware of the danger involved in maintaining such an isolated outpost. But after listening to his arguments, Herron refused to alter his troop dispositions.

In retrospect, it seems that illness may have affected Herron's behavior in this matter. The individual who had fought bravely and acted resolutely earlier in the war now suffered from an unidentified malady that prevented him from even journeying to Sterling's Plantation to appraise the situation. In the days to come, Herron's condition continued to deteriorate. Suffering acutely, he turned over his command to Major General Napoleon J. T. Dana on September 28; it is unclear from the official records whether Herron passed along, at that time, any cautionary information about the status of the force at Sterling's Plantation to his successor. In either case, Dana would have had little opportunity to make any changes; on the following day a Rebel force attacked the Union advanced guard.

The northern force included the 19th Iowa. Clayton was captured and would spend the next ten months as a prisoner of war. Upon his release, Clayton and his fellow captives of the 19th reported to camp in the New Orleans area to await reunion with the portion of the regiment that had avoided capture at Sterling's Plantation.

Although Clayton wrote only four letters during this period, he managed to convey the wide range of emotions that the experiences of battle and captivity brought out in him: anger, frustration, despair, and finally redemption. Although initially wary of the reception he would receive from his more fortunate comrades who escaped captivity, Clayton seems to have quickly made peace and begun preparing himself for his reentry into the prosecution of the war.

~

Point Coupee Parish, La.
September 21st, 1863
Dear Brothers:
Having a few spare moments & thinking that you will probably be getting out of patience waiting for a letter from me, I concluded to scratch a few lines.

We have been absent from our camp at Carrollton since the 5th of this month, having left there at that time leaving our tents standing, and also our *knapsacks*, which accounts for my not writing sooner. One of the boys happened to bring his port folio along in his *haversack*, and I was fortunate enough to get this sheet of paper & envelope. All that we have with us is the clothes upon our backs and a rubber blanket. It has been quite cool for a few nights & our *woolen* blankets would be quite acceptable if we could get them.

I received your letter of Aug. 29 day before yesterday and was glad to hear from you again, but sorry to hear that the season has turned out so unfavorable for farmers.

I also received a letter from Cousin George Smith about a week ago. He wrote that he had been *drafted* and was to report the first of this month.[1]

The day before we left camp there was another grand review of the 13th Army Corps by Maj. Gens. Grant & Banks. It passed off with much enthusiasm, the boys *cheering* their favorite general as he passed along the lines.[2] Herrons division embarked on steamers on the 5th and started *up* the river arriving at a point about 4 miles below a little town called Morganza about 35 miles above Port Hudson and 15 below the mouth of Red River. A squad of rebels had fired on a steamboat a few days previously.

Upon our landing 3 regts. of the 2nd brigade started out leaving our regiment and the 1st brigade at the boats. They found the rebels in considerable force (reported at 10,000) and were obliged to fall back after getting about 15 miles from the river. The next day Gen. Herron started with the balance of his force, excepting the 19th which was left to guard the boats. He run the rebs to their hole which is said to be a good one, being on the other side of a stream called the Atchafaylah[3] and which our forces could not cross. Finding that he could accomplish nothing he returned the next day to the boats. This was on the 9th; on the 11th our regt. & the 26th Indiana were ordered out with 3 days rations. We came out here and stopped on a plantation about a mile further out than our previous position.[4]

After remaining there three days, 5 more days rations were sent to us and we came back to this place on account of the water giving out at the other place. We have again received 5 more days rations & it is uncertain how long we will remain here. I think we are waiting for a force to get in the rear of the rebs, and we remain here to hold them where they are. We have all the sweet potatos here that we can eat and have plenty of sugar and molasses which we get from a sugar house on the plantation.[5] We have a great old time making candy & eating it.

Nincehelser is well, Stone & Buckles were left at Carrollton. Joseph

Norwood's Plantation, as it appears today.
Photo by Sue DeVille.

Paxton wishes you to tell his folks that he is well, if you see them. I am well.

I remain your affectionate,

W. H. H. Clayton

New Orleans

July 24th, 1864

Dear Father, Mother and Brothers:

It is with the greatest pleasure imaginable that I avail myself of a priviledge which for a long time has been denied me, that of writing you. I have written so very little during the last ten months that I hardly know how to go about it. I wrote two or three letters while in the Confederacy but do not know that either reached its destination.[6] We finally, after two unsuccessful trials, have been *exchanged*, and are enjoying again some of the pleasures of life. There was 28 of the company taken, 7 succeeded in escaping, the balance 21, here at present, are all in good health.

I expect that you wish to know how we were treated. I can hardly make use of words to express myself as I would like, but will give a short account of our treatment. I will have to begin with our capture

"We Held Them at Bay for Two Hours"

The Sterling's Plantation Battlefield, as it appears today.
Photo by Sue DeVille.

on the 29th of Sept. last.[7] The 26th Indiana and 19th Iowa & a small body of mounted men,[8] about 550 men in all had been holding an advanced position about 8 miles from the division, which was then at Morganza, 25 or 30 miles below the mouth of Red River. The morning of the 29th was rainy and the boys were laying around in quarters, some cleaning guns & some writing letters, etc. About noon the pickets between us and the river, were fired upon.[9] Every man at once knew what was up and rushed for his gun and into line as quick as possible. The line was formed in less time than it takes to write it and advanced to the fence, pouring deadly volleys into the rebels who were in a large field of cane.

We held them at bay for two hours and ten minutes repulsing them several times, then their cavalry finally charged down upon us and compelled us to leave our position behind the levee. The cavalry deceived us, many of them having on our uniform[10] so that they approached within 40 or 50 yards before we discovered who they really were. We then scattered out every one for himself, but were so completely surrounded that but few got away.[11] We knew that Lieut. Kent[12] was severely wounded but did not know that he was dead until this spring. We learned from one of the 3rd Iowa Cav., Thos. Pace of Pittsburg, that he died. The boys all mourn his loss, there was not one of the company but what liked him. He was always joking with some one, and would do anything in his power to please us. Abs. Nince-helser we know was wounded in the hand, we suppose that he got away safely. Crpl. Anderson [13] was mortally wounded. Several others were missing and we judged that they succeeded in getting away. Our knapsacks had just arrived from our camp at Carrolton, the evening before the fight, just in time for the rebs to get them. As soon as we were taken we were started for the Atchafalaya River which we crossed about dark. It rained hard all night, we had no shelter and were obliged to stand and take it. The next day about noon they brought us our rations, and such rations! We hardly think of feeding such stuff to cattle at home. It was corn ground into what might be called fine hominy and appeared to have been not more than half husked before grinding. We were hungry however and were glad to get it, many having had nothing since breakfast the day before. We had nothing to cook it in but 2 or 3 tin cups and made *mush*. After making we would empty it out on pieces of boards, so that others could use the tins, and then eat it with little paddles. I did not have my blouse on when the fight began and was taken with nothing on but pant, shirt, & hat, my shoes gave out before reaching the river, and from that on I had to march barefooted. It went rather hard, but others were in the same fix, and the roads being soft on account of the rains my feet stood it much better than I expected. They told that we would be paroled at Alexandria, but when we reached there the paroling officer was at Natchitoches. [When] we got there we found that they had again lied to us. We then marched to Shreveport and then to Camp Ford [14] 4 miles N.E. of Tyler, Smith Co., Texas. We reached Camp Ford about the 20th of Oct.[15] There was no shelter for us whatever and we went to work and built cabins and lived tolerably comfortably for 2 or 3 weeks.[16] About the 1st of Dec. we were paroled and started through for exchange. This march was the severest trial that we had while in the Confederacy. The ground was frozen 2 or 3 inches deep and ice in many places covered the roads. Many of the boys were barefooted and their feet were swollen and cut so that blood was left in their tracks as they marched along. Capt. Olford [17] who had charge of us was a per-fect tyrant and had no mercy upon us whatever. He put us through to Shreveport 110 miles in 4 days. I was fortunate enough to get an old

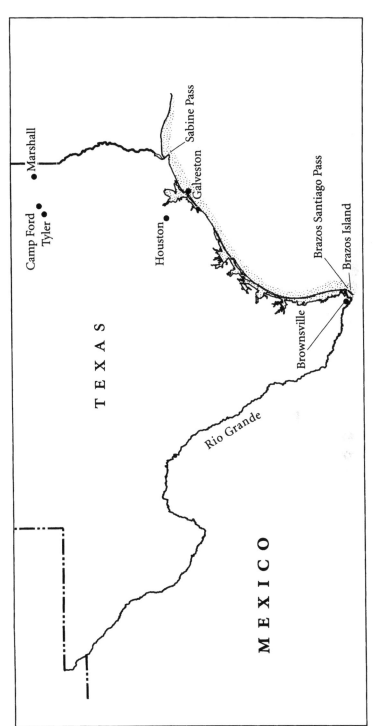

Texas, 1863–1864.

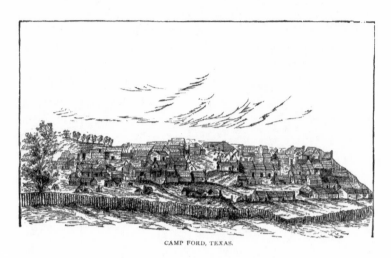

CAMP FORD, TEXAS.

Sketch of Camp Ford, Texas, by a Union soldier.
From *Camp-Fire Chats of the Civil War*, by Washington Davis.

pair of shoes before leaving Tyler, they blistered my feet all over but kept my feet off the ground. At Shreveport we were put in some open barracks. There was no place for fires and each squad built fires on the ground and huddled around to get what warmth we could. The smoke could not get out and it was smokey inside most of the time that we could not distinguish a person more than 10 or 15 steps. It ruined the eyes of many and [was] so disagreeable that we could not sleep at night. Many of the boys had no blankets and all suffered on account of the cold. We finally went to work and built good log cabins again. We had to carry all the logs for houses and all the wood we burned. Upon the approach of the Banks expedition [18] we were started back to Tyler on the 25th of March. We remained there 5 days, signed another parole, and started back for exchange again.

When we got to Marshall on the 8th we heard of the fight at Mansfield [19] and were stopped. They took us about two miles from the road and went into camp and remained there until May 25th when we again started for *Tyler*. When we got there we found the stockade enlarged and about 4,000 Yankees inside of it. There was about 400 of our command (Col. Leake's).[20] We renewed our paroles on the 6th of July, started the third time for Yankeedom on the 9th marching to Shreveport. We there took boats and came down Red River arriving

"We Held Them at Bay for Two Hours"

at the mouth early on the morning of the 22nd, when we once again beheld the Stars & Stripes floating on the gunboat *Choctaw*. The rebel prisoners arrived about noon and by night we were aboard the noble steamer *Nebraska*. We gave our flag three rousing cheers upon arriving at the boat. The rebs did not think their *rag* worth cheering I suppose. At any rate they did not do it. We got plenty of *hard tack* and *coffee*, the first genuine that we had tasted for ten long months. We started down the river Saturday morning, 23rd, reaching here about midnight. This morning (Sunday) after the people got to moving about the streets, we got off the boat and marched through some of the principal streets to show the citizens how Confederates treat prisoners. I will not attempt to describe our appearance, but will say that a more ragged set of men was never before seen. Soap was an article almost unknowed to us while in the Confederacy and you may reasonably suppose that we did not present a very cleanly appearance. Clothing has been issued to us since I commenced writing this. I never saw the appearance of a set of men so quickly changed. I can hard recognize those with whom I am well acquainted, when off a short distance. We have very comfortable quarters in a cotton press. We get "grub" ready cooked, and are marched to tables to eat. The light bread we get goes much better than our "*corn dodger*."

We got [in captivity] about a pound of meal a day and enough beef for one meal. We had to bake the most of our bread without sifting the meal, mixing it with water and a little salt. It was rather rough living, but a healthier set of men than Col. Leakes command could not be found anywhere. Out of 460 there was but 4 deaths during the ten months. For my part I never had better health than while in the Confederacy. There is about 3,500 yet at Tyler. Those captured this spring have a good deal of sickness and many have died. I hope that exchanging will continue until all are freed from their imprisonment.

I have not heard a word from home for more than ten months. I hope this will find all well. Excuse the confused manner in which this letter is written. I could say much more but space will not admit. Give my respects to all. Write as soon as this is received, direct to Co. H, 19th Iowa Camp of Distribution, New Orleans.

Yours as ever,

W. H. H. Clayton

Colonel Joseph B. Leake, 1864.
Courtesy of Roger Davis.

New Orleans

August 1st, 1864

Dear Parents and Brothers:

I wrote you on the 25th July, informing you of our release from captivity on the 22nd, which I hope has been received.

We have had quite a good time since our arrival, having plenty to eat and wear. The bread, pork, beef, rice, & dried fruit and coffee which we get here, affords a striking contrast to the everlasting corn-bread and beef of the Confederacy.

We are stopping at the camp of distribution, where soldiers arriving in the city are kept until transportation is furnished and they are distributed to their regiments. Three meals a day are *prepared* for us, all that we have to do is to help ourselves.

We received two months pay, Saturday, which we greatly needed.

We received the last two months pay at the increased wages — privates $16, corporals $18, sergeants $20 per month. Having lost everything except what we had on our backs, when captured, it takes considerable to procure an outfit — such as plate-cup-spoon, pocket knife, handerkerchief, pocket-book and other necessary articles.

The balance of the regiment is expected here in a few days from Brownsville, Texas, which point it is said, our forces are evacuating.[21] It will be a joyful meeting when we once again meet our comrades, from whom we have been so long parted. As it will be to the most of us, [but] from what we can learn there may be some ill feeling shown on the part of some. It appears that in some companies *promotions* have been made which those who are here do not approve of, and I would not be surprised if it caused a disturbance in some instances.

We claim to be the *regiment*, all who were fit for duty last fall were at the plantation and the greater part captured. Those now at Brownsville are the ones who were sick at that time, the few who succeeded in escaping, and recruits and playoffs. We the *best part* of the regiment do not propose being overlooked simply because we were at our posts and were so unfortunate as to be "gobbled up" by superior numbers, and retained so long in their hands. But we will likely see how things stand, before long.

Well, a few words in regard to the Confederacy. I did not think that they (the Rebs) were in quite as bad a condition as they are. I can not see how they maintain their ground as well as they do. Their army west of the river is poorly organized and equipped and very poorly fed. They all told us that they gave us the best they had while prisoners, I have every reason to believe it. We did not get so plenty as their own soldiers, but the rations in other respects were the same. They live on cornbread and beef, and it is literally a *corn-fed* army. We were corn-fed at a great rate, but they could not make *Confederates* of us, which they would like to have done.[22] We knew that Uncle Sam had plenty for us to eat and wear and that the good time would come some day.

You have read a great deal about the exorbitant prices of articles in the Confederacy and probably have doubted the statements, but we found everything as high as reported, in their Confederate currency. A loaf of bread costing 5 cts. here would sell for one dollar in Confederate at Shreveport. Corn is worth from 5 to 8 dollars per bushel, pork from 2½ to $3 per lb. & everything else in proportion. Clothing is so high that you would hardly believe the price if I told you. I have seen boots, worth about ten dollars here, sell for 100 & 150 dollars per pair. At Shreveport where we came through last a common sized watermelon sold for one dollar *greenback* or ten dollars *Confederate*. They like to get hold of the *greenbacks* although many of them seem glad to hear of the difference between them & gold. At Marshall Texas this spring I saw $400 in Confederate money given for $20 in gold. Greenback has ranged at from 5 to 20 for 1, that is one dollar greenback was worth from 5 to 20 in Confederate.

The rebs were considerably alarmed this spring when Banks started up the river. Many gave up Shreveport as lost long before the fight at Mansfield. That miserably managed affair has encouraged them greatly and put back our cause very much. A great many were preparing to go with our army as soon as it reached Shreveport and had it been successful many would have joined it & Louisiana would have given up without much more opposition & Texas also for the people of that state wish to keep the scenes of conflict outside their borders. There is a great many Union men there who only wait for a favorable opportunity to display their colors. Many of the men who guarded us during our imprisonment were Union men and prayed for our armies to be successful in the recent expedition.

The 26th Indiana left this afternoon to join the balance of the regiment at Donaldsonville. Those now at the place are veterans. Those who have been with us have but a few weeks longer to serve, then they go home.

Our two regiments combined presented a splendid sword this afternoon to Lt. Col. Leake, 20th Iowa regiment, who commanded the detachment of us who were taken prisoner, for his devoted attention to the wants of the men of his command. He always had a great deal of influence with the rebels & when marching generally received permission to march us as he saw fit to, and in many instances bettered our condition when there was any chance.[23]

Give my respects to all.

I remain ever yours obediently,

W. H. H. Clayton

New Orleans

August 8th, 1864

Dear Father & Mother,

I once more address you a few lines from this place. The regiment arrived here from Brownsville yesterday. I went down to the vessel and found the boys all well. It was a happy meeting having been separated nearly 11 months.

Buckles, Nincehelser, Mooney & Stone are looking well having enjoyed the best of health. From them I learned that the folks at home were well when they last heard from the neighborhood, which was good news to me, I assure you. The regiment has gone up to Carrollton to camp.[24] The balance of the division have gone, the supposition is, to *Mobile* and it is likely the 19th will soon follow. We expect to join the regiment today. We have yet to draw arms and camp equipments. It will go awkward with us to have a gun in our hands after being so long without them but we will soon become accustomed to it again.

The boys of our squad are all well. I was glad to see the boys who escaped from Shreveport early this spring.[25] They had a hard time getting through. The orderly, Wm. Byers,[26] got through just in time to prevent another one of the company being promoted over him. He is now 1st Lieut. and acting quartermaster of the regt. since his return. The position of orderly has been filled by a former corporal. His promotion occasions a good deal of dissatisfaction in this portion of the company.

I got several old letters yesterday, written Sept. 11th, 16th and Oct. 11th of last year. They were old but nevertheless I was glad to get them. Uncle Nide & Uncle Sammy Clayton wrote one of them. Give them my best respects. I will answer them as soon as I can.

I want John and George to write me a long letter and tell me how things have been going on, up on Chequest.

I believe that I have nothing more to write and will close.

I remain with respect your affectionate son,

W. H. H. Clayton

~

Camp 19th Iowa Vols. Inftry.

Carrollton, La.

Aug. 13th, 1864

Dear Brothers:

I once more write from *camp* having joined the balance of the regt. last Monday the 8th instant. We found the boys from Browns-ville, looking well, and as brown and sunburned as we did when we got back.

We are encamped nearer the town of Carrollton than last year but in nothing like so pretty a place, there being no shade trees here.

It will [be] one year tomorrow since the regiment arrived here from up the river. We remained until Sept. 5th and then started to Morganza on the, to us, rather unfortunate expedition.

Things do not wear the same appearance as then at that time the entire 13th Army Corps was here. Now there is but our regiment alone. Banks, by his various movements during the past year, has suc-ceeded in entirely breaking up the corps above mentioned and scat-tering the divisions & detailing them out as was done at Mansfield La.

The rebels themselves were surprised at gaining the victory they did there. The majority of them expected our forces to be successful in getting possession of Shreveport and I know of many who were disappointed because they did not succeed. Had Banks reached that place and taken it the whole trans-Mississippi department would have but little more show of resistance. I have heard many express their sentiments, while we were camped near Shreveport, and say that they would go over as soon as the Yankee army got that far [in] advance. But the victory at Mansfield and subsequent retreat of Banks has encouraged the hot-heads and discouraged the hopes of many true Union men, who would be glad to see the *old flag* wave over the states of Louisiana & Texas. A spirit of despotism and tyranny reigns tri-umphant in the Confederacy and a Union man dare not openly ex-press his sentiments. He would do so at the risk of his neck. We found many who would acknowledge their sentiments to us, but they dare not let their officers know it.

The colonel who commanded the camp near Shreveport, where we remained last winter, is now in New Orleans. His name is *Theard*.[27] He has resumed his former occupation attny-at-law. I and

A group of noncommissioned officers of the 19th Iowa after their release from Camp Ford, 1864. Courtesy of the U.S. Army Military History Institute, original owned by the Massachusetts Commandery, Military Order of the Loyal Legion.

another of the boys called upon him the other day. He was very glad to see us. I believe him to be sincere in his professions of devotion to the Union.[28] Many of us were almost sure that he would go to New Orleans when he was relieved of command at Shreveport.[29]

I stated in my last the portion of the division which preceded our regiment has gone to Mobile. We expected to go there too but the indications are at present that we go to *Pensacola*, Florida. I understand that we are under marching orders for that place. We draw *arms* today and will then be ready for the field.

Efforts were made, after we got out of the Confederacy, to get *furloughs* for us but they were unsuccessful as I supposed they would be.

There seems to be a good deal of dissatisfaction existing against the present commander for the regiment, Lt. Col. Bruce.[30] The boys wish that old Dan Kent was back.[31] He is as good a man for commander of a regiment as could be found if he only had a little more military talent.[32] He was always good to his men and did all that he could to make their duties light. The boys have seen a hard time of it at Brownsville having a great deal of guard duty to perform and being court martialled for the least offenses.

Well boys I guess that I will bring my letter to a close. I will send a photograph of the 19th as it appeared upon our arrival here from Camp Ford Texas, as soon as I can get an opportunity, also a kind of company history printed on a large card. The price is $2.00 per copy, but as I made out the list I get one free of charge.

Write and give me all the news.

From your affectionate brother,

W. H. H. Clayton

p.s. I sent a photograph picture in a box expressed to Thornberg, Keosauqua.[33] You will call and get it.

CHAPTER 6

" *If the North Would Remain United* "

Ulysses S. Grant had given the United States two victories of supreme importance in 1863. First, in July he had forced the capitulation of Vicksburg, receiving the surrender of 31,000 Confederates. And second, he had opened the way for a drive on Atlanta by dislodging the Confederates from strong defensive positions around Chattanooga, Tennessee, in November. Congress had responded by promoting Grant to the rank of lieutenant general in February 1864, thus making every other Union general subordinate to him. For the rest of the war, Grant would exercise command over all Union forces in every military theater.

Upon taking command, Grant decided that a campaign against Mobile, Alabama, would become a priority. A number of factors influenced Grant's thinking in this decision. After the fall of New Orleans, Mobile became the most important port still controlled by the Confederates. If the Union sealed it off, the Confederacy would find its ability to import badly needed foreign goods severely curtailed. Knowing that the Confederates would not suffer the loss of Mobile lightly, Grant recognized that thousands of Confederate troops would be sent to defend the port. This would keep them from being used to resist the other, more important, campaigns Grant envisioned, including offensives aimed at the Confederate Armies of Tennessee and Northern Virginia. And, if successful, the capture of Mobile would give the Union a base of operations to use for a strike deep into the heart of the Confederacy. For these reasons, once he mobilized the remnants of the force that Banks had used in his abortive Red River campaign, Grant ordered a combined army-navy force to move on Mobile.

One possible strategy for attacking the city involved an advance on Mobile from Pensacola, Florida. Since May 1862, the Union had controlled Pensacola and its protective fortifications, providing a potential springboard for an offensive. Gradually, in the fall of 1864, northern troops began to arrive in Pensacola in ever-increasing numbers. While they would make occasional forays into the interior of Florida, these soldiers initially failed to see any possible reason for their presence in Pensacola. Quickly, however, most sensed that they would sooner or later take part in a campaign against Mobile.

Clayton's regiment was one of those sent to Pensacola in 1864. In the eleven letters he sent from there, he once again provides a detailed commentary on his surroundings and his activities, including the combat his unit experienced. But what makes these letters so interesting is that Clayton wrote them during the period when the Union cause reached its most desperate moment — August 1864, when the Confederacy had apparently stymied both major northern offensives — and then scored some of its greatest triumphs, culminating in the reelection of Abraham Lincoln. Throughout it all, Clayton's letters demonstrate his unwavering faith in the cause in which he and his fellow soldiers had invested two years of their lives.

~

Camp of the 19th Iowa Vols.
Barrancas,[1] coast of Florida
Aug. 19th, 1864
Dear Father, Mother, & Brothers:
Having a few spare moments, I hasten to write you a few lines, as a vessel is to leave tomorrow for Philadelphia and take the mail.

I wrote from our camp at Carrollton, just above New Orleans, informing you that our destination was Pensacola. The regiment accordingly embarked on two small propellors,[2] the first one with 4 companies aboard started out and came on through without trouble. The one that the balance started on, our company being aboard, started on the 14th, we only passed the city and got below Algiers when it was found that the vessel had sprung a leak. We accordingly put about and landed at one of the docks at New Orleans and got another vessel.

"If the North Would Remain United"

It was found too small and another was added so that the regt. came over in three detachments. Three companies were left behind when the regt. left Brownsville. The companies were left on Brazos Santiago Island.[3] They have not yet joined us. We left New Orleans on the morning of the 15th, passed Forts Jackson and [St.] Philip[4] in the afternoon and crossed the *bar, S.E. Pass*, just at dark. As soon as the vessel got over the bar we could feel the swell and she rolled considerably, but not enough to make many sea-sick. The next day we had 2 or 3 squalls — more rain than anything else however. Got sight of land during the afternoon, it looked as white as snow. When we first [saw it] many thought it was camps stretching along the coast, but the seamen told us that it was white sand. We got in past Ft. Pickens[5] just after dark and remained aboard until the next morning when we disembarked. We now found that what we saw was sand. It is as white as snow and looks like it does up north after a light fall of snow with the grass showing in a few places. We are camped about ¾ of a mile from the bay. We get water out of wells and also springs.

There is not many troops here. Part of two or three white regiments and 2 or 3 "nigger" regiments[6] being all. There is no force whatever in the town of Pensacola. It is 7 or 8 miles up the bay. I was down in Warrenton[7] yesterday about ¾ mile from camp. I was in the navy yard and [saw] some of the destruction perpetrated by Bragg[8] while he was here. The ruined walls of many nice brick buildings are yet standing, giving one an idea of what it once was. Several of the buildings have been repaired and mechanics are working in them. From the navy yard the town of Pensacola is seen. It does not appear to be much of a place. One or two vessels are laying off the town. It is a kind of neutral ground neither party having any force there.

I do not know, nor does any one with whom I am acquainted, what we came here for. There is not force enough here to make any aggressive movements that would amount to much. Part of the 7th Vermont regt. has been here doing duty for more than two years. The greater part of the regt. has gone home on veteran furlough[9] and will not return to this place. It is likely that we take their place here. If so we may be put in the greater place of the balance of our time at this place. We will be tired of it if we do. There is no regularity in receiving mails at all. I have not received any letters yet since being exchanged. I will expect some before long.

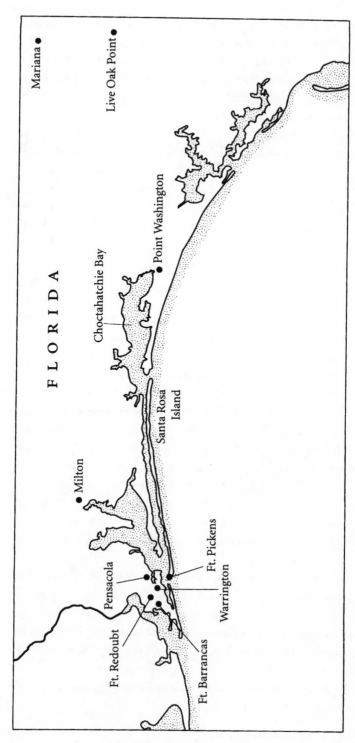

Florida, 1864.

We will soon have the regimental bakery in full blast and will then get along finely. We can buy bread in Warrenton, 3 loaves for 25 cts.

I have nothing more to write of interest and will accordingly close. Give my best respects to Uncle Nide, Aunt Rachel & Alice,[10] and also Uncle Sammy.

I remain yours affectionately,

W. H. H. Clayton

P.S. I forgot to mention the name of the general commanding. It is *Gen. Asboth*.[11] Direct Letters *via New Orleans* at present.

∿

Camp of the 19th Iowa Vol. Infantry

Barrancas, West Florida

Aug. 27th, 1864

Dear Brother:

Your truly welcome letter of the 6th was received last evening, and its contents eagerly perused. It was good news for me, to hear that you and the rest of the family were alive and well. I also received a letter from Cousin Mary Lighthill in answer to one written from New Orleans. The friends in that section were all well.

I suppose from what you write that great changes have taken place in the neighborhood. I think that it must be a kind of lonesome place, as all the young men, old enough, have gone into the army, and so many having left for other parts.

I was sorry to hear of Jonathan Pugh's death, but it is the way of all flesh, whether at *home* or in the *army*. It is a sad spectacle to witness death under any circumstances, but of all places that I have yet seen the "shuffling off of this mortal coil" in the stockade near Tyler, Texas, was the worst. This spring, after the prisoners captured from Banks and Steele[12] were placed there, they died off 5 and 6 a day. When they would get sick it was almost impossible to get medicine, and men would linger along without any one to care for them. It was impossible for a well man to keep rid of vermin, and a sick man after he became unable to help himself would become actually alive with lice. I have seen them so thick on a dead body that you could not touch it with your finger without touching one.

The corpse would be placed in a rough coffin in the same condition and deposited in the ground a short distance from the stockade.

The mortality seemed to be greater among eastern troops than among the western. They seemed to be more disheartened than we, and took no care of themselves at all.

I had heard a great deal said about the superiority of western troops over eastern troops, but was inclined to disbelieve it, but I think that there is in fact a great difference. For this there is several reasons — one great reason is that the men do not have confidence in their officers. Their officers do not associate with the men as ours do, and will not let any one go to their *tent* unless he has special business there. They are also much more strict and put on a great deal of *style*. More foreigners will be found in eastern regts. than western. Unless the officers are foreigners also they are not much of a force — merely soldiering for the day. The difference was plainly to be seen, in the stockade, in the habits & conditions of the two. I have seen these soldiers from Maine so lousy that (the lice) could be counted by the dozens on the outside of their clothing, while they had been prisoners but two or three months.[13]

But I have got out of that *scrape* and must think of something else. I am afraid however that it will be some time before I forget what a time we used to have baking our "corn dodger" three times a day. Some ate but twice a day, but my mess preferred making three meals of the tinful of corn-meal which was each man's allowance. We had meat, seldom more than enough for one meal.

At this place we get bread baked by men detailed for that purpose, plenty of beans, peas, coffee, tea, pork, fresh & salt beef, & occasionally pickles & dried apples.

We still remain in the camp from which I last wrote. There is not much guard duty to perform at present, but the *fatigue*[14] comes down pretty heavy occasionally. It is generally either loading or unloading vessels, a hundred men from this regt. and the same number from the 2nd Maine cav. were busy several days loading mortars, shell and ammunition for Mobile. They were taken from Ft. Pickens. The shell weighed 205 lbs. without being loaded or about 240 ready for use.[15] I did not get over to see the inside of the fort but have a pretty good view of the outside from here.

I was in Fort Barrancas a few days ago. It is not a very large fort but there is 25 or 30 guns mounted in it. It is manned by two companies of the 25th "Corps de Afrique."[16] There is two "nigger" regi-

"If the North Would Remain United"

The commissioned officers of the 19th Iowa after their release from Camp Ford, 1864. Courtesy of the U.S. Army Military History Institute.

ments here. They do all the picket and out post duty which makes it comparatively easy upon us. The negroes make better soldiers than I expected they would. They keep themselves in good trim and seem to be well drilled. Col. Allen [17] who commanded the post at Tyler [18] for a long time says that they will fight, for he knows it. He was wounded & taken prisoner in the fight at Millikens Bend above Vicksburg, last year.[19]

But for all that, I do not much like the idea of soldiering with them and believe that it would have been better never to have armed them. That is, I think, the principal reason why we were not exchanged sooner. The rebs will not recognize them as soldiers, and our authorities persist in retaining them as such.[20]

I went up a *notch* while in the Confederacy from 3rd sergeant to 2nd.[21] Pity that I did not know it while there. It might have afforded some consolation to think of such a promotion! Orderly Byers who escaped is now 1st Lieut. & what used to be Corporal Woods [22] is now 1st sergt.

I sent from New Orleans a printed *roster* of Co. "H" the names being put down as they were on the original roll. With the remarks stating what has become of each. It would look very well if put in a frame. I also sent a photograph picture, in a box with some other articles which the orderly was sending home. I thought that it was to be sent to Thornburg but it appears that it was sent to Games [23] in Keosauqua. I hope that you will get the picture. It will give some idea of how weak [we] looked when we got out of the Confederacy.

I am glad to hear that Uncle Sammy and Uncle Nide & Aunt Rachel are well. Give them my best respects!

The health of the regiment is good. Abner Buckles is working in the regt'l bakery. Mooney is one of the company cooks. John Stone is well, also Corporal Nincehelser. We have the wedge tent,[24] 4 occupying a tent. My messmates are James Akers,[25] Tho. Humphrey & Zerah Dean.[26]

My love to father, mother, & John. Hoping that you and John will write often.

I remain affectionately your brother,

Wm. H. H. Clayton

∼

Camp of the 19th Iowa Vols.

Barrancas, Florida

September 7th, 1864

Dear Brother:

With pleasure I seat myself to write a few lines in answer to your letter of August 13th which was received yesterday.

I was glad to hear from you, but sorry that John was unwell. I hope that he has recovered before this time.

I also received yesterday a letter from George Smith. He had been at Aunt Jane's and had seen my letter. He was well, as also were the rest of the friends.

You say that the new house is ready to occupy. I had supposed that you had passed last winter in it. At any rate I consoled myself last winter, when I had nothing to wear except a ragged shirt and pants that the folks at home were having a good time in a warm house. Last winter, in northern Texas, was the coldest known for many years. Of course it was no comparison to an Iowa winter, or we would have frozen to death. I had no idea that a set of men could stand as much exposure and dogging around as we did. People at home furnish better quarters and better food for their *dogs* than we got a good part of the time.[27] You doubtless have read the newspaper accounts of our appearance when we arrived at New Orleans. The statements that I have seen are correct in every respect excepting one. That in regard to our emaciated appearance, animated skeletons, etc. I must admit that

The parade ground of Fort Barrancas, as it appears today.
Photo by Andy Bennett.

there were some who were little more than living skeletons, but the majority of us looked well enough after we got our new clothing. That helped our appearance amazingly, the ragged clothes of some making them look thinner than they really were. I held my own during my imprisonment. I did not weigh myself until yesterday. I may have improved some but not a great deal — my weight is now 165 pounds.

I think that we are entitled to our ration money — I have others to get it but it is a difficult matter. Commutation rolls have been made out and will be sent off shortly. I don't believe that we'll get more than half ration or 15 cts. a day if we get any.[28]

I have made up my mind to not look for any favors whatever while in the army. Efforts were made by the regimental officers to get all of us furloughs. Gen. Canby[29] who saw us upon our arrival at New Orleans thought that we were entitled to them & so did Gen. Sherman[30] — indeed every one, nearly, who knew any thing about the case acknowledged that we ought to have leave of absence, & I believe that we would have got them had not Lt. Col. Bruce with the balance of the regiment arrived at the time they did. It is known that he refused to sign furloughs for those boys who escaped, when his signature was the only thing that prevented them from getting them.

This is a rather dull place, nothing of importance transpiring. We have got mails so far about once a week — we are away behind in regard to news having heard nothing of importance for some time. We do not even get news from Mobile, notwithstanding it is comparatively near us.

I was down in the navy yard yesterday and saw the *Monongahela*. Her nose is considerably "bruised up" just above the waters edge in consequence of her collision with the *Tennessee* in Mobile Bay.[31] There is at times 15 or so large vessels in the bay, mostly war vessels.

I cannot give much information in regard to Corporal Anderson[32] as I did not get to see him after the fight was over, being immediately started back to the rear. Christopher Mort, with whom Clinton messed before going to Morganza, says that he sold his watch while yet at New Orleans. I am confident that he had none at Sterling Farm[33] for he and I slept together there and I would have known it if he had one there.

Absalom Nincehelser says that his personal effects were taken care of by our regimental surgeon Dr. Sloanaker,[34] and that he wrote a letter to his mother, and he (Nincehelser) understood Sloanaker to say that he sent the articles to her.

I forget whether I mentioned in either of my letters about the "partnership letter" as you call it. I got it after my return to the company and was pleased, upon opening it, to find that Uncle Nide had written to me, and also Uncle Sammy.

I intended to have written to Uncle Nide before this time but have been delaying from one cause or another.

I can hardly get time enough to write a letter without being interrupted. I have been honored with the position of *company clerk* and do all of the writing pertaining to the company — which is no little I assure you. I am relieved from other duty (guard & fatigue). I have stopped twice while writing this and am now finishing by candlelight.

I was happy to receive the few lines in mother's familiar handwriting. I have no doubt but what my prolonged stay with the rebs gave her much uneasiness. I often thought while in their hands, of *home*, and often imagined that you would give up ever hearing from me.

The health of the company is good. This is considered a healthy locality but I can't see what makes it so. It is very hot both day & night.

One would think that there would be a sea breeze here, but on the contrary there is generally very little air stirring — especially back half a mile from the bay.

My respects to all,

William

P.S. Nincehelser got a letter from Emery Neal[35] stating that old Mrs. Neal[36] died about 14th of Aug.

~

Camp of the 19th Iowa

Barrancas, Florida

Sept. 14th, 1864

Dear Father and Mother:

Having a little spare time this afternoon, I have concluded to write you a few lines. I have nothing of much importance to write there being nothing of interest transpiring and having written, but a few days ago, to George.

I visited yesterday, in company with Abs. Nincehelser and Charley Wilber,[37] the *light house* out on the picket line. It is quite a structure built of brick in a circular form, I think about 30 feet in diameter at the bottom and gradually tapering towards the top where it is about 10 ft. in diameter. Its height is about 180 feet, the ascent is made up the winding stairway on the inside, the steps are iron, all that was used in its construction being brick and iron.[38] The lamp is a splendid concern, made of cut glass. The one used before the war, was carried away by the rebs when they left here.[39] The walls are very thick and substantial — several balls from Ft. Pickens struck it during the stay of the rebels, but they did not come near penetrating, merely scaling off the outside layer of brick for 2 or 3 feet around where they struck.[40]

An unobstructed view of the country for many miles around is had from the lookout. A sentinel is kept there constantly during the daytime to give notice of the approach of any one towards the picket line.

Father, I want you to give me some advice as to the best manner of taking care of my wages. I now have 12 months pay due me, $210.00. The paymaster is looked for (by many) with impatience almost. I expect to send the greater part if not all of it home and you can do what you think best with it. I lost my memorandum book at Sterling Farm when taken prisoner in which I had set down the amount sent home, but I don't remember exactly how much it was.

Have you ever got that Westcott debt?[41] If not and you think it is safe, probably it would be well enough to let it run on — provided he wishes to and there [is] no way in which it could be better invested. The value of the currency seems to have a still downward tendency, and if it continues as it has been for the past year it will not be worth a great deal when my time is out, (if I am so fortunate as to see that time).

The captain has written to G. W. Games of Keosauqua and others requesting them to send to him for Co. "H" — such articles in the eating line as would be desirable to "us fellows," such as pickles, saur kraut, and other pickled vegetables. A good many are getting something like the *scurvy*[42] — owing in a good measure to the lack of vegetable matter. If you can send anything of the kind, take it to the above mentioned person who will attend to it. If you cannot without trouble, it will be all right anyhow. I, myself, do not particularly stand in need of anything of the kind, although they would be quite acceptable. Cap. thinks that it would be best to not send any butter. It would not be good by the time it reached us. All articles sent must be considered for the *company*. Some have written home to their folks to send them certain things. Captain Sommerville wrote to Dr. Games, telling him to send nothing for any particular person. If such a thing was allowed some would take advantage of the opportunity and have a lot of stuff sent to them while others would get nothing at all.

The health of the company is tolerably good at present — but 4 or 5 on the sicklist — but a good many in the regt. report to the surgeon every morning.

Remember me to Uncle Nide, Aunt Rachel & Alice. I want John & George to write as often as they can conveniently. I am always pleased to get letters from them. My circle of correspondence is not very large and I do not get many letters except theirs.

This leaves me in the enjoyment of good health.

I remain your affectionate son,

William

Camp of the 19th Iowa Vols.

Barrancas, Florida

October 3rd, 1864

Dear Brother:

Having a little spare time this evening, I hasten to write a few lines, it having been some time since I last wrote. I last wrote to George on the 14th of last month.

On the 15th Companies "H" & "I" received orders to be ready for a scout with two days rations in our haversacks, and ten more days in bulk. We were to be ready to march at one hours notice. We did not know our destination for quite a while, but finally found that we were to accompany an expedition fitted out by Gen. Asboth for the purpose of making a raid up through Florida, we were to guard the steamer *Lizzie Davis* which carried supplies for the expedition.

The 2nd Maine cavalry and 1st Florida cavalry were landed at Live Oak Point about 8 miles from the Navy yard. It occupied 2 or 3 days transporting the cavalry to that point, and we did not get off until after dark on the 18th. The General and staff were landed at Live Oak and we then proceeded up the Santa Rosa Sound. We met the cav. about 40 miles up the sound and two days rations were issued to them. They then started across the country to *Marianna*. We proceeded on through the "narrows" and entered Choctahatchie Bay on the 23rd.

The water is very shoal[43] in the narrows in many place and we grounded several times and had to wait for high tide to get off. We had plenty of water in the bay and we passed up to the head of it and went up the bayou 4 miles. This bayou was very narrow and it was with difficulty that the boat got up. We went for the purpose of awaiting the arrival of the cavalry and delivering them more rations. We laid at the 4 miles landing 2 nights. One company of the cavalry came in while we were there bringing a lieut.[44] and 13 men in as prisoners. I did not feel very easy while we lay there. Had there been any force of rebels near they could have blockaded the bayou below us and kept us there, but fortunately there was none about.

I was glad when we started back, although it was an unpleasant way of getting out. The steamer had to back down more than a mile before she could be turned — running into the bank every few rods.

One snag punched a hole in the hull at the waters edge causing her to leak badly.

We finaly got into the bay and started back to East Pass — the eastern end of Santa Rosa Island — arriving there on the morning of the 26th, we here unloaded about 40 horses and 50 contrabands — repaired the boat and started back up the bay to Point Washington where we were to meet the cavalry again. Arriving near the place on the night of the 27th, we lay at anchor most of the time until the 30th. About noon of the 30th an aide of the general arrived giving notice of the approach of the general who was severely wounded in an engagement with the enemy on the preceding Tuesday at Marianna about 70 miles from where we lay. The general and cavalry arrived about 4 P.M. He is shot in two places — the left cheek and through the left arm breaking it above the elbow. He appears to suffer a good deal of pain. The genl. is quite grey-haired and looks as though he was about 60 years of age. He is a Hungarian — one of the Kossuth[45] staff during the Hungarian war, and speaks English brokenly. He appears to be a go-a-head sort of a man, and seems to think a good deal of his men. He was wounded while leading a charge in the town of Mariana.[46] His adjutant general — Capt. Young — was killed[47] and several of his staff wounded. We had 29 killed and wounded on our side, mostly in the 2nd Maine cavalry. I think that the general may consider himself lucky in getting off as well as he did. He did not have more than 650 or 700 men with him & part of them were armed only with sabers. He had a small detachment of negroes belonging to the 82nd infantry Co. I.[48] They did not show much quarters to the enemy from what we heard. The rebs when they seen them shouted "*no quarters*,"[49] and the niggers "went in." The rebel loss was 40 or 50 killed — but few wounded. About 20 prisoners were brought in,[50] including one col.,[51] one captain, and two lieutenants, also a general of militia named Anderson.[52] They were delivered to us on the boat and we had the pleasure of guarding them down to *Pickens* where we left them yesterday morning.

We had a tolerably good time, but were rather crowded being compelled to remain on the boat the greater part of the time. A sad accident happened shortly after our arrival at the landing at this place about midnight of the first, by which we lost one of the best men in the company. John McIntosh by some means fell overboard and was drowned. His parents reside south of Keosauqua. It will be sad news to them. His body was not recovered until today. It floated ashore near the navy yard. He was buried in the military cemetary here.

The prisoners captured were a hard looking set. About two-thirds of them were old men and boys, from 12 to 60 & 70 years old. They show plainly to what straits they are out to them such as these are compelled to fight.

They were a very innocent set of fellows to hear them tell it, and would hardly harm a "mice" if it would run in their way, but the Florida boys were acquainted with many of them and felt the effects of their persecutions towards Unionists, some having to leave the country on their account. Col. Montgomery looks like a vicious rascal. He is a tall portly fellow with moustaches reaching almost to his ears. He does not deceive [in] his looks any from what those say who deserted his regiment and are now in the Florida regiment. The 1st Florida cavalry and 1st Florida battery are made up almost wholly of deserters from the rebels. Quite a number who deserted from Atlanta while Sherman[53] was operating against the place, have come here & joined our service.

If the North would remain united, and not suffer itself to be divided by factions, it would tend greatly towards breaking the rebellion. The leaders of the south are encouraged *greatly* by the various parties at the North[54] who are using their utmost endeavors [to] divide the people and thus weaken the government. In fact I believe that the war would have been almost over by this time had it not been for some of the violent sympathizers, who have been encouraging them in various ways.

I have been very busy since our return making our returns etc. for the last month.

You must excuse the indifferent style in which this is written. I have to stop every little while and do something else in the writing line.

Give my respects to Uncle Nide & Aunt Rachel. Your letter of 26th August reached here on the 19th Sept. but I did not get [it] until we returned from the recent expedition. I was really glad to receive a letter from you and hope that you and George will continue to write *frequently*.

Hoping that this will find you all as it leaves me — in the enjoyment of good health.

I remain as ever your affectionate brother,

William

~

Camp of the 19th Iowa Vol. Infty.

Barrancas, Fla.

Oct. 13th, 1864

Dear Brother:

With much pleasure I seat myself this fine evening to write you a few lines in answer to yours of the 17th September mailed the 20th, and received today.

I need hardly tell you that I was glad to hear from you. You can judge that I was getting, as you say, "out of patience" for the letter previous to the present one was dated August 26th. It reached here about the 20th of Sept. But I did not get it until the 3rd of this month, upon our return from the recent expedition of which I wrote in my last, of that date.

I was glad to learn that the roster of the company, and the photograph of the prisoners, had been received.

That picture, while it gives a good outline of our apearance, does, in fact, give but a faint idea, leaving the imagination to work out the balance, the varieties in shape & color of the patches, many of which were sewed with yarn, some the ripples placed held together with leather strings, or strips of cotton cloth torn off and used as thread, and the non-use of soap for nearly ten months, gave us an appearance which could only be represented by some good picture painter.

Although we looked hard and suffered a great deal I pity the poor fellows who have been kept up there in Georgia.[55] I think that they see a much harder time than we did. There is so many of them that it cannot be otherwise, for we were in that portion of the Confederacy (so called) that supplied the army east of the river in great measure before the fall of Vicksburg, and I suppose that we got more & better to eat than they do in Georgia.

I have not got a picture here to look at now and cannot give my exact position. Co. "H" was pretty well to the rear when it was taken,

The men of the 19th Iowa after their release from Camp Ford, 1864.
Courtesy of the U.S. Army Military History Institute, original owned by the
Massachusetts Commandery, Military Order of the Loyal Legion.

excepting a few, the front rank if I mistake not is setting down, the
next is standing. We stood in the third rank. I was standing a little to
the right of center, and can be seen between two of Co. F who were
in the rank before ours. I had on a white (ought to have been) jacket,
and a gun boat cap, which have no rim. Jack Smith[56] of our company
is looking over my shoulder, having a tolerably broad rimmed black
hat on. The tall man you see is Silas Langford[57] of Co. "H." He was
6 feet 7 inches when he enlisted, and I think a little taller now. He lost
a piece of the hat that he had, while going down on the boat, and had
an old handkerchief tied around his head. Of the squad sitting directly
in front 3 belong to "H." The one on the right lower right hand corner
is Tom Humphrey, the one on the left is Joseph Lannum, whom father
saw when he was home on a furlough. He got back to the company
just in time to be gobbled with the rest of us.

About the center is Billy Smith,[58] a fat, chubby fellow with a cap
on. The one towards the left sitting down with a tall peaked white hat
on is Oscar Burch,[59] our sergeant major.

You ask if musquitos were not bad while in imprisonment. That
was a plague from which we were entirely free. The country in Texas
is high and rolling, very little swampy land to breed them. I have no

doubt that they would have been bad in the camp where we stayed last winter, but we left it in March, before the weather got warm enough for them.

We have the biggest musquitos here that I ever seen any place. They are or rather have been very bad out on the picket line, but in camp they have not been very troublesome. Perhaps you are not aware that soldiers can have the luxury of a musquito bar,[60] such is the fact, and the most of the boys have them. They are made to sleep under & cost $1.00 each.

It has been a long time since I heard from William Butcher.[61] I was glad to hear that he is doing so well.

We are so far from *anyplace* that we cannot hear the news until it has become quite stale. The rebs have been stirring things up quite lively in Missouri,[62] I see. It looks to me as though such an expedition would not have been undertaken had aid not been promised after they got [there], such as, assistance that certain *societies* proposed giving, certainly could have been the only inducement. I really do not understand why it is that men in the north act as they do, every action tending to produce a war at home. They certainly know not what they do.

The soldiers in the field are becoming more confident every day that the rebellion is on its last legs and were it not for Northern sympathies we would finish this thing in short order. That is their only hope (for I have heard themselves tell it), that the North will become divided and the strength of the government be weakened accordingly, but I hope there is enough patriotism yet, in the North, to sustain us in our endeavors to subdue this wicked rebellion.

We, (the soldiers) want *peace* as badly as any and one would think, much *more* than any one, not in the army, but I have yet to hear the *first* soldier desire a peace until the last rebel has laid down his arms and returned to his allegiance. That is the only peace that a true lover of his country can desire. For we can have no other without bending the knee to that arch traitor Jeff Davis,[63] and his clan. They began the war by taking up arms against the government, and they can end it very easily by laying down those arms. I am not in favor of giving them one inch until that is done, and it would not be long until such a thing would happen if it were not for the hope of a divided North.

That hope encourages them to hold out yet a while longer, waiting for some thing to turn up in their favor. I believe the people at home are despondent, principally on account of the efforts made by some in their *midst*, to undermine the government in various ways. They are led to believe that it is pretty much the same way in the army, but they are mistaken. The army is united in a determination to put down the rebellion, and it would put it down so much the sooner if all would give their support if it was no more than words. Nothing is so much calculated to discourage one who is battling for the rights of his country, than to hear of efforts of men, (who are at home, and enjoying all the benefits and comforts of life) using their utmost endeavors to weaken the strength of the government. There is [as] treasonable a set of men in the North as there is in the south. They can be known by their rejoicing at the defeats of our army. I think that I could point out some who are and have been residents of Van Buren Co. They never award any praise to us when successful, but condole with their southern friends in their troubles. I venture to say, that if a person of that stamp, of Vallandingham[64] for instance, and Jeff Davis were set up as targets any place before the army, that Jeff would live a short time the longest. Nothing is thought so dispicable by a Union soldier as are those hypocritical cowards who advocate the southern cause, but are afraid to come and fight us. A rebel in arms is one hundred times more honorable than such. But I have said more than I intended when I commenced writing, and must turn to another more pleasant topic—the *paymaster*. This individual, whose visits are always welcome, arrived a day or so ago. We have received our pay. Those who were prisoners, had 12 months pay due. My wages were $210.00, ten months at $17.00 & 2 months at $20.00. I had due for clothing in excess of what I have drawn, $13.35, making my pay $223.35. I have sent per Adams Express Co. $225.00.[65] The company sends in all nearly $4500.00. It is all sent to Geo. W. Games, Keosauqua. I will send an order so that father can get it upon calling for it. I don't know yet whether *cap* [Captain Sommerville] will give it yet awhile, I will see in the morning. The last money sent, the orders reached their destination before the money did, causing some trouble. We got two months pay soon after our exchange. I have part of that yet, enough to last until next pay day if nothing happens.

Give my best respects to Uncles Nide & Sammy and to Aunt Rachel. My love to Father, Mother, & John.

From your affectionate brother,

William

P.S. This leaves me in good health. I will send the orders in my next.

~

Camp of the 19th Iowa Vols.

Barrancas, Fla.

Oct. 21st, 1864

Dear Father & Mother:

Having a little spare time this evening, I have concluded to improve it by writing a few lines to you.

I answered George's letter of Sept. 17th, on the 13th of the present month. That is the latest that I have from home, and am looking anxiously every mail for a letter. It takes a letter 20 or 25 days to come from home.

I received yesterday a letter from Mary Lighthill, dated Sept. 30th. The friends are all well. She mentioned that Jeannette[66] had seen Ann Anderson a short time before, and that she was glad to hear that I had got out of the rebs hands. She had not enjoyed very good health for some time. This is the first time that I have heard from her for a long time.

I wrote in my last that the paymaster had been around and paid us up to August 31st. I sent by express $225.00 to you, in care of G. W. Games, Keosauqua. I inclose an order for that amount. The express agent is still here, and it is likely that the money has not yet started & the order may get there before the money so that it will probably be well enough to delay going to Keosauqua for it for awhile after receiving this.

I forget whether I mentioned in my last that I paid the expressage & insurance, $4.50.

We have not any very late news from the North. I would like to hear how things are going in Missouri.

We have had a change of commanders here. Brig. Gen. Asboth has been relieved and Brevet[67] Brig. Gen. Bailey[68] takes his place.

Maj. Gen. Granger[69] came over from Ft. Morgan[70] a few days ago, and made the change. From appearances this place will become the fitting out place for an expedition. Quite a large number of wagons have already arrived. The dock is being enlarged, and everything betokens lively times. There is one good saw mill here in running order, and another one came over from New Orleans a few days ago.

To get logs to supply these mills, it is necessary to make trips up the bay 25 & 30 miles. There the beach is covered with logs, which have been cut when times were better. It is not much trouble to roll them together & make rafts. 2 companies of our regt. went out last week to get a raft, and were attacked by a small party of rebs. The next day 200 of the regt. went up through St. Mary de Galvez Bay into Blackwater Bay, and proceeded to construct a raft. About 12 o'clock the raft was finished and it was being started out to the steamer to be taken in tow — when the rebs made an attack on the pickets, firing on them from the extreme right to the left and soon drove them in.[71] I happened to be on guard on the boat at the time, the *cusses* fired at the boat quite wickedly for awhile, leaving the bullet marks in many places. They had no artillery, and we had two pieces on the boat, which finally drove them off. One of the artillery men was wounded in the foot. On shore the bullets flew over the boys quite briskly. The boys lay along the beach waiting for the rebs to charge but the rebel commander could not make his men do so, and he cussed them unmercifully. The commander of the expedition had orders not to bring on an engagement, but to get logs. After shelling them out we hitched on to the raft. One of Company "I" was killed during the skirmish. We could not find out the loss of the rebs.[72] My space has about "played out" & I must close for this time.

I remain ever your affectionate son,
William

～

Camp of the 19th Iowa Vol. Inf.
Barrancas, Fla.
Nov. 1st, 1864
Dear Brothers:
Your welcome letter bearing date of Oct. 3rd and 9th was received yesterday. I was truly glad to hear from you. My last word from you

being the 17th of September. I wrote to father on the 21st Oct. sending an *order* for the money expressed home. I hope it has been received.

I am anxious to hear from you again, having learned through the papers and letters received by others that a band of rebels had entered Van Buren Co. and were committing their usual depradations.[73] I wish that every one of them would be taken, and executed on the spot. No quarters should be shown them whatever. If there is any force of the guerrillas, the militia will have an opportunity of exhibiting their bravery. It seems to me that it is part of the plot or scheme to revolutionize the northwest — the entrance of Price into Missouri, and the scattering of so many guerrilla bands over different sections of country.[74]

The opinions of the boys, upon hearing of this "invasion," were various. Many seemed to think that it would ultimately result in good, to give the folks at home a taste of war, for heretofore the people of Iowa, and other states distant from the field of active operations, know absolutely nothing of the miseries and actual suffering from that cause. Of course they miss those who have left their homes, and entered the army. They feel the increased taxation, and higher prices of articles of wear & consumption, but they cannot realize the destruction consequent from an invading force. When a hostile force comes along, and encamps, they do not hesitate to burn fences, pillage houses, run off horse and cattle, take what grain they want, and let the owner whistle for compensation. The ford at Uncle Nide's would, if an army of any size were marching through that section, be very apt to be one of the camping places, it being necessary to have plenty of water for man and beast, and an army could not be supplied with that article on the prairie. Judging from what I have seen, I imagine one stopping there, the advance of cavalry, generally as soon as they got there would pitch into the hay & oats stacks and secure forage for their horses, that is the first thing they look to, getting as much as they could tie on their saddles. The cavalryman would then think of his own wants, seeing a nice hog or sheep or chicken. He hauls out his revolver, and takes the best. The infantry finally comes up. They stack arms and having only themselves to care for, they make for the fence to get a supply of wood. I have seen strings of fence 300 or 400 yds. long disappear in an incredibly short space of time, there being a man for every 2 or 3 rails. The boys are very fond of poultry, and chickens

"If the North Would Remain United"

suddenly disappear on their approach, and there is always some who will go into houses and take whatever they see desirable.

I sincerely hope that Iowa will never be subject to such an invasion, but I believe that men are living there who would bring about such a state of affairs, or worse. I do not think that a small body of men, such as those who went through Van Buren, would be adventurous enough to try the like without the thought of finding friends who would probably assist them in their hellish designs.[75] I wish that the 19th was in that section awhile. I think that we could dispose of rebels, and some others who pretend to be loyal, but are the very traitors living.

I see that a number of soldiers have been murdered in different sections of the state.[76] If things do not alter, it will become more unsafe at home than in the army.

I hope to see the "better day" which is coming, I think, before a great while. Every thing before us looks encouraging and were it not for the eternal, infernal, peace howlers of the North, the war would soon end in our triumph over the rebels, and then we could have a *permanent* peace.

Nothing of interest has transpired since my last. Several expeditions for saw-logs went out and returned, safely.[77] We had an *alarm* a few nights ago, caused by our pickets being fired upon. We got in line (about 2 o'clock A.M.) but did not leave our camp.

You speak of finding shells along the coast. I expected to find them here, but there is none worth mentioning, nothing but white sand, as white as snow. It makes a noise similar to dry frozen snow, when walking through it.

We have been getting mail more frequently of late. I understand that the *Zephyr*, a small steamer is to make trips twice a week hereafter between this place and New Orleans. It is getting so dark that I can hardly see what I write and must close.

Give my respects to Uncle Nide, Uncle Sammy & Aunt Rachel, also to Walter Ferguson. My love to father and mother. Hoping this will find you all well.

I remain as ever your affectionate brother,

William

P.S. Father can do as he pleases or thinks best with the money sent home.

~

Camp of the 19th Iowa Vols.

Barrancas, Fla.

Nov. 8th, 1864

Dear Father, Mother, and Brothers:

I hasten to improve a few spare moments, this evening, by writing a few lines to you. My last was written on the 1st inst. in answer to your letter of Oct. 9th.

I have been busily engaged yesterday and today, having been selected for one of the clerks of the election,[78] which passed off quietly yesterday.

There was 515 polled by the regiment. Eight counties were represented, and it was a tedious business to count the vote. We got through this evening, and have everything ready for Mr. Commissioner Knox, of Warren County,[79] to deliver to the Sect. of State.[80]

As the result we have for Presidential Elector at Large C. Ben. Darwin, 466 votes and for Mitchell 38 votes. Van Valkenburg 465 and Miller 39, the number for electors ranging on one ticket from 466 to 455, and on the other from 39 to 24.[81]

On the county ticket, thinking it our duty to give a ex-soldier a *lift*, Bonney,[82] for clerk, has 72 and Miller[83] 19 votes. Goddard,[84] for recorder 69 — no opposition.

The vote in 2nd Maine cavalry was 230 Lincoln and 5 McClellan,[85] thus you see the manner in which soldiers of this section wish to procure a peace.[86] The 19th and 2nd ME. are the only white troops here, excepting a small detachment of the 7th Vermont, that voted, the 1st Florida did not vote there being no provision for it.[87]

I suppose you will have a pretty good idea, as to who the successful candidate is, by the time this is received, so enough of that.[88]

Another thing worthy of mention, since my last, is the arrival and issue to the regiment of a new set of guns. The *Springfield Rifled Musket*[89] — in place of our *Enfields*, which are about worn out.

I do not know that they are a better gun than the Enfield, but they *look* better, and that goes a great ways, on an inspection.

The duty continues very heavy, 5 and 6 on *guard* and *all* the rest on *fatigue*, 150 men from the regt. each day work on fortifications which are being erected.

Gen. Bailey seems to be a thorough going man, he is continually around, wherever any thing is being erected, or else visiting the picket guards, inspecting camps, etc. He has issued orders, which come down pretty heavily on officers. He expects every one to *know* his duty, and to *do it*.

We got news yesterday of *Prices* defeat[90] and retreat south, if true, it is one of the best things happening of late.

The weather for some weeks past was cool, frost being seen on the 5th instant in places, but for the last two or three days there has been a warm south wind, making the waters of the Gulf and Bay quite rough.

I have nothing more of much importance to write I believe, except, that all the boys of your acquaintance are well.

Tattoo[91] is now beating, so no more this time.

Yours affectionately,

William

~

Nov. 10th. It is quite cool this morning, the wind having shifted to the north last night.

After I stopped writing last night, I thought that you would, probably, like to know how we *live* here.

The company is supplied with the common (wedge) tent, more than half of the numbers have fixed up for the winter. We built a square enclosure of boards the size of a tent, say 6 or 7 feet square, and then put up the tent, which forms the roof.

As for eatables we have been well supplied. Two or three schooners from Boston & New York have arrived since payday, laden with supplies of vegetables, etc.

Potatoes sell at $6.50 per bbl. apples sell at $15.00. We have bake ovens, and some of the boys make a good deal of money, baking and selling pies made of dried apples, pies retail at 20 and 25 cts. each.

Condensed milk is one of the best things that the sutler keeps, [it] sells at from 50 to 80 cts. per can, eight about one pound. We can have milk at all times if we wish. All of the water is taken out of it by some process, leaving the other parts which is easily diluted by putting in warm water or coffee. We have all the sugar that we can use and light bread, pickled pork, mess beef, fresh beef 3 times a week. The U.S.

Sanitary Commission has kept us pretty well supplied with onions, and some potatos.

For the present adieu,

William

~

Camp of the 19th Regiment Iowa Infantry Vols.

Company "H"

Barrancas, Florida

November 27th, 1864

Dear Brothers,

Your welcome letter of October 22nd was received a day or two ago — I was glad to hear that you are all well.

The articles sent to the company by our friends arrived yesterday. They consisted of potatoes, onions, dried apples, and a few green apples, a barrel of "sour krout" and some canned fruits.

You spoke in the last letter of having sent some potatoes. The boys send their thanks to all who contributed towards sending. I am sorry to hear that the potato crop was so much of a failure. Since pay day we have been tolerably well supplied with potatos & onions. Several schooners[92] from New York have stopped here selling potatoes at $6.50 per barrel.

Our Sutler Cap. Paine[93] has been doing a big business in the apple line, for two or three weeks past, having brought on 3 different supplies. He brought over 80 barrels [of] apples a short time ago, and 20 bbls. oranges, selling them all in two days, the apples at $15.00 per bbl. and the oranges at $16.00 per bbl. They cost him about $5.00 per bbl. in New Orleans, so that his proffit was quite handsome.

I have nothing of much importance to write that would be interesting to you but must try and fill my sheet.

The duty performance by the regiment is very heavy as a general thing, every man is on duty daily. I was acting in the orderlies place for several days past, the orderly Amos Wood being unwell. It kept me busy filling details. First comes the picket guard, two men daily & occasionally a sergt. or corporal. Then wharf guard, headquarters guard, at the genls. quarters, and camp guard. This last is not like the camp guard when we first came out, which then would encircle the camp. Now there is but two sentinels on a relief, one at the colonels quarters and another to prevent riding across the camp ground. After all the details are filled the balance go on *"fatigue"* at Fort Redout [94] throwing up earth, or rather sand, works, for it is all sand. If there is no "fatigue at the fort" all of the available force is called upon for an expedition. Yesterday evening the boys were congratulating themselves upon resting today (Sunday) as the fort fatigue was not called for, but in a little while along came the detail — 1st sergeant, 4 corporals, and 14 men for "expedition."

They started this morning at 7 o'clock with one days rations, they have gone up the bay either for logs or else to tear down some old buildings to get lumber.

An immense amount of lumber is being used here now, since the present general took command a new wharf has been built here [with] about [a] 100 ft. front and running about 250 ft. A new bakery has been put up and they are now building a lot of large warehouses, and a large stable, over 400 ft. long for the mules belonging to post train.

Every man who ever sawed off a plank or drove a nail before he came to the army, is detailed as a *carpenter*. Mooney, Nincehelser, and 4 others are detailed from our company. Abner Buckles is working in the regimental bakery. John Stone has not been fortunate enough to get detailed and is with the company. Those mentioned above are all well, as also are George & Joseph Paxton.

We had some very cool weather a few days ago, turning cold on the 22nd. Ice was formed in places that night and on the night it froze considerably, the ice being ¼ inch in thickness. Today it is quite pleasant. A person would feel comfortable without a coat. I felt the cold almost as much the other day as I would if at home. It appeared to have as much effect as an Iowa winter. I do not like this southern climate near so well as the northern. Here it is warm enough to do without a coat, and next day, probably, clothing enough cannot be got on to make a person feel comfortable. We have all the clothing that we want, the most of us having more than we ever had before since entering the service. Speaking of clothing puts one in mind of the socks that mother was knitting for me, of course I would like very well to have them, but it would be rather difficult to get them here, they being apt to get lost if sent by mail. I can draw all the socks I need, although they do not last very well, but 35 cts. per pair is not much and I can afford to keep several pair.

If the duty was not so heavy we could enjoy ourselves very well here now, having plenty of every thing to eat and wear, which I could not say this time last year. It will be a year day after tomorrow since we started from Tyler the first time. The ground was fro.:en hard, many had no shoes, some nothing but pants and shirt. The morning before we started I succeeded in getting an old pair of shoes from one of the guards. They had no shape to them, the leather was hard, and they were a little too small for me. That morning I started off with them on, but they hurt my feet so that I had to take them off after going 3 or 4 miles. I then tried it barefooted about 5 miles, the road being very rough and in some places covered with ice. I thought that I would sooner stand the hurting of my feet by the shoes than the frozen ground, and accordingly put them on again. We were forced over 21 miles of road that day starting at 11 o'clock in the morning and reaching the Sabine River at dark. The next morning hardly a man could move upon first getting up. We were finally got out in line, and compelled to stand for some time, the ground froze hard, and covered with a heavy white frost, finally the guards got ready and by sun up we were on our way again. We thought then that we would be exchanged right away, but we found out different. My feet got blistered all over, and so sore that I could hardly bear it, nor would not had it been under any other circumstance.

But it is among the things that were, and I do not now feel much the worse of it, but I would not have believed that any person could stand what we did.

Give my best respects to Uncle Nide & Aunt Rachel. I must write to them some of these days. Also my regards to Capt. Ferguson[95] and Mrs. Ferguson.

As ever your affectionate brother,
William

~

Camp of the 19th Regiment Iowa Infantry Vols.

Company "H"

Barrancas, Florida

December 4th, 1864

Dear Brothers:

Your truly welcome letter of November 6th was received on the 29th.

I had written one only a day or two previously. But making it a point to answer letters received as soon after receiving them as convenient, I concluded to write a little this evening, not having much of importance to communicate I expect it will be short.

The usual routine of duty continued until a day or so ago. The wharf guard & head quarters guard was relieved, leaving only the usual detail for picket to be filled.

We began to think something was going to "turn up." It was not long until orders were received to be ready to march, upon short notice. No one knew where, exactly. The camp was soon full of rumors, some reported that we were to go back on the Mississippi, others that we would go around on the Atlantic Coast & operate at Savannah or some other point, with Sherman.[96] Still others that we were to go out by land, and draw the attention of forces in southern Alabama & Georgia to prevent them marching against Sherman.

I think the latter, about the nearest conjecture. I think that it was proposed to make a kind of demonstration, towards the railroad running from Mobile to Montgomery. But all of these are mere conjectures. Lt. Col. Bruce himself not knowing the exact destination.

Today I have not heard much about it, every one seeming to think that it will fall through with. The general (Granger, I suppose) was to have come here last night, but when the boat arrived he was not aboard, and sent word I heard, that he would not be here.

Brevet Brig. Gen. Bailey has been relieved, he taking command somewhere on the Mississippi of a cavalry force. A Col. Robinson[97] is commanding until a general (reports say McKean)[98] arrives.

I suppose that you have had some cold weather by this time. After the cool spell last week, we are now having some very pleasant weather. We have very comfortable quarters here, and if we are allowed to remain until spring, and get the benefit of them, it will be all right. But I would not be much surprised to be ordered away at any time, then again we may be allowed to remain the balance of our term of service, which expires on the 21st of August next.

I suppose from what you write, that you will be able to keep warm this winter without much trouble. About this time last year, and later, while near Shreveport, La. I would often think of the "new house" and how I would like to be in it, some of the cold days and nights.

About the last of December, last year, we were going on parole at the camp near Shreveport, and had the privilege of going one half mile from camp. The board sheds, in which we were quartered, were very cold, standing as they did in an open field, exposed to the cold north wind. Four of us having *three* excuses for blankets, took them, and went to the woods, kindled a big fire or rather log head, in a deep hollow where the wind could not get at us, raked together a pile of leaves, and slept [better] than we would have done in the quarters. We slept, these several nights when the bayou close by would freeze over during the night, the ice being from one to one and a half inches thick.

One of the boys got a letter the other day from one of the 19th Kentucky boys,[99] who were left there when we came through, about six hundred were exchanged this time leaving about 3000 there still.

We have been living highly since the sanitary supplies, from home, arrived, having plenty of pickles, sour krout, potatoes, etc. I have just eaten supper, we had some boiled corn, such as I used to get at home.

I want you to write as frequently as you can, give all the news. I would like to know how "Watch" and "Tiger"[100] have been getting along since I left home, also the horses. I have never heard how that colt father bought from Uncle Nide, turned out.

I have been thinking of writing to Uncle Nide but have had nothing to write about recently. Tell him that I will write to him some of these days. Give my best respects to him and Aunt Rachel, also to Uncle Sammy if he is there. I would like very much to get a letter from him. My love to father and mother, reserving a fair portion for yourselves.

I remain affectionately your brother,
William

CHAPTER 7

" We Will Be Apt to Wake Things Up in Alabama **"**

While a Union force under General Granger had succeeded in capturing the forts guarding the entrance to Mobile Bay by the end of August 1864, it soon became apparent that Granger lacked sufficient numbers to move on the fortifications defending the city of Mobile itself. Therefore, his superior, General Canby, decided to build up his troop strength gradually to prepare for that stage of the campaign.

A number of possible strategies for such an undertaking presented themselves, and Canby carefully weighed his options. He finally selected a plan that would utilize two converging approaches on the city. First, a force under his command would move against the city along the eastern shore of Mobile Bay from Dauphin Island, with Spanish Fort as its initial objective. And second, troops under the command of Major General Frederick Steele would advance overland from Pensacola against the Confederate fortifications around Blakely, Alabama, the major barrier along that route to Mobile.

The 19th Iowa became part of Canby's expeditionary force. Deployed initially on Dauphin Island at the mouth of Mobile Bay, the 19th soon joined a detachment that threatened Mobile with an assault from a position in southeastern Mississippi. After weeks of service there, the 19th Iowa rejoined Canby's main force on the shore of the bay for the final campaign against the defenses of Mobile.

Clayton's fourteen letters from this period once again cover a broad range of experiences. He would look upon his days on guard duty in Mississippi quite fondly; the same can hardly be said for his description of the siege operations around Mobile. Most important, during this period Clayton hears of, and comments on, the series of developments in the East that would bring the Civil War to its conclusion.

～

Camp of the 19th Regiment Iowa Infantry Vols.
Company "H"
Fort Gaines, Ala.[1]
Dec. 12th, 1864
Dear Brothers:

You will see by the heading of my letter that the "19th" has again changed its stopping place, this time for the worse.

We had just got ourselves well fixed over at Barrancas, each squad having either a stove or chimney to its quarters so that we cared little what kind of weather we had.

On the 6th however the steamer *Alabama* brought orders for us to move to this place shortly after we got our tents down. It commenced raining, and continued several hours, giving us a good wetting. We got aboard of the boat finally, and started about 2 o'clock P.M. The waters of the gulf were rolling considerably, and our boat pitched about a good deal, many of the boys were sea sick, but it did not affect me any. We arrived here about 10 o'clock P.M. and went into camp near the fort the next morning. There was but few troops here, the only ones being the 3rd Maryland dismounted cavalry, and a detachment of the 6th Michigan in the fort. Day before yesterday, however, two more regiments, the 69th Indiana and 97th Illinois, arrived from Morganza on the Mississippi.

Fort Morgan lays several miles across the channel, too far off to get a good view of it.[2] Fort Gaines is a very nice fort, larger considerably than I expected to see. It is on Dauphin Island.[3]

The weather since we came here has been very windy, and cold, the north wind sweeps down on us from off the Bay, and on the other side is the Gulf.

On the other side, in the vicinity of Morgan, are the 20th Wisconsin and 94th Illinois regiments, the ones that we were brigaded with while in Missouri.

A movement is expected soon, upon Mobile. That place is about 35 miles from here up the Bay.

A cavalry force left Baton Rouge a short time since, supposed to

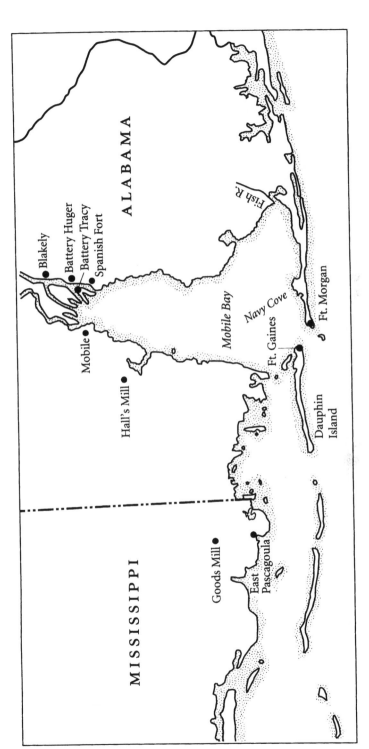

Mississippi and Alabama, 1864–1865.

The Ladies Sanitary Aid Society of Fairfield, Iowa, preparing a shipment of food, 1864. "Auntie" Woods leans against an apple press, resting her chin on her hand, to the left of center. Courtesy of the State Historical Society of Iowa, original owned by the Fairfield Public Library.

[be] destined for that place.[4] There is not force enough here yet to do much in that direction but more troops are looked for. Maj. Gen. Granger commands at this place.

We have been living highly for some time past. Another large supply of sanitary goods arrived, since we got here, for our regiment. They were in charge of Mrs. Woods[5] of Fairfield, and consisted of potatos, onions, apples, etc., about 30,000 pounds in all.

All of the detailed men joined the company when we left Barrancas, so that we now have a good sized company, 57 men. 4 are absent sick making a total of 61 men all told.

The boys are all well from your neighborhood, and there is but two on the sick list. I have written this in a hurry and you must excuse bad writing. It will soon be time for evening inspection and I must close.

Give my respects to all.

As ever your affectionate brother,

William

"We Will Be Apt to Wake Things Up in Alabama"

~

Camp of the 19th Regiment Iowa Infantry Vols.
Company "H"
East Pascagoula, Miss.[6]
January 4th, 1865
Dear Brothers:

I will attempt to write a few lines today in reply to yours dated November 25th, which I received on the 26th Dec. I was very glad to hear from you, also to learn that my money had arrived.

We have been on the *go* so much of late that I have had no chance of writing, my last letter being written at Ft. Gaines on or about the 12th December.

We received orders to march on the 13th but did not get off until the 14th when we embarked on the steamer *Alabama* bound for this place. All of the troops (excepting the garrisons) left Forts Morgan & Gaines at the same time. We landed here on the evening of the 15th, and marched out 5 or 6 miles, and the next day continued our march 5 miles further where all the troops went into camp. On the 17th the 19th moved 1½ miles further out to a saw mill where there was an immense lot of lumber, some of it rough and a good part of it, flooring boards, ready dressed. We guarded the lumber for several days, and skirmished with the Johnnies,[7] who began to appear in our front. They kept us constantly under arms for two or three days. The regiment went outside of the pickets as often as three times a day, and skirmished with them, without any loss to us however. The 20th Wisconsin went out one day to reccounoiter and the rebs attacked them with four pieces of artillery. Our regiment went to their support with two pieces of artillery, and we drove them away. The 20th had one man wounded, the only casualty on our side. The 20th Wisc. finally received orders to raft lumber. They worked at it four or five days, rafting a large lot of the flooring. We were only 30 miles from Mobile, and not thinking it safe to remain longer with our force (about 3500) we were ordered to fall back. We started at midnight Christmas night. The roads were *very* bad, and we only got about 2½ miles by daylight, it being almost impossible to get the artillery and train along. The water the greater part of the way stood from 3 to 6 inches deep all over the ground (the country being very level), and it was dark as *pitch*. There was no getting out of it, and we *waded* it through. The Army fell back to within 6 miles of this place, and went into camp on the 26th where they have since remained.[8]

On the evening of the 27th Capt. Sommerville received orders to proceed with his company to this place, and report for *Provost* duty.[9] We started at daylight next morning, and came here and have been on duty ever since. We have to guard prisoners arrested by the Provost marshal[10] and patrol the town, and protect the inhabitants and property. We do not get much rest, but I think it better than to be in the front, in the mud, and pine smoke, which makes a person look like a "nigger." We left "Gaines" in light marching, bringing nothing but a blanket and overcoat. After we came here we got permission to send for our clothing. I accordingly was sent to Ft. Gaines for the knapsacks on the 30th. Our camp is still standing there, 5 or 6 men from each company being left behind. I got back the next day with them, so that we had a change of clothing for New Years. The troops at the front have not had their clothing sent to them. This place is being fortified, and it appears to be the intention to hold it, probably as a future base of operations against Mobile.

From the accounts given by prisoners, we could have taken the place with little or no opposition if we had marched on immediately after landing but it is likely that they have a large force there by this time.

I suppose you had a good Christmas dinner. We happened to be short of rations that day, and had only a piece of salt beef and hard "tack." I have never been on an expedition when rations were as scanty as the present one.

There is any quantity of *oysters* here, that can be had for the picking of them up, at low tide, so that we will not starve while here.

Give my best respects to all. I would like much to get a letter from cousin Ellen. I will write to her when I get more time. I must quit, and see how the guards are getting along — so no more at present.

From your affectionate brother,

William

~

Headquarters Pro. Guard [11]

East Pascagoula, Miss.

Jan. 17th, 1865

Dear Brothers:

Your truly welcome letters of the 18th & 28th Dec. came to hand today and I assure you that I was glad to hear from you.

My last letter to you was written on the 4th of this month. I would have written sooner but nothing of importance transpiring I thought it hardly worthwhile.

Co. "H" is still here doing Provost duty, and have it a little easier at present, having been reinforced by a company of the 94th Ill.

The boys now are on duty every other day in place of every day, which is quite a relief. For my part, I have got so accustomed to being up until 1 or 2 o'clock that I cannot go to sleep much earlier now that I have the opportunity.

I would like very much to be up on "Old Chequest" a week or two about this time of year. I never was a very successful deer hunter but I think that I would be out after them "bushwhacking."

You speak of the weather being cold. Here it gets cold enough occasionally to freeze a little, and then it turns warm. I have heard the frogs in the swamps back of town every evening since we came here & an occasional mosquito sings around of evenings to let us know, I suppose, what we may look forward for in warmer weather.

All of the forces have fell back near town since I wrote last, no more troops have come here since I cannot determine what is to be done here, but I think that the place will be held. The rebs do not make much show in our front any longer.

Two deserters who came in last night from Mobile (having left there day before yesterday) report that they have but a small force at that not over 3 or 4000 at the outside, many of them being militia. Their advance post is 12 miles this side of the city at Halls Mills. [12]

From what these and others tell, we could easily have gone on when we first landed here, and taken the place, and I wish now that it had been done. [13]

Col. Bertram of the 20th Wis. commands the post, [14] General Granger being absent.

We have a great time here doing Provost duty, no officer or enlisted man is allowed to be absent from camp without written authority and the boys take delight in "coming (NO, CLOSING)" down on the officers, especially those belonging to the negro regiments. It is amusing to watch them when officers come along. They are required to salute officers according to rank. When a line officer[15] comes along the guard comes to a shoulder arms, and as the officer approaches, throws up his left hand, then brings down his gun, halts him and asks to see his pass.

I would like to know the address of John Brunson. I have heard nothing from him for so long that I would like to write him and get an answer from him.

Give my best respects to all and my love to father & mother. The bell rings for supper and I must close. This leaves me in good health.

Ever your affectionate brother,

William

~

Hd. Qrs. Provost Guard

East Pascagoula, Miss.

January 29th, 1865

Dear Brothers:

I again address you from this point, Co. "H" being still on duty here as Provost guards.

We have had a very pleasant time so far. We have our quarters in a dwelling house but have hardly enough room, but still it is so much better than being out in the mud that we are fully satisfied.

We have now been here on duty a month but I think it likely that we will soon be on the go again. Troops have been passing here going east, their destination is supposed to [be] Mobile but it is said that those that have passed, have gone to Barrancas. I heard today that the brigade to which we belong, is going to remain here for the present, with the exception of the 19th Iowa. It came from good authority, but I cannot say whether such will be the case.

This is a very desirable place to remain, at any rate every one seems loath to leave it.

Balls and dances have been the order of the day (or rather night), for some time past.

Ladies are quite numerous here, and as this has been the residence of many wealthy merchants of New Orleans and New York, the residents are of a different class, to what we have found generally in our travels, being educated, and look as though they know what civilization is.

All of the citizens have to be fed by our government. They got their supplies from Mobile before we occupied the place, but as a matter of course they could do so no longer after our arrival. Well that is enough about the citizens.

Our favorite general, F. R. Herron,[16] was here a few days ago. He is Inspector Genl.[17] of Canby's department.

My last letter from you was dated Dec. 28th. I answered it as soon as I received it. I also got a letter a short time ago from Cousin Mary Lighthill. They were all well.

We have not had much of importance transpiring here for some time. The 14th New York and 6th Mo. cav. regts. left here yesterday and the day before, their destination being New Orleans.

The weather has been quite cool for some days past, freezing a little every night. The health of the company and indeed of all the troops here, is good.

I have hardly time any more to write so that you must excuse the brevity of my letters.

Give my respects to all and my love to father & mother.

I remain as ever your affectionate brother,

William

⁓

Camp of the 19th Iowa Vols.

Fort Gaines, Ala.

Feb. 8th, 1865

Dear Brothers:

Here we are again on Dauphin Island, getting the full benefit of all the breeze that comes along. In my last letter from East Pascagoula Miss. I mentioned that we would not remain there much longer from appearances. The troops commenced leaving about the last of the month, the 19th Iowa and 20th Wisconsin being the only regiments left there on the evening of January 31st.

They embarked after dark, and by midnight the Yankees were all out of Pascagoula, the "Provost guards" being the last to embark.

We (the Provosts) were sorry to leave the place, having become acquainted with all the inhabitants, and having as good a time, for over a month, as we could wish.

We disembarked the next morning (Feb. 1st) at this place and fixed up our old camp.

Part of the troops went direct to Barrancas, Fla. from Pascagoula, some stopped over at Morgan, and two or three regiments stopped here.

Yesterday and today several thousand more troops have landed on the island, the 21st Iowa among the number. They came here from New Orleans district, but came from Little Rock, Ark., and Memphis, Tenn., not long since.

Preparations are being made, no doubt, to give Mobile a visit.

It has been reported that the place is being evacuated, but such is not the case, yet, although they might as well do so, as it will fall into our hands anyhow.

Some think that they will not make much resistance there, but make Selma and Montgomery their standpoints.

We have received no mail for over a week. The last letter I got from you was one written Dec. 28th, 1864. I shall look for another one, if we can get another mail.

We got ready for an inspection this morning, but the inspector not making his appearance, it has not come off yet. The boys dislike these inspections, more than anything else in the line of duty. The guns, equipments, and clothing have to be in the best of order or fault is found. Well, as we say when we get to talking about it, "*only seven months scant*" [18] and inspections will play out.

The weather here at present is rather cool, although I feel comfortable enough here in my tent without any fire.

The health of the company is good, while doing Provost duty at Pascagoula there was no one sick during the time we were there, now there is but one on the sick list.

I have written enough for the present and must quit. Give my respects to all.

I remain your affectionate brother,

William

Camp of the 19th Iowa Vols.

Fort Gaines, Ala.

Febr'y 19th, 1865

Dear Brothers:

I received John's letter of Jan. 25th, day before yesterday, and, as it had been so long since receiving any word from you, it is hardly necessary to say that I was truly glad to hear from home once more.

I suppose you have enjoyed yourselves *hugely* in that pleasant exercise — skating. Skates are an article unknown in this part of the world, there is an abundance of water, but no ice. I have not seen ice ¼ of an inch thick this winter.

Still when we have north winds, they have such an effect upon us that we need all of the clothing we have to keep us comfortable. We have had some very pretty weather of late, but it does not last long at a time.

Our number has been largely increased on this island within the last two weeks, there being now about 10,000 men here. A larger number have landed at Barrancas, Fla. They belong to what is called the reserve corps,[19] and have been (the greater part of them) commanded by Gen. Steele in Arkansas.

We will be apt to wake things up in Alabama some of these times, I learn that a force is organized in the northern part of the state, with which this force is to co-operate.

This is a remarkably dull place not withstanding the fact that so many troops have landed.

The wind is blowing constantly so that our ears are always filled with its noise, and that of the water upon the beach. There is three brass bands upon the island, but the wind blows all of the sound away, so that it is almost impossible to tell what tune is being played at the distance of fifty yards. In drilling company drill it is almost impossible at times for the commander to make himself heard from one end of the company to the other. 1st Lt. William Byers now commands the company, Capt. Sommerville having been detached. He, the capt., is now Provost Marshal, Dauphin Island, Ala.

I would like very much to get a *pop* at some of those turkeys which, I presume, are plenty in your section of the world.

Down here we have, (or had when at Goods Mills,[20] Miss. two months ago) what the boys termed "turkey hunts" when we were called out two or three times some days to skirmish with the rebs, this last mentioned kind is not so pleasant as they might be, if the feathered kind only was to be found.

Well, as I have said before this is a dull place & items scarce and I shall bring my scribbling to a close. All of the boys from Chequest are able for their rations.

I would like very much to receive a letter from Walter Ferguson. The boys frequently speak of Lieut. Ferguson, and wish that his health had permitted him to remain with us. My respects to him, and all friends.

Ever your affectionate brother,
William

~

Camp of the 19th Iowa Vols.
Fort Gaines, Ala.
Febry. 26th, 1865
Dear Brothers:
Again I scribble a few lines from this point.

We have remained inactive since I last wrote to you, (on the 19th instant) but there has been a considerable quantity of troops landed here, and at Ft. Morgan since that time. Part of Gen. A. J. Smith's[21] men have landed at Morgan, and they are arriving daily.

We have had very stormy weather for a week past, making it difficult for boats to land, but today is *very* pleasant, not a breath of air stirring, and the sun shining out brilliantly. It is no uncommon thing for the sun to be hid from view for a week at a time by the fog, and clouds. Today is the Sabbath, and it appears more like Sunday than any I have experienced for a long time, everything is so quiet.

There has been a good deal of excitement, in a quiet kind of way, in the regiment for two or three days past — occasioned by the presence among us of Mr. Ingalls[22] from Iowa, who is lecturing in favor of the Iowa State Orphan Asylum.[23] When the appointment to speak to the regt. was first given out little was thought about it, the boys thinking that it was some new fangled scheme to get a dollar or two, which, by the way, he has done. He is an able speaker and all soon became deeply interested in the subject, and the 21st Iowa and our reg't. have subscribed liberally to the Institution. The 21st subscribed upward of $6000, but ours goes considerably ahead. Co. "H" alone subscribing $1320.00 and is so far the "Banner Company" of the 16 Iowa regiments visited, and the 19th is also the banner regiment.

The boys have subscribed liberally thinking that the money so expended may in some way alleviate the suffering of some poor children left parentless on account, probably, of this war, and it is money too which if kept would, by many, be spent foolishly.

I made out a list of the names and the amounts subscribed by each, which will be forwarded to Keosauqua for publication.

Dauphin Island has been honored of late by the presence of many distinguished persons, Genls. Canby, Steele, Veach,[24] Dennis,[25] Stack,[26] etc. Genls. Granger & Steele passed through our camp a few minutes ago, being around visiting the different camps.

The move will doubtless be made before a great while from this point but as yet I have learned no particulars. The health of the troops at this place is very good.

All of the company of your acquaintance are well. I received a letter a few days ago from Cousin Mary Lighthill dated Febry. 2nd. They were all well.

Give my love & best respects to Uncle Nide & family. I am looking anxiously for a letter from cousin Ellen.

I remain your affectionate brother,

William

P.S. Write often & long letters.

∼

Navy Cove, Mobile Point, Ala.

March 6th, 1865

Dear Brothers:

My last letter to you was written from Ft. Gaines, a week ago yesterday. That same evening we received marching orders to be ready at daylight the next morning. We were ready accordingly and got aboard the *Mustang* — a steamboat captured on the Rio Grande River by our forces when they took Brownsville, Texas over a year since. Well after everything was ready we started across the bay to this place, about 8 miles distant. Here we joined the rest of the brigade, consisting of the 20th Wisconsin, 94th Ill., 23rd Iowa, & our regt. We were soon about as well fixed as we had been at Gaines. This — Mobile Point — is a peninsula about 5 or 6 miles long and from ½ to ¾ mile wide with the waters of the Gulf on one side & Mobile Bay on the other. At the end of the point stands Ft. Morgan. It is about 3 miles from our camp. A railway has been built from the fort to the landing at the cove, about 5 miles. I was down to the fort a few days ago. The effects of the bombardment are yet visible everywhere. The walls showing the marks of the shells [are] on all sides. There is only 12 or 15 guns in position at present but others are being mounted. The most of them are of rebel manufacture — made at the Tredegar Works,[27] Richmond Va. There is also a number of the Brooks[28] guns, which are nice pieces. Workmen are busy removing rubbish and rebuilding the shattered walls, it will be a long time before it is completed.

Troops still continue to arrive. There is now about 20,000 here and at Ft. Gaines. The division to which we belong, is all at Barrancas, excepting this brigade. It is rumored that we will move again in a day or two, and I think that is where we go too. Quite a number of vessels of war lay at anchor here in the cove. Three large double turretted monitors[29] are here, and one or two more up the bay toward the city. They have been provided with a kind of rake which is attached to the bow of each and is calculated to pick up torpedoes.

Before we left Gaines the boys sent off a good [part] of the surplus clothing such as overcoats & blankets. I sent one blanket in a box with some, belonging to the Smith boys and Wm. Holmes.[30] The box was sent to Thornburg, for Mr. Holmes who lives south of Bonners on the road leading to Ely's Ford.[31] Billy Holmes wrote to his father to send my blanket to Dr. Bergen,[32] at Lebanon, and you can get it there if the box gets through safely. It was expressed from New Orleans, & contained 4 woolen blankets & three overcoats—I did not think my coat worth sending — there was the seven articles in the box, the coats cost when new $8.50, and blankets $3.60 so that you can figure out about what part of this expense should be paid for the one blanket. If father will take the trouble to get it he can put it to any use he sees fit. It would make a good horse blanket or two saddle blankets, and it did not feel uncomfortable over a person some of the cold nights this winter. You will know it by its being a lighter color than the others, and by my name on one corner of it in ink.

The mail is very irregular of late and letters "few and far in between," the last from you was written Jan. 25th.

I believe that I have nothing more to write at present, and will close.

As ever your affectionate brother,
William

~

Camp of the 19th Iowa Inf. Vols.
In the Field
March 17th, 1865
Dear Brothers:

The chaplain[33] just came around and informed us that the *mail* would leave this evening, and as I have not written since the 6th Inst. I thought that I would again let you know of my whereabouts. We were encamped near Navy Cove when I last wrote. The next day (the 7th) I received George's letter dated Feb. 13th — Hello! There goes an orderly up to the Col's. H'd quarters, and I now hear the command "Fall in" so I must stop for the present. Well it is *over*. What, you will ask, why — *Review*. When the order to fall in was given, the drums commenced beating the "assembly" and everybody got on his "harness" as soon as possible, for we thought that probably the pickets had been attacked. The brigade was in line in a few minutes time, and we then saw that there was no fight on hand this time. Brig. Gen. Benton[34] & staff soon appeared and rode down the line accompanied by Col. Bertram our brigade commander. They [rode] down in our rear on a gallop and we were then dismissed. I do not think that we were out more than 15 minutes. It is the first time that we have been reviewed without previous notice, but I must go back to where I left off, and resume — On the 7th of March we received marching orders, and at 8 A.M. on the 8th we marched about 4 miles up to the point and went into camp where we remained until today. We received marching orders yesterday and started about 8 o'clock this morning, we have come about 8 miles today, over sand roads. This morning before starting I received John's letter of Feb. 26th mailed March 2nd. I was very glad to hear from you, and learn that all was well. I would like to be with you to help make sugar. I would be all right for a *sugar campaign* if I had [my] fixings up there. I could take my "dog" tent and pitch it almost any place, when I would have as good a shelter as I would wish. Fixed as I am at present I could go it three days, then my rations would be out. The rumors about the evacuation of Mobile are all false, for the rebs still have full sway up that way. Our gun boats went up the bay a few days ago and engaged some of their batteries at Dog River Bar. After thundering away nearly all day the fleet returned to Navy Cove. We are now about 15 miles from Fort Morgan. I do not know how long we will remain here. I think not long — we may advance further tomorrow. We have encountered no rebs yet but may expect to hear from them before we go much further. It is not far to Fish River, where I understand they will make some resistance. We are encamped on an arm of the bay, and can see a good deal of smoke further up which I suppose rises from some of their fires.

I am considerably fatigued and you must excuse this scribbling. I know you would do so if you were to see me writing. I am seated on the ground, beneath my shelter tent sort of tailor fashion with the paper on my port folio before me. Give my respects to all.

I remain as ever your affectionate brother,

William

P.S. This is the 1st Brigade, 2nd Division, 13th Army Corps, and is the *advance*. I understand that all the troops at Morgan left there this morning.

Camp of the 19th Iowa Vols.

On the Fish River, Ala.

March 22nd, 1865

Dear Brothers:

I again have a chance to write and hasten to improve it, although I have nothing of much importance to communicate. I last wrote to you on the 17th Inst. The next morning we resumed our march at daylight and marched about 14 miles, the roads the greater part of the way being tolerably good. The next day (the 19th) we did not make but 5 miles the roads being so bad. In one place the whole brigade turned out and made a corduroy[35] across a swampy piece of road, about 600 yards in length, making it almost entirely out of fence rails.

"We Will Be Apt to Wake Things Up in Alabama"

On the 20th we marched about 4 miles. That night it rained all night and continued until noon the next day. We pulled up stakes however about 8 o'clock, and started but we did not make much headway. Our regiment marched in rear of the battery (Co. "F" 1st Mo. Artillery, Capt. Faust's[36] battery). We had to pull them out of camp and about one third of the distance traveled. The pieces got along well enough, but 12 horses could not budge the caissons in many places, the ground being so soft and miry. In such places they would unhitch the horses, and attach ropes, and about 100 men would take hold, then it would move right along. We did not go more than 5 miles. Still we did not get into camp until long after dark, camping last night about a mile from here on the other side of the river. The 16th Corps effected a landing here the day before we arrived, and is encamped here now. It is about 12 miles from the mouth of the river. Boats run up to this place with the troops. A large number of troops are behind on the road by which we came, and I hardly see how they can come over the road and all. It seemed to have no bottom in places. We had no trouble coming up, from the rebs; very few were seen. We have been on rather scanty rations for two days past, it being impossible to get [and] keep the supply train up. This morning we got one cracker to the man, (of the smallest size) about 3½ inches square. 11 such crackers are the usual rations. We have plenty of meat, however, and are not starving yet, by a good deal.

I hear that the rebs drove in the pickets on our right, today. A division or two of Smith's[37] men were sent out after them. We are the first of 13th Corps to arrive here, our brigade keeping the advance all the way thus far. We do not hear much of the movements made by the rebs so that I cannot venture to say much in regard to our future movements. I hear however that they have a fort about 16 miles from here.

Paper is rather a scarce article so that you must excuse appearances. Some more troops are marching by, belonging to the 16th Corps, playing that old tune "We'll all drink stone blind, johnnie fill up the bowl."[38]

They boys are all well, from the neighborhood. My respects to all.
I remain as ever your affectionate brother,
William

~

In the rear of Spanish Fort, Ala.[39]

April 1st, 1865

Dear Brothers:

The mail leaves today & I have concluded to write a few lines. We are now seeing tolerably rough times besieging the fort named above. Our army took position about 2 miles from the fort on the 26th of March. On the 27th the lines were advanced and our work commenced. The 19th Iowa was the advance on the extreme left of our lines next to the bay. About noon we started carefully feeling our way for some distance. Finally we reached the top of a hill and found ourselves in full view of the fort on the bay, and only 1200 yards distant. We stacked arms and commenced throwing up a breastwork of the pine trees which they had fallen so as to have [the] range. They opened on us with their artillery. I have never seen men work as we did there. Men were posted to give warning when they fired and every man dropped to the ground until the shell passed over and then up and at it we went again. It was but a few minutes until we had a pretty good breastwork. Before we got it quite down a shell exploded over a portion of the company wounding Joseph Paxton in the foot. It had to be amputated. 2 others were wounded by the same shell. We advanced within 700 yards that evening. About 25 have been wounded & 4 killed since we commenced.

Our works are now advanced much farther. They have mounted more guns and have been reinforced. There was very heavy shelling yesterday and last night.

I have not time to write more at present.

As ever your affectionate brother,

William

~

Camp of the 19th Iowa Vols.

Spanish Fort, Ala.

April 10th, 1865

Dear Brothers:

I have the pleasure of penning a few lines to you from the *interior* of the rebel works at this place. The "Johnnies" evacuated last Saturday evening the 8th after dark, and our troops occupied the place by midnight. Saturday afternoon about 4 o'clock we opened upon their works around the entire line with artillery, and such a bombardment I never seen before. Our brigade occupied the extreme left of our line directly in front of the main fort which has ten guns mounted upon it, some of them are only field pieces. Our regiment was in the rifle pits during the firing, and was only about 150 yards from the fort. Behind us was our batteries, at about the same distance in our rear, consisting of 4 sixty-four pounder siege Howitzers,[40] 4 30 PDR Parrots,[41] and two 8 in., and two 10 in. mortars, 12 pieces in all, while the fort belched forth for a while from 4 or 5 guns. I never heard the like of it before, I have often heard of terrific cannonading but this was the first time that I could realize what it was like. Around to our right we had batteries in position which we [had] at work at the same time. Awhile before dark the firing slacked and the 8th Iowa and one or two other regiments made a charge on the extreme right where the rebs' works were very weak. They succeeded in capturing a lot of prisoners, and occupied their works for some distance. The Johnnies concluded to get out of the place then and went off in small boats. The bay is much cut up with islands. They have batteries on two of them which they still occupy. The water battery at this place has been firing all morning at them. One of our transports came up opposite the fort this morning (the first one that has ventured) when the rebel batteries opened upon it, they threw balls pretty close to it but did not hit it. Our gunboats have been unable to get close enough yet to do any good, on account of the torpedoes. One of our best monitors was sunk the first day they tried to get up. The rebels have planted land torpedoes all over "creation."[42] The first day 4 or 5 horses were killed by them and two or three men wounded. As yet none have been exploded since we came inside the fort, although they are known to be in the ground.

The loss in our regiment, after the first day, was small. During the siege, which commenced March 27th four were killed, and about 25 wounded. Yesterday, Sunday, was a busy day for us, and in fact we have been so ever since we got in sight of the fort. We were in the pits 24 hours and then off 24 hours. We went into the pits on the evening of the 7th remaining until after dark on the 8th. We then were relieved and went to camp, got our supper, and tried to get some sleep but were aroused by midnight to go to the fort. When it became daylight

Sunday morning we went back and brought up our camp equipage, and put up our shelter tents. About noon we received orders to take the prisoners, captured here, to the landing, 5 miles below on the bay. There was about 500 of them.

We did not get back until after dark last evening. Our brigade occupies the fort and adjacent works. The greater part of the troops have gone on to Blakely.[43] I have just heard that that place was taken last night, with 2 or 3000 prisoners.[44] I hope it is true. Yesterday we heard of the fall of Richmond which is good news.[45] I must close for the present. We put our camp in order this morning and we had to move our tent so that [I] have not had much chance to write. You must excuse the scribbling.

Ever yours affectionately,

William

P.S. 3 Monitors are coming up, having cleared the channel, and the rebs up in their battery will have some fun.

I received George's welcome letter of March 12th & 16th on the evening of the 7th and was truly glad to hear from you all. It is the only mail that we have received since we left Navy Cove March 17th. Also rec. one from cousin Mary Lighthill of March 13th. They were all well. George had enlisted and gone to Nashville Tenn. to join regt.

∽

Camp of the 19th Iowa Vols.

Spanish Fort, Ala.

April 18th, 1865

Dear Brothers:

We are still occupying the same camp from which I last wrote on the 10th Inst. We have been a good deal dissatisfied at our staying at this place, every person being anxious to go over to the city and see what kind of place it is. It lays about 7 or 8 miles north of west, across the bay. We have too [a] tolerably good view of it when the atmosphere is right clear. When I last wrote to you our batteries at this fort, and the rebel batteries "Huger" and "Tracy"[46] were exchanging compliments in the shape of 100 pound balls and shells. The next day the 11th, the firing was kept up with more severity than the day previously. Our camp was in fair range, and our position was anything but pleasant. Shell fell on each side of us, but fortunately none came into camp.

"We Will Be Apt to Wake Things Up in Alabama"

A storming party was to assault the batteries that night at 2 A.M. on the 12th. The troops belonged to some brigade at Blakely. They approached them in pontoon boats and found that they had been evacuated. The next morning we learned that the "Johnnies" had also left Mobile leaving everything in our possession. Right upon the heels of this comes the news of the surrender of Lee and his forces.[47] We thought this news too good to be true, and were rather slow to believe it, but as it has been officially announced, and a salute of 100 guns, from each of the batteries around Mobile, fired yesterday, we conclude that it must be so.

I anxiously await the arrival of Northern papers, to get the particulars of the many events of recent date. You will obtain the account in regard to operations here, and know the particulars of the evacuation of Mobile sooner than we. All the operations that we know anything about are those at this fort. At Blakely we know that 4 or 5000 prisoners were taken for a good part of them passed here, but we do not know what our losses were at that place. As to the city all we know is that it was evacuated, but we do not know which way the rebs went from there, nor what troops first occupied the place, nor anything, only the simple fact that it is evacuated.

I have omitted to mention in my last letters, about seeing Joseph Pollock and Ballard.[48] They hunted us up when we were at Fish River. I was much surprised at seeing them in this part of the world dressed in the Lincoln blue. They belong to the 12th Iowa Infantry. I seen Jr. last, while the siege was going on at this place, they appeared to be in good health, but did not seem to relish the shizzing of rebel bullets any better than other folks. The weather here is quite warm and inclines to make a fellow feel lazy. If the war should happen to stop, I do not know what some of us would do. We would miss our 16 & 20 dollars per month, and the *commissaries* would play out, with their supplies of hard "tack" coffee and sugar.

The health of the command is good. Very little sickness of any kind.

Our brigade (the 1st, of the 2nd Division, 13th Army Corps) is all the force now here. We hold the works known as Spanish Fort. Boats pass here daily (now that the channel is clear of torpedoes) going and returning from Blakely & Mobile. We lost several gun boats by the explosion of torpedoes. The rascals were not content with placing them in the water but have them stuck around thickly on land. They had a line of them around the works here, and had them planted in the roads leading to the fort. Quite a number of horses were killed, and several men wounded, some mortally, but considering the number of torpedoes, we have been very fortunate. They are a common shell fixed with a cap,[49] so that a mans weight upon it will cause it to explode.

But enough for the present. My love to all.

Yours affectionately,

William

CHAPTER 8

❝I Long to Get upon Old Chequest Again❞

The combination of Lee's surrender and the loss of Mobile convinced virtually all the Confederates still active in the field that they had lost the war. Consequently, throughout April and May of 1865, the commanders of the various departments of the Confederacy made their peace with the Union. As a result, the victorious northern army began the process of demobilization. While some Union regiments would remain in federal service as occupation forces in the former Confederacy, most units prepared for an early release from their enlistments.

The members of the 19th Iowa who had enlisted in 1862 fell into the early-release category. They remained in Mobile, awaiting the orders that would send them back to their homes in Iowa. Clayton wrote five letters home before he returned to Van Buren County; in them he gives his favorable impression of Mobile and expresses his fervent hope that the War Department would spare the veterans of his regiment from a campaign back in Texas, the state of his captivity. His wish came true, ending his letters on July 9, 1865.

~

Spanish Fort, Ala.
April 30th, 1865
Dear Brothers:
You will doubtless begin to think that I am negligent about writing, it being nearly two weeks since I last wrote, but I think you will pardon me this time. I have not had anything of importance to write about, and if that is not a sufficient excuse, the fact that "letter pa-

per" was "played out," certainly will be. There has been no chance of getting any since we left Navy Cove, no sutlers being allowed with the army, until recently. One arrived here today, and others will soon follow.

I was much pleased at receiving your letter of the 8th and one from cousin Ellen written on the 2nd. They both reached here in the mail of the 26th. I ought to have written to Ellen before this time, and would have done so had I known that she would remain so long. I supposed that she had returned to Council Bluffs some time since. I will write, and direct to that place.

This is a rather stale place for *news* at present. The forts at this place and Blakely have been partly disabled, all of the guns found in them have been sent over to the city. It is the general opinion that the greater part of the force here will leave soon, probably a battery of field artillery and a regiment of negroes will hold the post. Two regiments of our brigade have occupied Blakely for over a week past, Col. Bertram having command of both points.

But I think that we will be on the move again, before a great while, our destination, as usual, being a matter of dispute. Some think that Montgomery is the place, others talk of an expedition to Texas, Galveston being the point designated,[1] and still others think the Mississippi the place. Well, in three months from June this time we will have a better idea of the destination aimed at. Those of us, who are fortunate enough to see that time will have a *serious* notion of travelling northward. Many seem to think that we will be home by the Fourth of July but I cannot *see it* exactly in that light, though I sincerely hope that their predictions may come true.

The news of the assassination of the President[2] cast a deep feeling of sadness in the minds of all. Coming as it did, so soon after the cheering news of the surrender of Lee, and of our own successes at this place, we were not prepared for it, and when the chaplain made it known that he would make a few remarks in regard to it (on the evening of the receipt of the news) every man in the regiment went to hear him, all being anxious to know all the particulars concerning the affair.

I must take back part of what I said when I told you that we had no *news*. The *paymaster* has arrived at Mobile bringing money to pay off the troops. That is about the best news that a soldier gets. We have

8 months pay now due us, but do not expect to get more than 4 or perhaps 6 months pay, at present.

I will write soon again. My regards to all of the friends.

As ever yours affectionately,

William

~

Camp of the 19th Iowa Infantry

Fort Gaines, Ala.

May 10th, 1865

Dear Brothers:

Here we are again on Dauphin Island enjoying the pleasant breezes, which are wafting to us from beyond the grand old Gulf of Mexico.

When I last wrote to you from Spanish Fort, I mentioned that we expected to move from that place but did not know to what point we would go.

On the 2nd Inst. orders were received to proceed to this place. We did not get off until the 4th. We then embarked on the steamer *Landis* and after a three hours ride arrived here safely.

On the next day (5th) we relieved the 3rd Maryland Cavalry (dismounted), who have been on the island for nine months. They had a very good camp, of which we have taken possession. "Our mess" of four have a "nice little shanty," (so called here) but if seen at home it would be called a "poor excuse" for a *hen* house, nevertheless we feel perfectly at home, and do not wish for anything better so long as we are in the army. At present, there is no troops on the island excepting the 19th and two or three companies of the 6th Michigan heavy artillery, who are in the fort. I like the place much better than Spanish Fort. It was so lonesome there. Nearly all the boats running between New Orleans and Mobile touch at this place so that we get the news tolerably regularly. The latest Northern news comes now, via Mobile by telegraph from the north.

You will have learned, long before you get this, that Dick Taylor has been added to the list of rebel Genl's. who have found it useless to contend longer with the Yankees, so that there is no considerable force of Johnnies, now in existence east of the river.[3]

It seems however that Kirby Smith[4] intends to give us trouble awhile longer, but I hope that he will see the folly of doing so, before *it is* too late. I learn that the greater part of the 13th and 16th corps, are returning to Mobile, and it is said that an expedition is being fitted out for Texas. If it becomes necessary for it to go there, the whole country should be laid waste, to show the Texans that they cannot do as they think they can — have everything their own way.

I have no particular fondness for that section. For my part I have seen enough of Texas to do me.

We have a good time of it here so long as we remain. Lieut. Col. Bruce is post commander, and Capt. Sommerville, Provost Marshal. Quite a number of men are permanently detailed as Provost & commissary guards, the balance of us in camp have but little to do, principally *fatigue* such as coaling boats, from vessels in the bay.

Lieut. Byers has just returned from Mobile to which place he went, in charge of about 200 convalescents from the hospital here.

He says that it is a much nicer place than New Orleans, the streets are shaded with live oak trees and others, giving it a pleasant aspect in this warm weather.

I received your welcome letter of April 23rd yesterday, and was glad to hear that all were well. We had cool weather here about the time it snowed with you.

It rained all day the 21st and that night the wind turned to the north, and it was almost too cool to be pleasant for several days, but it has got bravely over that now, and if it was not for the breeze which is almost constantly blowing the heat would be unbearable.

Our paymaster has not yet made his appearance. The troops in Mobile, and those up the Alabama River have been paid. I think it will be our turn soon. The one who pays our regiment is west of the Mississippi River, paying off detachments at Thibodeaux and Brashear City.

We hear a good deal about being discharged before our term of service expires. Many are confident that we will celebrate the coming Fourth of July at home. Well I am willing to do so, and am ready to start at any time, still I make no calculations upon starting for a month or two yet.

I long to get upon old Chequest again and see my friends again, but I suppose that I would be a stranger to all but a few families.

I think that I could dispose of some of your maple molasses if I had the chance, and I think that my case is worse than that of the conscript who was helping to guard us at Marshall, Texas. Last spring, he said, (in talking with some of us) that he "had been in the service now two weeks, and hadn't had any furlough nor any *milk* yet." — the Johnnies are great fellows for milk.

Well, I have been in the service longer than that, and have had no furlough, and but precious little milk, I assure you.

We are now getting soft bread instead of "hard tack" which we had to use since leaving here before. We also have *potatoes* which are purchased here from the commissary at $3.50 per bbl. The Chequest boys are all well. We have not heard from Jo. Paxton since the middle of April. He was then nearly able to go around on crutches, and expected to start for Keokuk soon.

My love to father and mother. Remember me to Uncle Nide and Aunt Rachel & Alice.

Your affectionate brother,
William

∼

Camp of the 19th Iowa Inft'y
Fort Gaines, Ala.
May 28, 1865
Dear Brothers:

Your welcome letter of the 12th Inst. was received last evening, and as it had been three weeks since receiving one from home, I was truly glad to hear from you.

As you will perceive by the heading of my letter, we are still on Dauphin Island.

Nothing has transpired since my last letter of the 10th worthy of mention, so that I have been waiting to receive a letter before writing.

The weather for some time past has been very warm, but yesterday we had a cool bracing wind from the north which continues this morning.

We have been expecting for some time past, to be ordered into the field, having instructions to be ready for active service, but I do not think that it will be necessary now.

The rebel generals Price & Buckner have come to New Orleans to negotiate for peace, and terms have no doubt been agreed upon, at least we have a rumor to that effect.[5]

I hope it is true, for a trip through Texas at this season of the year would be anything but desirable.

There is a great scarcity of water in many portions of the state, making the advancement of a large army very difficult. They used to tell us while we were prisoners that they was not afraid of an army advancing far into their country on that account, and we know that it was difficult to get water for 600 or 800 of us, at all times.

A terrible calamity occurred at Mobile last Thursday the 25th, by the explosion of a large quantity of ammunition, about 300 persons are supposed to have been killed and many wounded.[6]

I heard the report of the explosion here very distinctly, and supposed at the time that it was the report of a heavy gun fired from some of the vessels in the bay, close by.

I have wondered that such explosions were not more frequent. While at Spanish Fort ammunition of all kinds was piled up on the wharf, having been taken from the magazines for shipment. Some of the packages would break open and powder was lying around loose everywhere.

Several of the regiment were injured after we had occupied the fort some time, by the explosion of shells, one bursting while a crowd were standing around a fire one evening, wounding 6 men. I was glad when we got away from there on that account. A person did not know when he was safe.

Since I last wrote to you we have received 6 months pay. I concluded not to send any of it home this time. I paid my subscription to the Orphan Asylum Fund, and as I do not know that we will get pay again until our muster out I thought that I would keep the balance for future use.

Well as news is scarce I must bring my scribbling to an end for this time. Give my best respects to all of my friends. My love to father, mother, and yourselves.

Your brother,
William

"I Long to Get upon Old Chequest Again"

Camp of the 19th Iowa Infantry
Mobile, Alabama
June 21st, 1865
Dear Brothers:

Here we are at last in this, the *Bay City* of the south. We had almost given up the idea of seeing this city after being as near as Spanish Fort and then going away to Dauphin Island. Fort Gaines got a be rather a *drag* on our hands. It was a very pleasant place when we first went there, but it got so warm that it would almost suffocate a person. There was no shade trees within a mile of our camp, and at times it was very sultry. Accordingly we were all glad when marching orders came on the 13th Inst. We had to remain for want of transportation until the evening of the 14th. The *General Banks* came in from New Orleans, and four companies embarked on her. The *James Battle* soon hove into sight, and to the channel for Mobile direct, but two shots from the fort brought her to, and we all embarked after dark. We laid at anchor below the obstructions from about 2 A.M. until daylight. We then steamed up to the city. It is very low along the river front, the streets being not more than 5 feet above the water level for several squares back, the ground then ascends gradually. The streets are all well shaded excepting some of the principal business streets, and it is a pleasant way of passing the evenings to promenade some of the fashionable thorough fares. The stores are being opened with good stocks of goods and everything begins to wear a business aspect. This city, I suppose, has felt the effects of war the least of any other southern city & everything is in tolerably good condition. The town is not very compactly built excepting the business portion. The private residences are generally got up in good style, many of them are magnificent, and all have spacious yards filled with nice trees and shrubbery. Our camp is on Government Street, about a mile and a half from the landing. This is one of the best streets in the city, and reminds me of Fourth Street, Cincinnati. It is about a quarter of a mile out to the inner line of works surrounding the city. These are very heavy and if there had been sufficient force here to man them, and the outer line, many would have fallen to rise no more, this side of eternity.

There is a large number of troops here yet, nothwithstanding many have left for Texas. Our old brigade has had marching orders for some time, and the 94th Illinois and 23rd Iowa left several days ago. They started for Galveston but I learn that they stopped at New Orleans. We have been detached from the brigade and attached to the provisional brigade for the "post and district of Mobile" — consisting of the 20th and 19th Iowa, 37th Illinois, 69th Indiana, and 31st Mass. Mounted Infantry — commanded by Lieut. Col. Leake of the 20th Iowa. We are doing duty in the city, furnishing *patrols* every other day, one company ("E") is detailed at General T. Kilby Smiths[7] head qrs. He is the commander of this post.

Quite a number of the regiment are also detailed as permanent guards at cotton presses in the city. I was over the ground where the great explosion took place. It beats anything that I ever seen before. The block in which the building stood is completely leveled, not a brick scarcely left on top of another, and the timbers are torn to splinters, not a piece more than a foot long to be found for some distance. Roofs have caved in, at three squares distance and the glass in windows has been broken out of sash at the distance of 6 or 8 squares. It is likely that we remain here until we start northward. I do not expect now to get out of service until our term of service has expired, which is two months yet. I was at the theatre a few nights ago, the first time since I was at the one in Cincinnati. Spalding & Rogers[8] have a show here but I have not been to see it. Two papers are now published here daily, so that we have the news, but it is very scanty now.

I was at the Episcopal church last Sunday evening and heard a good sermon and some good music. Churches are plenty, one at almost every turn.

Enough for this time from your affectionate brother,
William

∼

Camp of the 19th Iowa Infty.
Mobile, Ala.
July 9th, 1865
Dear Brothers:
Here we are, still in the same place from which my last letter was written.

I did think that I would write no more from this place, but we have remained longer than it was supposed we would. It seems to be a very hard matter to get us out of the service, but it was no trouble to get us into it.

Well, the long looked for event (our muster out) will certainly take place soon. We have been ready for several days, but the mustering officer belonging to the 20th Iowa,[9] he seen fit to muster them out first, notwithstanding the fact that our time would expire previous to theirs. They were mustered out yesterday but have not left yet. He is now examining our papers and I suppose that we will be mustered out tomorrow or the next day.[10]

But I can not say when we will get away, likely about Wednesday or Thursday the 12th or 13th.

One year ago today we left Camp Ford Texas for Yankeedom. It was a joyful day to us, and I think that we were more eager to get back to our regiment, at that time, than we are to start *home* now, and you may rest assured that we are all counting the minutes as almost hours in this seemingly unnecessary delay, which prevents us from being at that much talked of place.

The 23rd Wisconsin was mustered out on the Fourth of July and started next day for home. The 69th Indiana also is gone. Our discharge papers are all made out here and will be dated twelve or fifteen days ahead, that length of time being allowed to get to the state. When that time has expired our day will cease, whether we get there within the time allowed or not.

There was not much of a celebration here on the Fourth. Gen'l Andrews[11] commanding 2nd Division 13th Army Corps, reviewed the regiments of his division on their respective parade grounds. He made a neat little speech to our regiment at the conclusion of the review.

The "niggers" had a big time in town. They collected together to the number of several thousand on the public square and was having a fine time. They tried to run the thing their own way, one or two negro regiments acting as guards. They could not get along without coming in contact with the white troops however, and were compelled to leave for their homes about the middle of the afternoon to prevent a serious disturbance. They scratched one or two soldiers with their bayonets, and two or three of the "nigs" were killed and thus ended the celebration.[12]

As I have nothing more worth writing I will close. You need not look for Co. "H" much before the 1st of August.

Hoping that this will reach you and find all well.

I remain ever your affectionate brother,

William

P.S. I forgot to mention that I received your letter of June 17th a few days ago.

EPILOGUE

While Clayton's letters ended on July 9, 1865, his odyssey as a Union soldier had not yet quite ended. After their muster out of Federal service on July 10, the men of the 19th Iowa had to wait until July 12 to depart. They were informed that morning that they could board the steamer *White Cloud No. 2* to begin their journey home. When they arrived at the wharf, they found that they would have to share the boat with the 77th and 91st Illinois, two regiments that had already gone on board. The Iowans squeezed their way on, only to be informed by the quartermaster of the post at Mobile that they would have to disembark so that the *White Cloud* could take on a shipment of mules. Colonel Bruce argued against this but could not dissuade the quartermaster. Bruce then offered to help move the mules on board if the quartermaster would let his men stay, a suggestion that was accepted.

At this point, Colonel Henry M. Day, commander of the 91st Illinois, left the boat and went to complain about the delay in departure to General Smith, commandant of the post at Mobile. Smith heard the colonel out but was inclined to allow Bruce's compromise to proceed. When the quartermaster's men received notification of this decision and attempted to move the mules on board, however, the men of the 19th Iowa interfered with the process — an obstinancy that, according to observers from the 77th Illinois (the other regiment on board), may well have been alcohol induced.

In the face of this insubordination, the quartermaster had no choice but to send for the provost guard to restore order. When these troops arrived, however, most of the men of the 77th and 91st Illinois

Colonel John Bruce, 1864.
Courtesy of the Lincoln Memorial Shrine Collection.

joined with their fellow Midwesterners to resist the efforts of the provost guard. Finally, Colonel Bruce saw no other way to quell the disturbance than to order his troops off the *White Cloud*. His men obeyed, and the boat soon sailed away.

Because of this incident, the 19th Iowa was punished by having to wait until another day to find transportation. Captain Sommerville, Captain Norvill Powell, and Lieutenant John Bonnell received further punishment: they were arrested for their role in the disturbance and only released after a period spent in incarceration. Finally, on the morning of July 16, the 19th Iowa received permission to board the *Warrior* and cheered as the lines were cast off. But at that moment the boat's boiler burst, forcing the Iowans to spend one more night in Mobile.

At last, the next morning, the 19th Iowa boarded the *Landis*, which had taken the regiment from Spanish Fort to Fort Gaines, and traveled uneventfully to New Orleans. Transferring to the *R. J. Lockwood* at that location, the 19th Iowa then sailed up the Mississippi to Cairo, Illinois. There they disembarked, and boarded a northbound train. Reaching Moline, Illinois, the 19th Iowa changed trains, and rode across the Mississippi River into Davenport in their home state. On July 31, 1865, at the McClellan Barracks in that community, the men of the regiment received their discharge papers, and headed home.

Clayton returned to the family farm, as he had informed his family he would. However, he did not remain long. After helping with the harvest, he decided to leave his home and family, and moved back to his birthplace of Pittsburgh, Pennsylvania. There he combined his high-school education and his service as a clerk with the 19th Iowa to find employment as a bookkeeper. His motivation seems to have come less from a desire to seek gainful employment than to foster a developing romance, however. In his letters to his family during the war, Clayton had spoken often of corresponding with his cousin, Elizabeth Cooper; after moving to Pittsburgh, he began to court her. The two were wed in 1869 and moved into a house at 429 Carson Street, settling into the routine of domestic life.

Unfortunately, sorrow came to Clayton in Pittsburgh. On July 31, 1876, Elizabeth passed away. Clayton tried to carry on with his life but found it empty. In addition, for some time he had found little satisfaction, or chance for advancement, with his employer. For these reasons, in 1879 Clayton decided to leave his birthplace. He chose to relocate in southern California, moving to an unincorporated community known as Orange, south of Los Angeles.

In California Clayton became a farmer again. He originally planted barley but soon turned to growing raisins, grapes, and oranges on his 10-acre ranch. Events would soon put him on the path to a different occupation, however. The skills that had prompted Clayton's designation as company clerk in the 19th Iowa quickly brought him a similar responsibility in his new locale; his neighbors, upon forming the Orange Fruit Growers Association in 1880, asked Clayton to become its first recording secretary. After a number of years spent dividing his time between farming and his clerical responsibilities, in 1887 he decided to sell most of his acreage and go into business as a notary public. He soon added selling real estate and insurance to his business endeavors.

Clayton also found time to fall in love again, marrying twenty-three-year-old Ora A. Clayton in January 1883. Here again, he chose a cousin for a bride. On June 2, 1881, Ora had written to Amos Clayton from Douglas County, Oregon, informing him that she was the daughter of his brother, Ashford, and had just learned that she had an uncle in Iowa. No correspondence exists to establish what transpired next, but it is probable that Amos or Grace had a hand in getting Ora and William together. In their first seven years of marriage, William and Ora had two daughters, Anna Grace and Margery; unfortunately, both died in infancy. Their third child, a son, was born in September 1890. Christened William Henry Harrison Clayton, Jr., he would survive a serious childhood illness to grow into adulthood. Known as Harry, he eventually attended the University of Southern California and went into the furniture business in Los Angeles. Harry married Florence Emma Dowland in 1912, and the two presented Clayton with a granddaughter, Dorothy, in 1913.

As Clayton began his life with his new family, the lives of three of his old family members soon came to an end. His younger brother John Quincy Adams Clayton died in 1884 at the age of thirty-six. His mother Grace passed away at the age of seventy-eight in 1888, and his father Amos died at the same age in 1890. Only George Washington Clayton remained of his immediate family. George had married Minnie Mussetter, a neighbor ten years his junior, and had purchased a

William Henry Harrison Clayton, seated far right, at the Southern California Veterans Association Convention at Huntington Beach, California, August 1910. Courtesy of Christine Clayton Turner.

farm of his own near Lebanon in Van Buren County. The two brothers corresponded at least once a year, but Clayton's connections to Iowa had definitely begun to fade.

As time went on, more of Clayton's early life passed away as well. As the 1800s progressed, the communities of Clayton's home area in Iowa began a slow, steady decline in population, a trend that has prevailed to the present time. Davis County, which had 13,000 inhabitants at the start of the Civil War, had only 8,000 in 1990. Troy, the community that had grown so rapidly in the decade before the war, has fallen today to a population of around one hundred again. It lost most of its businesses and witnessed the closure of its famous Troy Academy. Van Buren County has seen an even more dramatic decrease, from 17,000 residents in 1860 to 7,600 in 1990.

While his old home of Troy declined in importance, his new one gained in vitality. One year after Clayton made the transition from agriculture to business, his community incorporated as a city. His work on behalf of the Fruit Growers Association had brought Clayton favorable attention from his neighbors, and, in the first election held in Orange, Clayton received 109 of the 116 votes cast for city treasurer. The voters of Orange reelected him in 1890, and in 1894 Clayton won

William Henry Harrison Clayton, after his retirement.
Courtesy of Phil Brigandi, original owned by Dr. G. Abbott Smith.

election to the city council. After one four-year term in that capacity, he ran again for city treasurer. In all these elections, he won with virtually no opposition.

While engaged in these activities, Clayton also became involved in the social life of Orange. He actively supported the Orange Fraternal Aid Union, and on May 23, 1887, Clayton and nine other Union army veterans chartered a Grand Army of the Republic Post in the community. During the rest of his life, he proudly held a number of offices in this organization. He also attended Union army reunions in Southern California well into his seventies.

In 1904, at the age of sixty-two, Clayton retired from public service after completing his fifth term as city treasurer. A history of the city of Orange reveals that in the years to follow Clayton attempted to continue to influence the decision-making process in his community but found his opinions almost entirely ignored by the new civic leaders.

Clayton tried to keep a hand in his business affairs after leaving public office but found this increasingly difficult. Rheumatism — no doubt exacerbated by his years of service in the Union army — had already earned him an Invalid Pension from the federal government in 1896, and other maladies soon began to plague Clayton as well. This combination of ailments finally ended Clayton's life at age seventy-seven on December 18, 1917. Two days later, Clayton's body was interred in a cemetery at Santa Ana, California. Fittingly, he chose the Grand Army of the Republic Post of Orange to conduct the ceremony that put him to rest in the soil of a nation that the Civil War had insured would remain under one flag.

1. *"We Were Mustered into the Service Yesterday"*

1 At the start of the Civil War, the U.S. War Department directed Iowa Governor Samuel J. Kirkwood to have volunteer regiments from his state gather for training at Keokuk. Camp Elsworth in that community hosted many of Iowa's first soldiers, and in the following months the state opened a few other training facilities. But when Iowa began to muster new volunteer regiments into service after President Lincoln's call for troops in the summer of 1862, state officials recognized the need for even more camps. Accordingly, on August 11, 1862, Iowa Adjutant General Nathaniel B. Baker announced the opening of Camp Lincoln, in Keokuk. The 19th Iowa regiment would be the first to occupy the camp, which was located on 18th Street just south of Lexington Grove.

2 Grace Smith Clayton. A native of Ireland, she had emigrated to the United States in 1817, settling in Pittsburgh.

3 A station on the Keokuk, Fort Des Moines & Minnesota Railroad line, three miles north of Keosauqua in Van Buren County. The location is currently known as Mount Zion.

4 George G. Wright, a native of Indiana, had become a member of the State Supreme Court of Iowa in 1855. He would later serve Iowa in the U.S. Senate.

5 The Simpson House was a combination hotel and boarding house, used during the Civil War as a temporary billet for troops who could not be quartered in a barracks.

6 A unit of the Union army, the company officially consisted of eighty-two privates, thirteen noncommissioned officers, two lieutenants, and one captain. It could contain a maximum of 101 men. Ten companies normally made up a regiment.

7 A community founded by John A. Drake in 1846 in the middle of Davis County. Francis M. Drake, the son of the founder, became a major general in the Civil War, was elected governor of Iowa in 1895, and helped found the university in Des Moines that bears his name today.

8 The 19th Iowa was officially enlisted, or mustered, into federal service on August 21, 1862, by Lieutenant Charles J. Ball of the 13th Regiment of the Regular U.S. Army.

9 Abner J. Buckles, a twenty-eight-year-old neighbor of Clayton's and his best friend.

10 The ten companies in a Union regiment were designated by the letters A, B, C, D, E, F, G, H, I, and K.

11 A group of four to eight soldiers, one of whom would prepare food for

the others. All the individuals in Clayton's mess listed Troy as their residence when mustered into service.

12 Merrett Mooney, age twenty-nine.

13 Absalom Nincehelser, age twenty-nine.

14 Ages twenty-two and nineteen, respectively.

15 Age twenty-one.

16 Norville Utt, the oldest member of the mess at thirty-two.

17 Charles Leach of Troy.

18 Captain Theodore W. Richmond of Keosauqua.

19 Clayton listed himself as five feet, seven and one-half inches in height and gave his weight as 165 pounds — one inch shorter but twenty pounds heavier than the average Union soldier during the war.

20 A bonus paid to enlistees in the Union army. Clayton did not realize that Congress had appropriated funds for a $100 bounty, to be paid in installments. His regiment had received only a partial payment at Camp Lincoln.

21 These were .577 caliber rifled muskets, manufactured at the Royal Small-Arms Factory at Enfield, England. Over 800,000 were purchased by both sides during the Civil War.

22 Starting on April 19, 1861, the Union navy attempted to prevent supplies from other countries from reaching the Confederacy by patrolling the waters off the southern coastline.

23 Colonel Benjamin Crabb of Washington had been a captain of the 7th Iowa early in the war. Although taken prisoner at the Battle of Belmont on November 7, 1861, he had distinguished himself in action at that engagement before his capture. He had later returned to his regiment but had been discharged in August 1862.

24 This would become the 30th Regiment of Iowa Volunteer Infantry.

25 The county seat of Davis County.

26 Business Corners was a community in Van Buren County, located one mile north of Douds. It no longer exists.

27 John Strang, twenty, of Portland, a community in northern Van Buren County. After the war, the residents of Portland decided to change the name of their town to Leandro.

28 An enlisted person assigned to do various duties for an officer.

29 Samuel Bonney, twenty-two, of Keosauqua.

30 Clayton had had more formal education than many Americans of the time, having attended Hughes High School in Cincinnati before his move to Iowa. His education and superior penmanship earned him an official appointment as company clerk on September 1, 1862.

31 Andrew Tanneyhill.

32 Garrett and Tanneyhill joined the 13th Iowa Infantry. In becoming a part of an established regiment, the two individuals deviated from the stan-

dard practice used for Union volunteers during the Civil War. Usually, enlistees would go to a new regiment being formed rather than to an existing regiment as replacements. Indeed, only 50,000 of the 420,000 enlistees in the Union army after Lincoln's call in 1862 went to old regiments.

33 At the time Clayton was writing this letter, General Robert E. Lee was preparing to take his Army of Northern Virginia out of that state and move into Maryland. At the same time General Braxton Bragg had advanced his Army of Tennessee into Kentucky.

34 As Union troops converged on St. Louis in August 1861, Major General John C. Frémont began the construction of a training facility on the western edge of, and adjacent to, the St. Louis fairgrounds. Buildings, each 740 feet long and 40 feet wide, were constructed to house the troops. Fremont named the facility Camp Benton, after his late father-in-law, Thomas Hart Benton, a former Missouri senator, and the housing units became known as the Benton Barracks. Private Timothy Phillips of Company A, 19th Iowa, whose diary is in the possession of the Wisconsin State Historical Society, described the buildings as "white-washed and kept in good repair."

35 One of the most distinguished of all Iowa regiments, the 2nd Iowa counted many residents of Davis and Van Buren Counties among its ranks.

36 A Confederate fort in southern Tennessee on the Cumberland River. Union forces under Major General Ulysses S. Grant captured Fort Donelson, along with 11,500 prisoners, on February 16, 1862.

37 Most steamboats of the time were propelled by a wheel with projecting wooden paddles. These were placed either at the stern or, as in the case of the *J. L. McGill*, on the side of the boat.

38 The daguerreotype and ambrotype were both early methods of making photographic prints. A daguerreotype print was made on a silver iodide–coated copper plate in a very time-consuming process. The ambrotype was simply a glass photographic negative placed over black paper or velvet and was therefore much less expensive than a daguerreotype.

39 Jane Lighthill, an aunt of Clayton's who lived in Pittsburgh.

40 At this stage of the Civil War, a captured soldier could sign a document giving his word that he would not bear arms against his captors unless exchanged for a soldier held prisoner by his own side. This document was known as a parole paper. Paroled Union soldiers from the western states who had not yet been exchanged were required to wait at the Benton Barracks.

41 Another name for the battle that took place around Shiloh Meeting House in Tennessee on April 6–7, 1862.

2. "We Are in the 'Army of the Frontier'"

1 Named for Major General Franz Sigel, an immigrant from the German province of Baden, who had fought at the Battles of Wilson's Creek and Pea Ridge.

2 The U.S. Army Commissary Department was the branch of the military charged with supplying food to the troops.

3 Heavy artillery pieces firing 32-pound projectiles. During the Civil War, artillery pieces were described either by the weight of the projectiles they shot or the diameter of their barrels at the muzzle.

4 A unit of the Union army, usually consisting of from three to five regiments, and commanded by a brigadier general.

5 Annanias H. "Nide" and Rachel Pugh, Clayton's sixty-one-year-old uncle and fifty-six-year-old aunt, who lived on the farm adjacent to that owned by Amos Clayton.

6 A cousin of Clayton's, who lived in Pittsburgh.

7 Wagons belonging to the Union army.

8 Crabb had actually been relieved of command because of the manner in which he had resigned his commission in his previous regiment. On September 8, 1862, U.S. Army Adjutant General Lorenzo Thomas had informed Governor Kirkwood that because Crabb had resigned due to his health, the War Department would not allow him to re-enter the service.

9 Indeed, the members of the 19th Iowa would circulate a petition asking for the retention of Crabb as their colonel.

10 Moved perhaps by the entreaties of the 19th Iowa, Governor Kirkwood had implored the War Department to reinstate Crabb. On September 27, 1862, Iowa's adjutant general received word that Crabb could keep his command.

11 Major Daniel Kent of Keosauqua.

12 Lieutenant Colonel Samuel McFarland of Mt. Pleasant, who had been a delegate at the organizational conference for the Iowa State Republican Party in 1856. During the Civil War, McFarland had previously served as a captain in the 11th Iowa Infantry. Throughout his diary, Clayton would spell his lieutenant colonel's last name "McFarlane" instead of "McFarland."

13 Captain Emanuel E. Mayne of Keosauqua, who had served as one of Iowa's eight delegates to the first Republican presidential nomination convention in 1856. The fifty-six-year-old Mayne, who had served as a judge in Van Buren County before the war, was one of only twelve Union fatalities at the Battle of Kirksville.

14 The Battle of Kirksville was fought on August 6, 1862. It resulted in a Union victory that severely hampered Confederate efforts to recruit new soldiers in northeast Missouri.

15 Alfred Morris of the 3rd Iowa Cavalry.

16 A resident of Pittsburg in Van Buren County.

17 A resident of Troy.

18 Brigadier General Francis Jay Herron of Dubuque. A lawyer by profession, Herron had started the war as a captain in the 1st Iowa, participating in the Battle of Wilson's Creek. Promoted to lieutenant colonel and assigned to the 9th Iowa Infantry, he had fought at the Battle of Pea Ridge, where he had been wounded and taken prisoner. After being exchanged, he had received a promotion and this new command.

19 Paper packets containing a premeasured amount of gunpowder and a lead bullet (known as a "minie ball," after the inventor, French Army Captain Claude E. Minié). A soldier would bite the top off this packet, pour the contents down the barrel of his rifle, drop in the bullet, then tamp the charge down with a device known as a ramrod.

20 Sutlers were civilians, under the jurisdiction of the U.S. Army's Inspector General Department, who were allowed to accompany Union forces and sell them goods. Each regiment could have one sutler. A man by the name of Higgins had originally served the 19th Iowa in this capacity but was soon replaced by Charlie Lewis.

21 Nide and Rachel Pugh.

22 On June 11, 1861, the Lincoln Administration had authorized General Lyon to recruit "loyal citizens" of Missouri for temporary federal service. In the summer of 1862, General Schofield enlarged upon this concept by requiring all male residents of the state eligible for military service to register for enlistment in an organization known as the Enrolled Missouri Militia. Union authorities would eventually enroll eighty-five regiments, sixteen battalions, and thirty-three independent companies for temporary service in Missouri.

23 Clothing dyed with natural ingedients, giving the garment a brownish hue. As gray dye became increasingly difficult for the Confederacy to procure, most Confederate soldiers wore clothing of this color.

24 Clayton is partially correct about Union troops holding their ground, then forcing the Confederates to "skedaddle," or run away. On September 30, 1862, Confederate forces had actually compelled units of the Union army to retreat after a battle at Newtonia, Missouri. But on October 4, after receiving reinforcements, the Union troops drove the Confederates out of that town.

25 These two regiments had simply advanced farther into southwest Missouri; the 19th Iowa would meet the 20th again at the Battle of Prairie Grove.

26 The Chequest is a small river that runs through Davis and Van Buren Counties; it is a tributary of the Des Moines River. The Clayton family farm lay alongside the Chequest in, appropriately, Chequest Township.

27 Melton Dysart and James Miller were residents of Troy who had both originally lived in Tennessee.

28 Major General Sterling "Pap" Price, at the time commander of the Confederate Army of the West, had been forced to retreat after suffering heavy losses while attacking Union forces at Corinth, Mississippi, on October 3–4, 1862.

29 The Battle of Wilson's Creek was fought on August 10, 1861, in southern Missouri. It was a Confederate victory, but Union soldiers, including the 1st Iowa, had performed well in the engagement.

30 Robert B. Rutledge, the 42-year-old sheriff of Van Buren County, had been delegated to find the 19th Iowa and record the votes of the regiment in the election of 1862.

31 Rutledge reported to the *Keokuk Gate City* that the 19th Iowa advanced so rapidly that he could never catch up with it. He therefore telegraphed voting instructions to them, and four companies — a total of 269 men — succeeded in casting ballots.

32 Many counties in Iowa offered bonuses to enlistees who answered Lincoln's call in the summer of 1862. For example, Lee County, which had provided a number of volunteers for the 19th Iowa, had given all individuals joining federal service a $75 bounty. No evidence exists in the extant Van Buren County newspapers from the period to corroborate Clayton's assertion that county officials had offered a similar bonus there.

33 Lieutenant Lafayette Bunner, twenty-six, a neighbor of the Claytons in Chequest Township.

34 Volday Solliday, a resident of Chequest Township.

35 Volunteer regiments would occasionally recruit individuals from an adjacent state. The 7th Missouri Cavalry employed this process when it enlisted recruits from Upton, a town in Van Buren County located on the border with Missouri, where the Fox River crosses into that state. Upton was later abandoned.

36 During the Civil War, officers conveyed commands to their soldiers by having drummers beat a certain cadence. The "long roll" called the infantry to be ready for battle.

37 Clayton means that they put on their equipment.

38 Composed of Union troops deployed in Missouri and Kansas, this army came into existence on October 12, 1862.

39 A malarial fever with recurring hot spells and chills.

40 Lieutenant Walter Ferguson, thirty-two, of Troy.

41 A rifled cannon had a groove engraved inside its barrel, making it superior in range and accuracy to smoothbore brass artillery pieces.

42 The Battle of Pea Ridge was fought in northern Arkansas on March 7–8, 1862. It resulted in a Union victory.

43 This alarm developed when sentries of the 19th Iowa, returning to camp in the early morning hours, discharged their rifles to clear gunpowder dampened by the mist out of their barrels.

44 A forward lookout watching for an approach of enemy forces.

45 A two-story building on the Springfield–Fayetteville Road, Elkhorn Tavern had been the scene of desperate fighting during the Battle of Pea Ridge. Confederate accounts usually referred to the two-day conflict as the Battle of Elkhorn Tavern.

46 Major General John McAllister Schofield, at the time commander of the Army of the Frontier. Schofield was later commander of the United States Army from 1888 to 1895.

47 Harris Neal, his brother James Emery, his father William, and his mother Abigail lived on a farm near the Clayton residence in Chequest Township.

48 Brigadier General James Totten, commander of the 2nd Division of the Army of the Frontier.

49 Brigadier General Nathaniel Lyon had given this nickname to the 1st Iowa in recognition of their speed while marching.

50 The University of Wisconsin sports teams are today called the Badgers.

51 The Battle of Pittsburg Landing.

52 Documents attesting to the loyalty of the bearers to the Union.

53 Major General James Gilpatrick Blunt had commanded the Department of Kansas until it was assimilated into the Army of the Frontier. He then received the command of a division in that unit.

54 Blunt was actually conducting operations in northwest Arksansas at the time.

55 Colonel William Orme, commander of the 2nd Brigade, 3rd Division, Army of the Frontier.

56 This term originally was used to describe the tendency of Union soldiers from Kansas to take property from suspected Southern sympathizers. By the time Clayton used the word, it meant a person taking any property without permission.

57 Named for Major General Samuel Ryan Curtis of Iowa, the victorious commanding general at the Battle of Pea Ridge.

58 The wagons carrying the food, forage, and equipment for the force Clayton was a part of.

59 These food products were known during the Civil War as "hard tack."

60 A bugle call sounded at night to indicate the time to put out all lights.

61 After the Battle of Wilson's Creek, the Confederates had used a ravine located in the middle of the battlefield to bury a number of the Union dead. Within a short amount of time, much of the dirt used to cover the grave had settled, exposing the skeletons to attacks by wolves.

62 The 30th Iowa, which contained the company raised at Business Corners, had spent a longer period at Camp Lincoln than had the 19th, then had been transported by boat to Helena, Arkansas. The regiment would remain there until late December 1862.

3. "It Was a Perfect Slaughter Pen"

1 The Illinois River crosses the Fayetteville–Cane Hill Road one-half mile north of the ridge upon which sat the Prairie Grove Church.

2 A rifle bullet in flight that has lost the velocity necessary to penetrate the human body.

3 Captain Theodore Richmond.

4 Lieutenant Colonel McFarland.

5 Age nineteen, of Pittsburg.

6 A tactical unit of field artillery pieces during the Civil War. Six-gun batteries were common in the Union army, while Confederate batteries usually contained four guns. The battery charged by the 20th Wisconsin was an Arkansas unit commanded by Captain William D. Blocher.

7 A measured rate of advance in the Union army. According to the infantry manual, a soldier should cover 109 yards in one minute at double-quick speed.

8 Official Confederate losses were put at 164 killed, 817 wounded, and 336 missing.

9 Clayton is correct. The official record reports that the 19th Iowa suffered 45 killed, 145 wounded, and 3 missing — far more than any other Union regiment involved, and more than fifteen percent of all Union casualties in the battle. In a later letter Clayton would quote slightly higher losses for the 19th Iowa at Prairie Grove.

10 Initially deceived by Hindman's ruse on the morning of December 7, Blunt deduced the Confederate's plan after hearing gunfire emanating from the Prairie Grove battlefield. Blunt quickly ordered his troops to march to Herron's aid but chose an indirect route to the battlefield that would allow his force to continue to protect his supply train located at Rhea's Mill. Fortunately, this approach brought his troops to the battlefield in a position to launch a punishing assault on the exposed left flank of the Confederate line just as Hindman prepared to attack Herron. Therefore, Clayton's assertion that Blunt's arrival prevented Hindman from delivering a crushing blow to Herron is quite correct.

11 In all, the 19th Iowa covered 117 miles in three and one-half days to get to the battlefield at Prairie Grove, a feat that all histories of the battle note as an extraordinary accomplishment. Understandably then, perhaps, a number of the Union deaths at Prairie Grove were later found to have been caused by exhaustion rather than Confederate action.

12 This regiment, recruited in the fall of 1862 near Fayetteville, was merely one of many raised for the Union in the South. Indeed, during the Civil War over 100,000 whites from Confederate states served the federal cause.

13 Soldiers sent out in advance of the main battle line to deliver nuisance fire into an enemy formation.

14 The 20th retreated so precipitously that they left behind their regimental

flag, which was considered a disgrace during the Civil War. During their advance, the men of the 19th Iowa recaptured the flag, returning it to the Wisconsin soldiers after the battle.

15 An apple orchard owned by Archibald Borden.

16 The 19th Iowa was fired upon by an infantry brigade to the west and south, and a brigade of dismounted cavalry to the east.

17 Major General Thomas Carmichael Hindman, the commander of the Confederate forces at Prairie Grove.

18 Brigadier General John Sappington Marmaduke.

19 There were a number of other Confederate generals at Prairie Grove, but considering where Richmond was captured it could well have been Brigadier General Daniel M. Frost, who commanded a brigade of Missouri Home Guards at that engagement.

20 The Second Division of the Army of the Frontier. Totten had left his unit before the battle due to illness, giving Herron temporary command of both the Second and Third divisions.

21 Charles B. Buckingham of Abingdon, the top-ranking noncommissioned officer in the regiment.

22 Lieutenants Thomas Johnson and Loammi Smith.

23 Samuel Payne of Bentonsport, Joshua Wright of Abingdon, and Harry Jordan of Fairfield.

24 Harrison Smith of Abingdon and William S. Brooks of Brookville.

25 Reports made after the battle did give special recognition to the 19th Iowa. General Herron asserted that while all "the Iowa regiments fought nobly, the Nineteenth particularly distinguish[ed] itself," and Colonel William Orme, commander of the Second Brigade, said "I cannot speak too highly of the gallant conduct of the officers and men of the Nineteenth Iowa."

26 Official records reveal that the Confederates suffered 1,317 total casualties at Prairie Grove — only 66 more than the Union reported.

27 Actually, Hindman brought only 11,500 men to the Battle of Prairie Grove.

28 Herron had 6,000 infantry and cavalry, while Blunt had close to 8,000.

29 Company H did have nine men killed — the most of any in the regiment.

30 Clayton's War Department record indicates that he was so ill that he spent time in the infirmary.

31 Pursuing Hindman's retreating force, Blunt and Herron had come upon the Confederates at Dripping Springs, Arkansas, and destroyed their camp. They then occupied the nearby town of Van Buren.

32 Many accounts of the aftermath of Prairie Grove relate a story of Schofield's anger toward his subordinates. According to these sources, when Schofield heard of the Battle of Prairie Grove, he had immediately returned from sick leave and journeyed to rejoin his army. Meeting his generals at the scene of the battle, Schofield had reprimanded Blunt for

not falling back on his reinforcements. He also criticized Herron for committing his soldiers to battle after their exhausting march.

Nothing in the official records of the Civil War supports this story, however. Moreover, in a paper written immediately after the war Blunt made no mention of such an incident. It would appear, then, that Schofield did not discipline either officer in the manner in which Clayton had heard. In fact, both Blunt and Herron were promoted to major general soon after the battle, an advancement that made Herron, at age twenty-five, the youngest person of that rank in the Union army.

33 In November 1862 Major General Ambrose Everett Burnside, commander of the Army of the Potomac, initiated a campaign in Virginia that resulted in a disastrous loss at the Battle of Fredericksburg on December 13, 1862.

34 A cousin of Clayton's, who lived in Pittsburgh.

35 A distant cousin of Clayton's, who resided in Pittsburgh. She would later become a closer relative, as the reader will see.

36 Captain Richmond had been released on parole after Prairie Grove, but his papers had not yet been exchanged for those of a Confederate held by the Union. He could not, therefore, legally rejoin the 19th Iowa as a combatant.

37 Lieutenant Silas Kent of Pittsburg.

38 Sergeant Samuel Baker of Keosauqua.

39 On December 31, 1862, General Marmaduke had led a Confederate force into Missouri, hoping to either capture or destroy the Union supply depot at Springfield. On January 8, 1863, the Union defenders of that city, led by, among others, Colonel Crabb of the 19th Iowa, repulsed a determined Confederate attack.

40 A river which runs through Davis and Van Buren Counties in southeastern Iowa.

41 Although the Clayton family had moved from Pittsburgh in the early 1840s, they had visited their relatives there often before the war. Clayton was therefore speaking from firsthand experience of the river ferries in the Pittsburgh area.

42 Captain John Bruce of Keokuk. He would later command the 19th Iowa.

43 Clayton required medical treatment on January 20th and 22nd for his fever.

44 Crabb had assumed command at Springfield on December 2, 1862. He had for that reason missed the Battle of Prairie Grove.

45 The *Dollar Times Weekly* was a newspaper published in Cincinnati, Ohio, where the Clayton family had resided on Hopkins Street in the southwestern part of the city before moving to Iowa.

46 Clayton is referring to the Emancipation Proclamation, announced in its preliminary form by President Lincoln on September 22, 1862.

47 The Republicans and Democrats.

48 "Butternut" was a term used in the nineteenth century to describe residents of the southern Midwest.

49 Curtis had indeed occupied Forsyth in early 1862 on his march to Pea Ridge, but the damage Clayton refers to in that town had occurred much earlier in the war. On July 20, 1861, Brigadier General Nathaniel Lyon, at the time the commander of the Union forces in Missouri, ordered his subordinate, Brigadier General Thomas W. Sweeny, to drive a force of approximately 150 Confederates out of Forsyth. On July 22, the Union force of 1200 men succeeded in its mission in short order, but after the Confederates evacuated the town a misinterpreted order caused the commander of the Union artillery, Lieutenant George D. Sokalski, to fire three shells from a twelve-pound howitzer into the courthouse building.

50 The store Clayton refers to was owned and operated by Josiah I. Earhart, who had helped found the community of Troy.

51 The *Missouri Democrat* was a popular daily St. Louis newspaper of the time.

52 A local resident loyal to the Union, listed in the official records only as "Hopper."

53 A line of fortifications, constructed to the height of a man's breast.

54 On April 16, 1862, the Confederate Congress had passed a law allowing men between the ages of eighteen and thirty-five to be drafted into military service.

55 A regiment of Arkansas conscripts in Colonel Robert G. Shaver's brigade did desert in its entirety during the Battle of Prairie Grove. Many other conscripts at the battle either refused to fire at the Union soldiers, or deliberately loaded their weapons with a charge of gunpowder insufficient to give their bullets a lethal velocity. This may help to explain how Clayton could have been hit by a spent bullet while fighting at close range.

56 Thousands of people in Iowa did not agree, privately or openly, with the Union war effort. Opposition was particularly strong in, as historian Robert Dykstra has described them, the "culturally southern, Missouri border areas, such as Davis County" (*Bright Radical Star*).

57 Northerners, usually Democrats, who opposed the Union war effort.

58 Samuel R. Stewart and John N. Pearson, both of Georgetown, Texas, enlisted in the 19th Iowa on March 14, 1863. Pearson deserted on February 25, 1864, while the unit was serving in Texas.

59 Lieutenant George W. Sommerville of Keosauqua.

60 William M. Hartson of Keosauqua had been one of the first enlistees in the 19th Iowa. He had been on detached duty, returning to Company H in March 1863. Obviously, he was not Clayton's favorite person in the world!

61 Clayton's cousin Jeannette Lighthill.

62 During the 1850s, William Robinson had lived in Cincinnati on Hopkins

Street, a neighbor to the Claytons. After the Claytons moved to Iowa, Robinson soon followed suit, buying land in Chequest Township only a short distance from the farm owned by his former neighbors. William Robinson was fifty-two at the time that Clayton wrote this letter, while Hannibal Robinson was twenty.

63 During the 1850s, Jacob Moyer had been a tailor in Cincinnati. He lived on Hopkins Street, a neighbor to the Claytons and Robinsons. Before the Civil War, he had moved his family to Olathe, Kansas, where he enlisted in the 10th Kansas Infantry on July 24, 1861. He was discharged due to disability on February 2, 1862.

64 John Moyer, a son of Jake Moyer, had enlisted in the 12th Kansas Infantry on August 16, 1862. When his regiment was mustered into service on September 30, however, he received a discharge. According to a report of the Kansas Adjutant General, this action was ordered "by civilian authority" rather than by the medical examiners.

65 Peter Moyer, another son of Jake Moyer, enlisted in the Second Kansas Battery, Light Artillery, on August 20, 1862. He is listed incorrectly in the *Roster of Officers and Enlisted Men of Kansas Volunteers* as Peter Mayer.

66 Located in the eastern part of the state of Kansas, Fort Scott had been constructed in 1842, decommissioned before the Civil War, and reactivated on March 29, 1862. Pete Moyer's battery was stationed there from December 10, 1862, to May 1, 1863.

67 Sergeant James A. Russell of Milton in Van Buren County. Each company in a regiment of the Union army included a first, second, third, fourth, and orderly sergeant. Clayton had therefore become the third highest-ranking noncommissioned officer in Company H.

68 Clayton fails to mention it, but when they abandoned Forsyth, the soldiers of the 19th Iowa burned the buildings of the town to the ground.

69 The 9th Wisconsin was made up exclusively of soldiers either born in German provinces or of Germanic descent.

70 The name of this town is now Hartville.

71 Colonel William Weer, commander of the 10th Kansas. At this time he held temporary command of the First Division, Army of the Frontier.

72 After General Marmaduke's attempt to secure Springfield was thwarted on January 8, he then sent his forces east, where the next day they captured the Union garrison at Hartville. On January 11, Marmaduke learned of the approach of Union forces and deployed his troops outside the town to the west. Union Colonel Samuel Merrill led his forces into action upon reaching Hartville, and in the ensuing action many Confederate rounds landed in the community. After driving Merrill from the field, Marmaduke returned to Arkansas, having inflicted 250 casualties and captured 300 Union soldiers during his expedition.

73 "Spondulicks" is a nineteenth-century slang expression, meaning cash or money.

74 Colonel Weer had in fact asked General Schofield on April 25 if his troops could be paid soon.

75 The Quartermaster Department of the U.S. Army was charged with providing quarters, clothing, and equipment for soldiers.

76 In April 1863 Major General Joseph Hooker led the Army of the Potomac across the Rappahannock River into an area of Virginia known as the Wilderness. He met Confederate resistance on May 1 and in three days of fighting suffered heavy losses. As a result of this engagement, known as the Battle of Chancellorsville, Hooker decided to pull his forces back across the river.

77 As Clayton wrote this letter, Major General Ulysses S. Grant was advancing his forces on Jackson, Mississippi; he would then turn west and move on Vicksburg.

78 Abner Buckles had recently received a furlough.

79 On April 17, 1863, General Marmaduke had launched another raid into his home state of Missouri; this time he had the Union supply depots at Cape Girardeau and Pilot Knob as his goal. He was repulsed at the former on April 25, however, and left the state soon after.

80 A rubber blanket.

81 While it is impossible to tabulate the number of individuals who at one time lived in Iowa and eventually moved to California, the 1870 census does reveal that by that year 5,361 individuals born in Iowa resided in California. This makes Clayton's assumption seem plausible.

82 Cranston Allen, a resident of Chequest Township.

83 This rumor came about as the result of a cavalry raid toward Richmond, conducted by Major General George Stoneman in conjunction with Hooker's campaign, which had culminated in the Battle of Chancellorsville.

4. "Vicksburg Is Ours"

1 Lieutenant Silas Kent.

2 After the debacle at Fredericksburg, Lincoln had removed Major General Burnside from command of the Army of the Potomac. He had become commander of the Department of the Ohio, and in the spring of 1863 Grant drew troops from Burnside's jurisdiction for his Vicksburg campaign.

3 After the capture of Forts Henry and Donelson, the attention of Union commanders in the West had turned to the Confederate positions guarding the Mississippi River south of Belmont, Missouri. Major General John Pope, commander of the Army of the Mississippi, began the task of eliminating the bottleneck by forcing the Confederates to abandon their defensive works along the river at New Madrid, Missouri. After occupy-

ing these fortifications on March 14, 1862, Pope then turned his attention to Island No. 10, situated near the Tennessee shore in a bend of the Mississippi. Pope's army and a Union fleet commanded by Flag Officer Andrew Foote soon managed to isolate the defenders of that position, forcing the Confederates to surrender on April 8.

4 Island No. 10 actually lies in the Mississippi River just south of Kentucky's border with Tennessee.

5 Vicksburg.

6 On December 26, 1862, as part of General Grant's initial attempt to capture Vicksburg, Major General William T. Sherman had landed four divisions on the banks of the Yazoo River north of that city. The point at which the Union forces disembarked was actually known as Johnson's Landing, at the base of Chickasaw Bluffs.

7 Mortars were artillery pieces that threw shells in a high trajectory. The Union navy built a number of flat-bottomed boats that mounted one mortar apiece.

8 On June 7, 1863, Confederate forces under the command of Brigadier General Henry E. McCulloch attacked a detachment of white and black northern soldiers at Milliken's Bend, Louisiana. After compelling the Union soldiers to flee to the banks of the Mississippi River, the Confederates were themselves forced to retreat when federal gunboats directed deadly artillery fire upon them. This battle drew a great deal of attention in the North because it represented the first test of black soldiers on a large scale during the war.

9 Frustrated in his initial attempt to capture Vicksburg in the fall of 1862, Grant had embraced a plan to divert the waters of the Mississippi away from that city by digging a canal for a new river channel. Brigadier General Thomas Williams had begun an excavation to that end earlier in 1862; Grant's forces attempted to complete the project. The plan had not succeeded, and Grant abandoned the effort in March 1863.

10 Erasmus W. Tatlock and John Grinstead were residents of Troy. Dan Bell was from Chequest Township; he, along with forty other members of the 3rd Iowa Cavalry, had been captured during a skirmish at LaGrange, Arkansas, on May 1, 1863.

11 Clayton is blending two separate engagements into one. On March 25, 1863, the U.S.S. Switzerland and the U.S.S. Lancaster had attempted to run past the fortifications at Vicksburg; the Switzerland took a number of hits, while the Confederates succeeded in sinking the Lancaster. After being repaired, the Switzerland again sustained extensive damage while participating in a naval expedition on June 3 to the mouth of the Atchafalaya River.

12 The ironclad U.S.S. Tuscumbia was at the time undergoing extensive repair work as a result of battle damage suffered when the vessel supported a Union assault on the Confederate lines guarding Vicksburg on May 22.

13 Guard rails posted around the deck of the ship.

14 Grand Gulf was located on the Mississippi River south of Vicksburg and had been fortified by the Confederates. After the Union victory at Port Gibson on May 1, 1863, threatened to isolate the defenders of Grand Gulf, the Confederates decided to abandon the fortifications the next day. Union forces then took possession on May 3.

15 Known during the war as the "dog" tent, later generations of American soldiers would call it the "pup" tent.

16 At that distance the Enfield rifle had a radial deviation of 4.2 feet, thus making Clayton's chances of hitting a Confederate slim.

17 An opening in the wall of a fort to permit a gun to be fired.

18 General Joseph Eggleston Johnston, commander of the Confederate Department of Tennessee, who was trying to gather a force in central Mississippi to lead to the relief of Vicksburg.

19 A river approximately ten miles from the Union lines around Vicksburg.

20 Lieutenant General John Clifford Pemberton, commander of the Confederate forces in Vicksburg.

21 In recognition of this unusual flora, the members of the 19th Iowa informally nicknamed their encampment "Camp Pipestem."

22 These insects are called "chiggers."

23 Mosquitoes.

24 Heavy artillery pieces used in the reduction of fortifications.

25 "Sortie" originally meant a sudden attack by a besieged force on the forward lines of the besiegers, but by the nineteenth century it also had the meaning of an offensive action undertaken by a small detachment.

26 In this case, camp rumors were correct: all of Clayton's letters from Vicksburg are postmarked "Memphis."

27 This "rebel raid" was in fact the Army of Northern Virginia moving through Maryland on its way into Pennsylvania.

28 By this stage of the siege, Grant's lines extended for over fifteen miles.

29 At the start of the Civil War, women in Lee County, Iowa, formed the Keokuk Ladies' Soldiers Aid Society, a voluntary association to provide food and medical supplies for state regiments in federal service. Thirty-seven-year-old Annie Turner Wittenmyer, a wealthy widow, had become the secretary of the group. Wittenmyer soon began to visit Iowa regiments in the field and earned a reputation as a tireless champion of the common soldier. Her efforts on the behalf of these individuals earned her an appointment in August 1862 as one of Iowa's two agents for the United States Sanitary Commission. An effective organizer and lobbyist, she gained great fame during the war for creating special diet kitchens for Union hospitals.

30 A voluntary organization founded at the start of the Civil War to help the U.S. Army Medical Bureau provide for the needs of sick and wounded soldiers. In June 1861 the Sanitary Commission had become a part of the

federal government, under the aegis of the War Department. On October 13, 1861, Governor Kirkwood had created the Iowa State Army Sanitary Commission to serve as the local representative of the national organization.

31 Actually, on June 28, 1863, Hooker had ceased to command the Army of the Potomac in its attempt to repel the Confederate invasion of Pennsylvania. Major General George Gordon Meade had replaced Hooker at that time.

32 The 19th Iowa actually had two regimental flags. The first featured one red and one navy blue diagonal stripe on a white field, with a navy blue stripe across the top. The other flag had gold stars on a navy blue field, with the inscription "19th Iowa" embroidered across the bottom of the banner in gold letters with red trim. The regimental flags of the 19th Iowa and its national flags can still be seen among the 135 Civil War battle flags on permanent display in the rotunda of the Iowa State Capitol Building in Des Moines.

33 Field artillery refers to cannon that could be moved quickly by teams of horses around the battlefield, while heavy guns were intended for use in permanent emplacements.

34 Thomas Pender, a resident of Bentonsport and a member of Company "I."

35 Greenbacks were treasury notes, printed by the federal government beginning in February 1862. They derived their name from the fact that the reverse side of the bills had been printed with green ink.

36 The citizens of Vickburg did not feel this way about the Fourth of July. Because Pemberton surrendered their city on that date, the residents of Vicksburg would not have a Fourth of July celebration until the 1940s.

37 On July 4, 1863, Confederate forces under Lieutenant General Theophilus Hunter Holmes had attacked the Union defenses around Helena, Arkansas, and had suffered a bloody repulse. Price fought at Helena but was not in command.

38 Port Hudson was a fortified Confederate position on the Mississippi River in Louisiana, 100 miles up the river from New Orleans and 250 miles downstream from Vicksburg. Since May 26, 1863, Union forces had been engaged in siege operations against Port Hudson.

39 Artillery batteries placed on the banks of the Mississippi River at Vicksburg to harass Union naval vessels.

40 The smallest military unit, usually made up of eight soldiers.

41 On July 9, 1863, Union forces had formally taken possession of Port Hudson.

42 The U.S.S. Baron DeKalb carried fourteen guns.

43 The DeKalb survived this encounter with Confederate artillery but later that day was sunk by explosive devices left in the river by the retreating force.

44 Major General Benjamin Franklin Butler had used this term while in Virginia in May 1861 to describe slaves who had run away from their masters and sought refuge inside Union lines. By the time Clayton was writing this letter, the term was in general use to describe all slaves who had left their masters.

45 Here Clayton means the planter class.

46 While participating in the siege of Vicksburg, the 38th Iowa Infantry's position rested along a swamp. The health of the regiment gradually deteriorated, worsening as the soldiers moved into camp near Port Hudson. At one point only eight officers and twenty enlisted men of the 38th Iowa could answer the morning roll call.

    The experience of the 38th Iowa, while extreme, was not that uncommon for Iowa regiments. Close to thirteen percent of all Iowa soldiers died of disease during the Civil War, the highest percentage suffered by soldiers of any state in the Union. Many experts attribute the susceptibility of Iowa soldiers to debilitating disease to two factors. First, residents of a predominantly rural state would not have been exposed to as many diseases during their lives as their urban counterparts in federal service. And second, many Iowa regiments did an extended tour of duty in the lower South, thus experiencing prolonged exposure to malarial maladies. Indeed, Clayton's regiment would soon find itself beset by illness much as the 38th Iowa had.

47 Ellen Tucker, a cousin of Clayton's who lived in Council Bluffs.

48 While fighting in Algeria in 1831, the French Army had incorporated into their ranks colorfully dressed soldiers of a Berber tribe known as the Zouaves. During the Civil War, a number of volunteer regiments on both sides adopted the style of their uniforms.

49 Started in 1857, *Harper's Weekly: A Journal of Civilization* was a weekly illustrated newspaper. It was one of the most popular journals of the Civil War.

50 Joseph Lannum lived in the Keosauqua area, while the seventy-one-year-old Johnny Spencer resided near Sammy Clayton on a farm outside Pittsburg.

51 Age twenty-two of Milton. His name is incorrectly spelled as "Umphrey" in the *Roster and Record of Iowa Soldiers in the War of the Rebellion.*

52 Major General Nathaniel Prentiss Banks, who had commanded Union forces at Port Hudson.

53 New Orleans.

54 In 1835 the New Orleans and Carrollton Railroad had begun trolley car service between those two cities.

55 The inscription actually reads "THE UNION MUST AND SHALL BE PRESERVED."

56 Clayton was obviously unaware that the inscription on the statue had not existed before the Union occupation of New Orleans in April 1862. Major

General Benjamin Butler, who had become commander of the Department of the Gulf, had ordered the inscription engraved on the statue in May of that year.

57 On January 8, 1859, city officials of Memphis officially unveiled a bust of Andrew Jackson in that community's Court Square. The pedestal bore the inscription "Our Federal Union! It must and shall be preserved." During the period of the Civil War before the occupation of Memphis by Union forces, someone chiseled off the word "Federal" and the first two letters of the word "Union."

58 The corps was an army unit of organization, usually consisting of three divisions. The United States Army used roman numerals to designate the various corps, but Clayton consistently used arabic numbers when writing of them.

59 Major General Cadwallader Colden Washburn, first commander of the reconstituted XIII Corps.

60 Joseph W. Jones, age twenty-five, lived near Troy.

5. "We Held Them at Bay for Two Hours"

1 On March 3, 1863, President Lincoln had signed into law the Enrollment Act, which created a complex system by which states could draft individuals to fill troop level requirements set for them by the federal government.

2 Soon after the review, Grant suffered serious injuries in an accident involving the horse he was riding and a carriage.

3 The Atchafalaya River.

4 Norwood's Plantation.

5 This belonged to Mrs. Lucella Sterling, a free person of color. The plantation consisted of approximately 3,000 acres.

6 They never did.

7 This action is officially known as the Battle of Stirling's Plantation, although the plantation owner's last name was Sterling.

8 A detachment of the 6th Missouri Cavalry.

9 In his official report Confederate Brigadier General Thomas Green, commander of the attacking infantry force, stated that he commenced the battle at 1:00 P.M. His cavalry force, however, had actually engaged Union pickets near the Fordoche Bridge at 11:30 A.M., thus supporting Clayton's recollection of the timing of the battle.

10 It was quite common during the Civil War for Confederates to replace their tattered clothing with uniforms taken from dead or captured Union soldiers.

11 At Stirling's Plantation, the 19th Iowa would lose 10 killed, 23 wounded,

and 210 taken prisoner. The total Union losses were 16 killed, 45 wounded, and 454 prisoners. The Confederates lost 26 killed, 85 wounded, and 10 missing, statistics that bear out Clayton's remarks about the severity of the fighting.

12 Lieutenant Silas Kent.

13 Corporal Webster Clinton Anderson of Troy.

14 Camp Ford was the largest Confederate prisoner-of-war camp west of the Mississippi River. It received its first shipment of prisoners on August 25, 1863, and remained active until the end of the war.

15 According to the history of Company H written by Captain Sommerville, the prisoners reached Camp Ford on October 23, 1863.

16 Camp Ford did not even have a stockade to contain the prison grounds until the arrival of the prisoners captured at the Battle of Stirling's Plantation.

17 Captain A. M. Alford, Jr., of the 6th Louisiana Cavalry.

18 In March 1864 General Banks had at last set off on his expedition up the Red River in Louisiana.

19 On April 8, 1864, Confederate forces under the command of Lieutenant General Richard Taylor defeated the expedition of General Banks at Mansfield, Louisiana, forcing the Union to abandon the expedition up the Red River.

20 Lieutenant Colonel Joseph Bloomfield Leake of Davenport, the commander of the 20th Iowa Infantry. He was on detached duty from his regiment at the time of the battle, acting as the commanding officer of the detachment at Stirling's Plantation.

21 The soldiers of the 19th Iowa who had escaped capture at the Battle of Stirling's Plantation had participated in the expedition that captured Brownsville, Texas, on November 6, 1863.

22 The records of the 19th Iowa indicate that only one prisoner, George Tucker of Company G, switched allegiance to the Confederate cause while in captivity at Camp Ford.

23 On June 7, 1864, Colonel Leake had received permission from Confederate authorities to send a letter to the Union commander of the Department of the Gulf asking for supplies for his men. This request was honored, and soon goods began to arrive at Camp Ford.

24 Camp Parapet.

25 The Confederates had captured twenty-eight members of Company H at Stirling's Plantation, seven of whom managed to escape at one time or another during the period of captivity.

26 William Byers of Portland.

27 Paul E. Theard, age thirty-six, had been a major in a Louisiana militia regiment at the start of the Civil War. He had risen to the rank of colonel by the time of Clayton's capture.

28 Clayton is correct. Theard took an oath of loyalty to the government of the United States and on April 3, 1865, was appointed judge of the Fourth District of Louisiana by Reconstruction Governor James M. Wells.

29 In January 1864 Theard had received word that the state of Louisiana had not followed proper procedure in giving him his commission as an officer. This resulted in his removal from command of the camp at Shreveport. Rather than wait for official action to restore him to his rank, Theard had abandoned the Confederate cause and returned to his home in New Orleans.

30 Lieutenant Colonel John Bruce had temporarily replaced Lieutenant Colonel Daniel Kent in command of the 19th Iowa in the summer of 1863 because of Kent's health problems. Bruce had been in New Orleans on the day of the Battle of Stirling's Plantation, thus avoiding capture. Captain William Adams had been in command of the 19th Iowa on the field of battle.

31 The officers of the 19th Iowa obviously did not share Clayton's opinion on the relative merits of these two individuals, having petitioned Governor Kirkwood on January 4, 1863, to have Bruce assume command of the regiment. Instead, that honor and promotion to lieutenant colonel had gone to Dan Kent. After Kent received that position, he had hoped to get his regimental officers to recommend that he be promoted to full colonel. In a vote on that subject held on April 2, 1863, however, the officers had given seventeen votes to Bruce and only two to Kent. Because of his health and this lack of confidence among his subordinates, Kent resigned his commission on March 9, 1864.

32 Timothy Phillips of the 19th Iowa stated in his diary that Kent was "about as fit to command as a donkey would be."

33 Forty-two-year-old Lewis W. Thornberg of Keosauqua owned a hardware store and a half interest in Burns & Thornberg, a grocery and produce business in his community.

6. "If the North Would Remain United"

1 To defend Pensacola, the U.S. Army had in the years before the Civil War built fortifications on the site of Fort San Carlos de Barrancas, originally constructed by the Spanish. Renamed Fort Barrancas, it had fallen into Confederate hands on January 10, 1861, after Florida seceded from the Union, but was regained by Union forces in May 1862 when the Confederates evacuated Pensacola.

2 Small vessels using propellers rather than paddle wheels for propulsion.

3 Federal reports from the Civil War often refer to a Brazos Santiago Island, situated at the mouth of the Rio Grande. It is actually called Brazos

Island, while the strait of water between Brazos Island and Padre Island is known as Brazos Santiago Pass.

4 On April 24, 1862, Union Flag Officer David Glasgow Farragut had run the ships of his fleet up the Mississippi River past these forts. Recognizing that they could no longer do anything to help defend New Orleans, the garrisons of the two forts surrendered on April 28; the city followed suit the next day.

5 Along with Fort Sumter, Lincoln had refused to hand over this installation to Confederate authorities after he became president. Situated on Santa Rosa Island, Fort Pickens had remained in Union hands throughout the war.

6 While no blacks were allowed to serve in the U.S. Army at the start of the Civil War, Union authorities had by this time in the conflict begun enrolling blacks in both state volunteer and regular U.S. Army regiments.

7 This town is actually Warrington, Florida.

8 General Braxton Bragg had commanded the Confederate Army of Pensacola from the fall of 1861 until the spring of 1862. The arrival of a strong Union naval force in May 1862 prompted the Confederates to evacuate Pensacola. Consequently, on the night of May 9–10, the Confederates had burned the naval yard there.

9 In the summer of 1864, the Lincoln administration sought to encourage soldiers in regiments whose terms of enlistment were about to expire to reenlist. One inducement offered was a furlough to those veterans who chose to do so.

10 Alice A. Jones, born in 1854, had been orphaned before the Civil War. The Pughs had then taken her into their household. Clayton family records yield no evidence that either the Claytons or Pughs were related to anyone named Jones; this suggests that the Pughs may have taken in Alice because she lived near them when she lost her parents.

11 Brevet Major General Alexander Sandor Asboth.

12 On March 15, 1864, General Grant had ordered Major General Frederick Steele to advance his force from Little Rock, Arkansas, to Shreveport, Louisiana, in conjunction with the expedition led by Banks. Repelled by the Confederates, Steele had returned to Little Rock on May 3, losing over 2,000 men killed and captured.

13 Clayton has identified a theme commonly found in the letters of diaries of Union soldiers. Western troops often derided their Eastern counterparts as only half-hearted warriors, more interested in creature comforts than in campaigning. They quickly reminded any soldiers sent west from the Army of the Potomac that the troops from the trans-Appalachian theater had given the Union the majority of its victories against the Confederacy. Soldiers from Eastern states, on the other hand, maintained that Westerners enjoyed their military successes against inferior compe-

tition. The rivalry remained until the end of the war, when on the eve of a Grand Review planned for Union forces, soldiers from Eastern and Western armies camped on opposite sides of the Potomac to avoid altercations.

14 Nonmilitary labor done by soldiers.

15 The standard 13-inch mortar fired a 220-lb. shell, propelled by a 20-lb. charge.

16 On August 22, 1862, General Butler had called Louisiana militia units known as the Native Guards into federal service. All members of these units were black. After assuming command of the Department of the Gulf, General Banks had enlarged upon this concept, calling on May 1, 1863, for "the organization of a Corps d'Armee of colored troops, to be designated as the Corps d'Afrique." The 25th Corps d'Afrique, one of the units raised under this plan, had its designation changed later in the war to the 93rd Regiment, United States Colored Infantry.

17 Colonel Robert Thomas Pritchard Allen of the 17th Texas Infantry.

18 Camp Ford.

19 Clayton referred to this battle in his letter of June 12, 1863. The commander of the attacking Confederate force in his official report gave credit to the tenacity with which the black soldiers resisted the attack, while insinuating that a number of soldiers in the white regiment — the 23rd Iowa — ran away at the beginning of the battle.

20 Clayton is correct. In many instances, Confederate authorities returned captured black Union soldiers who had been slaves back to their southern masters. Lincoln refused to allow prisoner-of-war exchanges to continue unless the rights of captured black soldiers were respected, informing the Confederate authorities on July 2, 1863, that "it is the duty of the United States to afford equal protection to all persons duly received into the military service." When the the Confederate government persisted in its treatment of captured blacks, the Lincoln administration decided to suspend the practice of exchanging prisoners-of-war.

21 According to the records of the 19th Iowa held at the Iowa Department of History and Archives, Clayton was promoted on June 1, 1864, to 2nd sergeant. He would end the war with this rank.

22 Sergeant Amos Woods.

23 Dr. George W. Games, age forty-seven, of Keosauqua.

24 The wedge tent was triangular in shape like the pup tent, but at seven feet by seven feet it was much larger.

25 A resident of Pittsburg.

26 A resident of Mt. Sterling.

27 Colonel Leake said of Camp Ford that "no great city presents scenes of more squalid destitution."

28 The Revised Army Regulations of 1863 stated that "the rations of prisoners held in rebel States shall be commuted for and during the period of

imprisonment, the commutation to be rated at cost price." The commutation rolls that Clayton referred to were statements regarding his regiment's imprisonment, which were required before the soldiers could be recompensed.

29 Major General Edward Richard Sprigg Canby. After successfully defending the New Mexico Territory from a Confederate invasion in 1862, he had become commander of the Military Division of West Mississippi in May 1864.

30 Brigadier General Thomas West Sherman, stationed at New Orleans as the commander of the Southern Division of Louisiana.

31 On August 5, 1864, Admiral Farragut led a Union flotilla through a mined channel into Mobile Bay. Confederate hopes inside the bay rested on the C.S.S. *Tennessee*, an ironclad warship. After a furious battle, in which the ironclad U.S.S. *Monongahela* had rammed the *Tennessee*, the combined might of the Union vessels forced the Confederate vessel to surrender, securing the bay for Farragut.

32 Corporal Anderson was killed at Stirling's Plantation.

33 This is the name used in correspondence by many of the individuals actually involved in the Battle of Stirling's Plantation.

34 Dr. Lewis M. Sloanaker of Montrose had started the war as the assistant regimental surgeon of the 19th Iowa. By 1864 he had become the head surgeon.

35 Clayton's neighbor James Emery Neal, age thirty-two, the oldest of the Neal children.

36 Abigail Neal, age fifty-six.

37 A resident of Lebanon in Van Buren County.

38 The Pensacola Light House, finished in 1858, had a measured height of 171 feet.

39 Confederate authorities had actually dismantled the lighting apparatus early in the war to make it difficult for Union ships to blockade the port. To make it difficult for the Union to recapture the equipment, the Confederates took it to Montgomery, Alabama.

40 This damage resulted from an artillery duel which took place between the Union and Confederate forces on November 22–23, 1862.

41 Alvin Westcott, a merchant in Troy.

42 A disease caused by a vitamin C deficiency.

43 Shallow.

44 Lieutenant Francis Gordan of the 15th Confederate Cavalry.

45 Lajos Kossuth, a Hungarian nationalist, led a revolt against the Austrian Empire in 1848. The state of Iowa honored Kossuth by naming a county in the northern part of the state after him.

46 Two bullets struck Asboth in this engagement: one broke his left arm, while the other fractured his cheek bone and lodged in his sinus cavity. Although the second wound did not prove fatal immediately, it troubled

Asboth into his postwar career as U.S. Minister to Argentina and Uruguay. Asboth finally succumbed to the effects of this wound in Buenos Aires in 1868.

47 Captain Mahlon M. Young of the 7th Vermont Veteran Volunteer Infantry.

48 This was a detachment of a Regular U.S. Army regiment of black soldiers, the 82nd Colored Infantry. The regiment was originally designated as the 10th Corps d'Afrique.

49 On a number of occasions during the war, Confederate soldiers refused to give quarter, or the right to surrender, to black Union soldiers.

50 In his official report, Asboth claimed the capture of eighty-one prisoners.

51 Colonel A. B. Montgomery, commander of the District of West Florida.

52 Brigadier General William E. Anderson.

53 General William T. Sherman had maneuvered his army toward this city from early May 1864 until its capture on September 1 of that year.

54 During the Civil War, a number of groups organized in opposition to the Union War effort. Although discounted today, a report given to President Lincoln during the war asserted that the antiwar Knights of the Golden Circle had members in every township of the state of Iowa.

55 Clayton is referring to Camp Sumter, the Confederate prison camp at Andersonville, Georgia. First opened in February 1864, over 13,000 Union prisoners-of-war would die there before the camp was abandoned in 1865.

56 Andrew Jackson Smith of Lebanon.

57 A resident of Keosauqua.

58 William Henry Harrison Smith, Jack Smith's brother.

59 A resident of Keokuk.

60 A nineteenth-century form of mosquito netting attached to a frame.

61 A cousin of Clayton's, who lived in Linn County, Iowa.

62 On September 19, 1864, General Price led a Confederate force of 12,000 men into Missouri, hoping to capture supplies stockpiled for the Union army at St. Louis. By the end of the month, he had advanced to within thirty miles of that city.

63 Jefferson C. Davis, president of the Confederate States of America. Clayton, and many other Northerners, considered him a traitor because he had left the United States Senate to offer his services to his secessionist home state of Mississippi.

64 Clement Laird Vallandigham had been a Congressman from Ohio until he was defeated in 1862. He became then gubernatorial nominee of the Democratic Party in that state in 1863 and toured Ohio denouncing the Lincoln administration in his campaign speeches. Arrested by General Burnside, Vallandigham had been sent to the Confederacy as punishment. He had remained there briefly before journeying to Canada. In

June 1864 he violated his sentence by returning to Ohio, but Union authorities chose to ignore his presence.

65 A Philadelphia-based shipping company, established in 1852.

66 Jeannette Lighthill.

67 A "brevet" was a temporary wartime promotion in rank. After the war, the officer's rank would return to its regular status.

68 Brevet Brigadier General Joseph Bailey.

69 Major General Gordon Granger, commander of the District of South Alabama.

70 Fort Morgan, built on the site of Fort Bowyer from the War of 1812, guarded the main ship channel leading into Mobile Bay. Farragut's flotilla had had to run past it to do battle with the Confederate fleet arrayed in the bay. Union forces under General Granger captured Fort Morgan on August 23, 1864.

71 This engagement, which took place on October 18, 1864, is known as the Battle of Pierce's Point.

72 In his official report regarding the expedition, Lieutenant Colonel Andrew B. Spurling of the 2nd Maine Cavalry claimed that the Union force killed six Confederates and captured eight others.

73 On October 12, 1864, twelve mounted Confederate guerrillas dressed in Union uniforms crossed from Missouri into Iowa at the town of Upton in southernmost Van Buren County. They then rode into Davis County and proceeded to rob a number of individuals along their route. While in Davis County, they killed in cold blood one civilian, Thomas Hardy, and two Union soldiers home on leave, Eleazer Small of the 3rd Iowa Cavalry and Captain P. H. Bence of the 30th Iowa Infantry. News of the raid reached Bloomfield, where the Davis County Fair was occurring, and a force was organized to pursue the guerrillas. The individual who commanded the pursuit was Colonel James B. Weaver of Bloomfield, who in 1892 would garner twenty-two electoral votes as the presidential candidate of the People's Party.

74 At the time that Clayton was writing, guerrilla leaders Bill Anderson and William Quantrill were striking fear into the hearts of Unionists in the area west of the Mississippi River.

75 Clayton is correct. On August 26, 1864, as General Price was advancing his force through Arkansas, he had received a letter from Missourian B. P. Van Court, a member of the Order of the American Knights, promising the full cooperation of his group when Price reached his state. Actual fifth column support for Price in his campaign proved negligible, however.

76 After the state of Iowa had implemented procedures for drafting individuals, a number of residents left their homes to avoid conscription. Often they banded together, sometimes joining with deserters and/or members

of antiwar groups. In September 1864, just before the Davis County raid, Iowa Adjutant General Nathaniel B. Baker had detailed two officers of his department, Assistant Provost-Marshal John L. Bashore of Centerville and Special Agent Josiah M. Woodruff of Knoxville, to seize a number of draft evaders reported to be in hiding in the vicinity of Grinnell. An armed band of twelve intercepted these two men between Grinnell and Oskaloosa on September 30, killing them both. Clayton is partially correct in describing the slain individuals as soldiers; Bashore had served in the 6th Iowa Infantry earlier in the war, while Woodruff had been a member of the 3rd Iowa Infantry.

77 While on a logging mission on October 26, 1864, the 19th Iowa had skirmished with a body of troopers from the 8th Mississippi Cavalry near Milton, Florida. The Union soldiers captured nine Confederates while suffering no casualties.

78 The presidential, state, and local elections of 1864.

79 James H. Knox of Warren County, Iowa. At the time, Knox was a writer for the Iowa newspaper the *Burlington Hawk-eye*.

80 Dr. James Wright of Delaware County.

81 In the election of 1864, Charles Benjamin Darwin, a lawyer from Burlington, was an at-large candidate for presidential elector of the Iowa Republican Party; Ira C. Mitchell, an Iowa City newspaperman, was his counterpart in the Democratic Party. John Van Valkenberg, a Fort Madison lawyer, was the Republican candidate for presidential elector in Iowa's First Congressional District, which included Clayton's home in Van Buren County. Daniel F. Miller, a lawyer from Keokuk, had been selected by the Democrats of that district as their choice for that position.

Because Iowa had eight electoral votes in the 1864 election, each soldier had to cast a ballot in eight separate contests for presidential elector. Clayton's report to his parents on the outcome of these elections is not quite correct: the number of ballots cast by the 19th Iowa for the Republican candidates for elector actually ranged from a high of 466 to a low of 445, while the votes received by the Democratic hopefuls ran from 39 to 22.

82 C. L. Bonney of Keosauqua, running on the Republican ticket.

83 John A. Miller, the Democratic candidate.

84 Edwin Goddard.

85 The Democrats had chosen Major General George McClellan as their candidate for president in 1864.

86 Because many states in the 1864 election tabulated the votes of soldiers separately from those cast by civilians, historians have been able to calculate that seventy-eight percent of those soldiers chose Lincoln over McClellan. By giving the president ninety-two percent and ninety-eight percent of their votes respectively, then, the 19th Iowa and 2nd Maine had

gone even more convincingly for Lincoln than the average for the army as a whole.

87 Florida had not yet been readmitted back into the Union, so there was no state mechanism in place for administering a voting procedure.

88 Clayton obviously had not heard how his home area had voted. While Van Buren County as a whole had supported Lincoln over McClellan by a count of 1,577 to 1,015, Chequest Township had stood solidly for the ex-general, casting sixty-eight ballots for him as opposed to thirty-nine for Lincoln.

89 "Springfield" was a term that was applied to the U.S. Model 1861 Rifle-Musket and to subsequent modified versions in 1863 and 1864. The Union obtained 1.5 million of these weapons, many of them manufactured at the federal arsenal in Springfield, Massachusetts. The Springfield had a range and accuracy very similar to that of the Enfield.

90 After initially holding his own against converging Union forces pursuing him, General Price was defeated at the Battle of Westport in Missouri on October 23, 1864. After the engagement, Price retreated, suffering another defeat at Newtonia, Missouri. Relentless Union pressure forced Price to withdraw all the way to the Indian Territory before stopping.

91 A drum signal sounded at night to call soldiers back to their quarters.

92 A sailing vessel having two or more masts.

93 Captain Samuel E. Paine of the 19th Iowa, a resident of Bentonsport, had been discharged from military service on April 1, 1863, and had become the regiment's sutler.

94 Fort Redoubt, located north of Fort Barrancas to help guard against an attack from the landward side.

95 Lieutenant Walter Ferguson.

96 General Sherman had left Atlanta on November 15, 1864, and had embarked on his famous "March to the Sea." By the time Clayton was writing this letter, Sherman's force was approaching the city of Savannah.

97 Colonel George D. Robinson.

98 Major General Thomas J. McKean, who in fact did eventually assume command of the district.

99 The 19th Kentucky Infantry had participated in the Red River Campaign. At the Battles of Mansfield and Pleasant Hill (April 8–9), Confederate forces had captured seventeen officers and 214 enlisted men from that unit, sending the prisoners to Camp Ford.

100 Dogs belonging to the Clayton family.

7. "We Will Be Apt to Wake Things Up in Alabama"

1 Fort Gaines guarded the lesser-used channels leading into Mobile Bay. The Confederate garrison had surrendered on August 8, 1864, after an

extremely brief defense. The rapidity with which the Confederates capitulated remains a controversial aspect of this campaign to this day.

2 It is five miles between the forts.

3 In 1821, the United States Army had begun construction of Fort Gaines on Dauphin Island, at the mouth of Mobile Bay. Work on the fort was finally finished during the Civil War — after Alabama state troops had seized it and Fort Morgan (which, in a similar fashion, the Federal government had not completed before the war) on January 5, 1861.

4 On November 27, 1864, Brigadier General John W. Davidson had led a force of 4,000 cavalry out of Baton Rouge into Mississippi with the object of destroying track of the Mobile & Ohio Railroad. Muddy roads and determined Confederate opposition prevented Davidson from accomplishing his goal.

5 Mrs. Mehitable "Auntie" Woods, a resident of Fairfield, volunteered as a nurse early in the war. She soon expanded her activities to include arranging for the delivery of food and supplies to Iowa soldiers. Because of her tireless efforts on their behalf, she received an appointment as an agent of the Iowa State Army Sanitary Commission on February 11, 1863. Governor Kirkwood recognized her outstanding contributions by giving her an honorary commission as a major.

6 East Pascagoula is just across the border from Alabama and is about thirty-five miles from Mobile. General Granger had landed troops in this area in early December 1864 as part of General Canby's overall strategy for the capture of Mobile. Canby reasoned that the Confederates would react to Granger's presence by moving troops from Mobile against him, thus reducing the force Canby would confront in his main thrust.

7 A slang phrase meaning "Confederates," short for "Johnny Rebs."

8 The skirmishes that took place between December 16 and December 25, 1864, are known collectively as the Battle of Good's Landing.

9 In the Union army, soldiers on provost duty had police responsibilities.

10 A provost marshal was a Union army officer given the power of a police chief within a certain area.

11 Provost Guard.

12 Halls Mill Creek, southwest of Mobile.

13 Major General Dabney H. Maury, the commander of Confederate forces at Mobile, certainly agreed with Clayton. After the war, Maury stated that had Canby approached Mobile up the west side of Mobile Bay, "an early evacuation would have been inevitable."

14 Colonel Henry Bertram had been the commander of the 20th Wisconsin earlier in the war. At the time Clayton was writing this, Bertram had assumed command of the 1st Brigade, 2nd Division, XIII Corps.

15 A line officer in the Union army held the rank of second lieutenant, first lieutenant, or captain.

16 Francis Herron's middle initial was "J" rather than "R."

17 An inspector general is an army officer who investigates conditions affecting the quality of military life. The officer operates under the auspices of the U.S. Army's Inspector General Department.

18 In August 1865 the 19th Iowa's term of enlistment would expire, and Clayton would be free to leave the army.

19 On February 12, 1865, the War Department had created an organizational unit called the Reserve Corps of the Military Division of West Mississippi. It consisted of the 19th and 23rd Iowa, 20th Wisconsin, 60th Indiana, and 94th Illinois.

20 The site of the camp of the 19th Iowa when stationed to the north of East Pascagoula.

21 Major General Andrew Jackson Smith. He and his troops had just come from Tennessee, where they had participated in the Union victory at the Battle of Nashville on December 15–16, 1864.

22 The Reverend Pearl P. Ingalls of Keokuk, who at the start of the war had been the regimental chaplain of the 3rd Iowa Cavalry.

23 While acting as sanitary agent for the state of Iowa, Annie Turner Wittenmyer had become involved in a project to establish a home for children orphaned by the Civil War. Largely due to her efforts, a group of influential residents of the state had succeeded in creating an Orphans Home, which had opened in July 1864 in the Van Buren County community of Farmington. After resigning from her position as state sanitary agent, Wittenmyer began to campaign for the establishment of an auxiliary home in Cedar Falls, to be followed by a much larger facility in Davenport. This main site, which Ingalls was raising money for, would be located after the war on the grounds of Camp Kinsman in that city at 2800 Eastern Avenue. Opened on November 16, 1865, it was later renamed the Annie Wittenmyer Home.

24 Major General James Clifford Veatch, commander of the 1st Division of the XIII Corps.

25 Major General Elias S. Dennis, commander of the 2nd Brigade, 1st Division, XIII Corps.

26 Major General James Richard Slack, commander of the 1st Brigade, 1st Division, XIII Corps.

27 This was the major iron works in the Confederacy.

28 The Brooke was a heavy rifled artillery piece. It had been invented by J. M. Brooke, the Chief of Confederate Naval Ordnance.

29 Most Union ironclads — except those used in inland waterways — were built along the distinctive pattern of the first such vessel, the U.S.S. Monitor. By the latter stages of the war, ironclads were therefore generally called monitors.

30 Jack and Billy Smith, and William Holmes, all of Pittsburg.

31 Ely's Ford was the most popular crossing point on the Des Moines River for travelers moving across the southern part of Iowa. It is currently lo-

cated inside the confines of Iowa's Lacey-Keosauqua State Park and is marked by a monument commemorating the crossing of the Mormons there in the 1840s.

32 Dr. S. R. Bergen.

33 The Reverend John D. Sands of Keosauqua. A Congregationalist minister, he had become regimental chaplain of the 19th Iowa on March 22, 1864.

34 Brigadier General William P. Benton, commander of the 3rd Division, XIII Corps. On March 26, 1865, he would be promoted to major general.

35 A name usually applied to a road made by sawing logs in half, then placing them with the round side up next to each other.

36 Captain Joseph Foust, commander of Battery "F" of the 1st Missouri Light Artillery.

37 General A. J. Smith.

38 This was a song quite popular with sailors of the time.

39 In 1780 Count Bernardo de Galvez, Viceroy of Mexico, constructed a fortification to guard the land approach to Mobile Bay from Pensacola. The American settlers of Alabama remembered the founder's nationality when giving a name to the site.

40 Artillery pieces that fired projectiles at a high angle of elevation.

41 Invented by Robert Parker Parrott, superintendent of the West Point Iron and Cannon Foundry, the Parrott was a muzzle-loading rifled artillery piece. Parrotts were designated by the weight of shell they were capable of firing; the 30-pounder Clayton refers to was the largest.

42 Later generations would know these devices as land mines.

43 Blakely, Alabama, once a thriving community, had become virtually a ghost town by the start of the Civil War. Located a few miles northeast of Mobile, at the head of the Apalachee River, it was defended by a four-mile line of fortifications, known as Fort Blakely. Union forces under Steele had begun the process of beseiging this position on April 1, 1865.

44 On April 9, 1865, Union forces took Fort Blakely, capturing 3,200 Confederates.

45 On April 3, 1865, units of the XXV Corps under the command of Major General Godfrey Weitzel occupied Richmond, which the Confederates had abandoned the night before.

46 Battery Tracy, named for Brigadier General Edward D. Tracy, stood on the west bank of the Apalachee River, while Battery Huger, named for Lieutenant Commander Thomas B. Huger, guarded both the Apalachee and Blakely Rivers from the northern tip of Blakely Island. The Confederates had five cannon at Battery Tracy and eleven at Battery Huger.

47 On April 9, 1865, General Lee surrendered the Army of Northern Virginia to General Grant at Appomattox Court House, Virginia.

48 Joseph Pollock and Strawder Ballard. Both, like Clayton, had a mailing

address of Troy while actually residing in Chequest Township in Van Buren County.

49 A small explosive device used to ignite a larger charge.

8. *"I Long to Get upon Old Chequest Again"*

1 Many units of the XIII Corps would indeed be transferred to Galveston in 1865 to pressure the French into withdrawing their support for Emperor Maximilian of Mexico, including those members of the 19th Iowa who had not been among the original enlistees in the regiment. The troops sent to Texas would be mustered out of service at Galveston on July 20, 1865.

2 President Lincoln was shot on the night of April 14, 1865; he died the next morning.

3 General Richard Taylor had become the commander of the Confederate Department of Alabama, Mississippi, and East Louisiana in September 1864. He surrendered all troops under his command to General Canby on May 4, 1865.

4 General Edmund Kirby Smith, commander of the Confederate Trans-Mississippi Department.

5 On May 26, 1865, Lieutenant General Simon Bolivar Buckner had signed papers agreeing to the surrender of all Confederate forces in the Trans-Mississippi Department. The document was agreed to by General Kirby Smith on June 2.

6 On May 25, 1865, the Marshall Warehouse, used as a temporary ordnance depot, exploded, killing and wounding hundreds.

7 Major General T. Kilby Smith, commander of the District of Mobile.

8 In 1851 impresario Gilbert R. "Doc" Spalding had joined with the noted equestrian Charles J. Rogers to create one of the most famous circuses of the antebellum period. The Spalding & Rogers show had appeared in Mobile annually before the Civil War and resumed performances there after the capture of the city. According to the Bloomfield *Western Gazette*, the circus had performed in that city in July 1858, so the Clayton family in all likelihood had some familiarity with the show.

9 Lieutenant J. O. Stewart.

10 Brevet Major A. L. Hough, Chief Commissary of Musters for the U.S. Army, had in fact issued the papers to discharge the 19th Iowa on June 30, 1865. Lt. Stewart was therefore either overworked or quite slow in handling the discharges.

11 Major General Christopher Columbus Andrews.

12 Black residents of Mobile had hoped to commemorate their first Fourth of July as free citizens with a public celebration but had faced determined

resistance to the idea on the part of the town's white civic leaders. The blacks had then turned to General Andrews, who gave them permission to use Bienville Square, a large park in the center of Mobile, for their intended purpose. To guarantee that white citizens would not interfere, he provided the 96th and 97th regiments, United States Colored Infantry, for security at the celebration. The white regiments still at Mobile conducted their usual patrols in the rest of the city.

In all accounts of this event that I have come across, from both northern and southern sources, I have seen no evidence to corroborate Clayton's assertion about the end of the celebration. All accounts state categorically that the heat of the day, rather than an altercation between white soldiers and blacks, convinced the blacks to curtail the festivities at around 3:00 P.M.; the history of the 19th Iowa, written in 1865 by J. Irvine Dungan, attributes the few casualties that occurred as the crowd dispersed to "evil disposed citizens."

Perhaps all the sources who wrote about the Fourth of July in Mobile had reasons to gloss over an incident of racial animosity. This seems unlikely, given the mixed nature of the reporting individuals. It may be that Clayton, no great admirer of blacks, simply took the story of the blood that was spilled and turned it to fit his opinions about the newly freed men and women.

Transforming a group of letters into a coherent whole requires a historian to consult a vast array of sources, both primary and secondary. I started, of course, with the Civil War letters and diary of William Henry Harrison Clayton, which can be found in the Manuscripts Collection of the Lincoln Shrine in Redlands, California. Christine Clayton Turner, in an incredible act of kindness, gave me the letters that Clayton wrote to her grandfather, George Washington Clayton, after William had moved away from Iowa. These letters provided the basic material for my book.

More primary information about Clayton and the 19th Iowa came from the Iowa Adjutant General's file on the regiment, found in the Iowa Department of History and Archives in Des Moines. In addition, the National Archives in Washington, D.C., houses the official War Department records relating to Clayton, including his medical file and his pension applications. Both sources yielded valuable information.

Secondary sources also supplied information about Clayton. Phil Brigandi, an expert on the history of Orange County, California, shared with me a biography of Clayton found in his *A New Creation: The Incorporation of Orange, 1888* (Orange, 1988). He also made me aware of another biography found in J. M. Guinn, *History of Southern California* (Los Angeles, 1902). Finally, he gave me a number of obituaries about Clayton found in Southern California newspapers.

While these sources gave me a fairly good picture of Clayton's life experiences, I found that I could present a much more coherent story because a number of other members of the 19th Iowa had their Civil War letters and diaries preserved as well. In 1963, the University of Texas Press published *Federals on the Frontier: the Diary of Benjamin F. McIntyre, 1862–1864* (Austin, 1963). McIntyre served in the 19th Iowa, rising to the rank of lieutenant. While he ceased to record his observations in 1864, his entries to that point proved very informative about the early history of the regiment. Timothy Phillips kept a diary while serving in the 19th Iowa; this document is in the possession of the Wisconsin State Historical Society. The Military History Institute at the Carlisle Barracks, Pennsylvania, holds the diary of Lieutenant John Bonnell of Company E, which covers the period from August 1862 through August 1863. And finally, a diary bearing no name, picked up on the Prairie Grove battlefield, came eventually to the Iowa Department of History and Archives; it is without question one kept by a member of the 19th Iowa. These first-hand accounts allowed me to corroborate names, dates, and places discussed by Clayton.

Twenty-five years after the Civil War, George W. Sommerville wrote *A History of Company "H," 19th Regiment, Iowa Volunteer Infantry* (Ottumwa, 1890). Sommerville gives an occasionally acerbic, but always interesting, account of the activities of Clayton's company. While not totally accurate in regard to names and dates, his book still proved extremely valuable to me.

At the end of the war, J. Irvine Dungan, a member of Clayton's regiment, wrote *A History of the 19th Regiment Iowa Volunteer Infantry* (Davenport, 1865). His book is not as conversational in tone as is Sommerville's, but Dungan still manages to make some important points about the war from the viewpoint of the common soldier in the regiment. Dungan's book is especially valuable because he had been captured at Stirling's Plantation, thus providing corroboration for Clayton's observations about Camp Ford.

More substantiation can be found in "The 19th Iowa in Battle and in Prison," an essay written by J. E. Houghland of the regiment. The Lincoln Shrine in Redlands has a copy of this narrative, which was written after the war had ended. In addition, Donald M. Anderson, the grandson of a member of the 19th Iowa, wrote an article about the regiment for the journal *Palimpsest* 58, no. 6 (1977). Entitled "The Adventures of the Nineteenth Iowa," the article is especially informative about the Battle of Stirling's Plantation.

Brief, but useful, accounts of the 19th Iowa can be found in a number of books. Lurton D. Ingersoll's *Iowa and the War of the Rebellion: A History of the Troops Furnished by the State of Iowa to the Volunteer Armies of the Union, Which Conquered the Great Southern Rebellion of 1861–1865* (Philadelphia, 1866) gives a summary of the activities of every regiment supplied by Iowa during the war, as does *Roster and Record of Iowa Soldiers in the War of the Rebellion, Together with Historical Sketches of Volunteer Organizations, 1861–1866* (6 vols., Des Moines, 1908–1911), prepared by the Iowa Adjutant General's Office. The latter book also allowed me to establish the residences of the members of the 19th Iowa. A more modern work of this type is Edith Wasson McElroy's *The Undying Procession: Iowa's Civil War Regiments* (Des Moines, 1964), as is Scharlott Goettsch Blevins, *Iowa Volunteer Militia* (Davenport, 1995). *Boys in Blue: Van Buren County in the Civil War* (Bonaparte, Iowa, 1963), by Theodore W. Cook, while discussing all the regiments in which Van Buren County soldiers fought, gives special attention to the 19th Iowa. Finally, A. A. Stuart's *Iowa Colonels and Regiments: Being a History of Iowa Regiments in the War of the rebellion and Containing a Description of the Battles in Which They Have Fought* (Des Moines, 1865), while focusing on those individuals from Iowa who attained the rank of colonel, does provide a useful account of the activities of Clayton's regiment as well.

A number of books based on the letters and diaries of individual soldiers from Iowa provided useful specific information and gave me ideas about how to present the accounts of Clayton. These include: Barry Popchock, ed., *Soldier Boy: The Civil War Letters of Charles O. Musser, 29th Iowa* (Iowa City, 1995); Mildred Throne, ed., *The Civil War Diary of Cyrus F. Boyd, Fifteenth Iowa Infantry, 1861–1863* (Milwood, N.Y., 1977); Almon Wilson Parmenter, *1864 and 1865 Diaries of Almon Wilson Parmenter: A Union Civil War Soldier Mustered Out Aug. 24, 1865, in Company C, 32nd Iowa Volunteer Infantry, 3rd*

Division, 16th Army Corps (San Jose, 1994); Kenneth Lyftogt, ed., *Left For Dixie: the Civil War Diary of John Rath* (Parkersburg, Ia., 1994); Kathleen Davis, ed., *Such Are the Trials: the Civil War Diaries of Jacob Gantz* (Ames, 1991); Harold D. Brinkman, *Dear Companion: Civil War Letters of Silas I. Shearer* (Ames, 1995); Edwin C. Bearrs, ed., *The Civil War Letters of Major William G. Thompson of the 20th Iowa Infantry Regiment* (Fayetteville, Ark., 1966). Steve Meyer's *Iowa Valor: A Compilation of Civil War Combat Experiences From Soldiers of the State Distinguished as Most Patriotic of the Patriotic* (Garrison, Ia., 1994) is a fascinating anthology of accounts left by soldiers from a large number of Iowa regiments. These works all aided immeasurably in my research.

Two documents made available to me by Roger Davis proved especially valuable. Mr. Davis showed me a copy of the diary kept by Lieutenant Colonel Joseph Leake during the Civil War, and he also gave me a copy of "Some Recollections of a Southern Prison," a paper that Leake read on March 3, 1886. These documents gave me a much better appreciation of the experiences of Union prisoners-of-war at Camp Ford.

In gathering information about the campaigns in which the 19th Iowa participated, I have used a wide range of histories about the Civil War. Any historian writing about that conflict must start with the 128-volume *War of the Rebellion: A Compilation of the Official Records of the Union and Confederate Armies* (Washington, D.C., 1880–1901), and the thirty-volume *Official Records of the Union and Confederate Navies in the War of the Rebellion* (Washington, D.C., 1897–1927). A useful general history of the Civil War is Shelby Foote's trilogy, *The Civil War: A Narrative* (New York, 1958–1974). Bruce Catton's three-volume work, *The Centennial History of the Civil War* (Garden City, New York, 1961-65), also proved helpful. The Confederate side is covered in great depth in Frank Moore, ed., *The Rebellion Record* (New York, 1977). Finally, although not as lengthy as the other works I used, James McPherson's *Ordeal by Fire: Volume II, the Civil War* (New York, 1993) did add greatly to my understanding of Civil War matters.

Works that focus exclusively on particular aspects of the Civil War as they pertained to the 19th Iowa include: Reid Mitchell, *The Vacant Chair: The Northern Soldier Leaves Home* (New York, 1993); Michael Fellman, *Inside War: The Guerrilla Conflict in Missouri During the American Civil War* (New York, 1989); Michael E. Banasik, *Embattled Arkansas: The Prairie Grove Campaign of 1862* (Wilmington, N.C., 1996); Steve Cottrell, *War in the Ozarks* (Wilmington, N.C., 1995); Henry Steele Commager, *The Blue and the Grey: The Story of the Civil War as Told by Participants*, two volumes (New York, 1950); Christopher Phillips, *Damned Yankee: The Life of General Nathaniel Lyon* (Columbia, Mo., 1990); Robert Shalhope, *Sterling Price: Portrait of a Southerner* (Columbia, 1971); Frederick Phisterer, *The Army in the Civil War, Volume XIII: Statistical Record of the Armies of the United States* (New York, 1885); Eugene C. Murdock, *One Million Men: The Civil War Draft in the North* (Madison, 1971); Hondon B. Hargrove, *Black Union Soldiers in the Civil War* (Jefferson,

N.C., 1988); Washington Davis, *Camp-Fire Chats of the Civil War: Being the Incident, Adventure, and Exploit of the Bivouac and Battlefield, as Related by Veteran Soldiers Themselves* (Chicago, 1889); Alonzo Abernethy, ed., *Dedication of Monuments Erected by the State of Iowa* (Des Moines, 1908); Arthur W. Bergeron, Jr., *Confederate Mobile* (Jackson, 1991); James C. Coleman and Irene S. Coleman, *Guardians of the Gulf* (Pensacola, 1982); Robert L. Kerby, *Kirby Smith's Confederacy: The Trans-Mississippi South, 1863–1865* (New York, 1972); Elmo Ingenthron, *Borderland Rebellion: A History of the Civil War on the Missouri-Arkansas Border* (Branson, 1980); Jay Monaghan, *Civil War on the Western Border, 1854–1865,* (Boston, 1955); Chester Barney, *Recollections of Field Service with the Twentieth Iowa Infantry Volunteers, or, What I Saw in the Army* (Davenport, 1865); Wiley Britton, *The Civil War on the Border 1861–1862* (New York, 1899); Alvin M. Josephy, *War on the Frontier* (Alexandria, Va., 1986); W. H. Bentley, *History of the 77th Illinois Volunteer Infantry* (Peoria, 1883); James A. Fowler, *History of the Thirtieth Iowa Infantry Volunteers: Giving a Complete Record of the Movements of the Regiment From its Organization Until Mustered Out* (Mediapolis, Ia., 1908); The Iowa Sanitary Commission, *Report of the Iowa Sanitary Commission: From the Organization of the Sanitary Work in Iowa to the Close of its Service at the End of the War* (Dubuque, 1866); Margaret Brobst Roth, ed., *Well, Mary: Civil War Letters of a Wisconsin Volunteer,* 2nd edition (Madison, 1994); Sharon Lee DeWitt Kraynek, ed., *Letters to my Wife: A Civil War Diary From the Western Front* (Apollo, Pa., 1995); Norman W. Haines, *Letters From Pensacola: the Civil War Years* (Pensacola, 1993); and "The Battle of Prairie Grove," a booklet that Don Montgomery of the Prairie Grove Battlefield State Park gave me.

A number of states had books written about the course of the Civil War within their boundaries. The best of these include: John D. Winters, *The Civil War in Louisiana* (Baton Rouge, 1963); William Watson Davis, *The Civil War and Reconstruction in Florida,* two volumes (Gainesville, Fla., 1964); Walter L. Fleming, *Civil War and Reconstruction in Alabama* (New York, 1949); Edwin C. Bearrs, *Decision in Mississippi: Mississippi's Important Role in the War Between the States* (Jackson, Miss., 1962); and B. P. Gallaway, *The Dark Corner of the Confederacy: Accounts of Civil War Texas as Told by Contemporaries* (Dubuque, 1968).

Information about military affairs in general came from a number of different sources. Bell I. Wiley's *The Life of Billy Yank: The Common Soldier of the Union* (Indianapolis, 1952), although forty years old, still provides an excellent overview of the military experience for Union soldiers. Specific details about the Union military were gleaned from William B. Edwards, *Civil War Guns: The Complete Story of Federal and Confederate Small Arms: Design, Manufacture, Identification, Procurement, Issue, Employment, Effectiveness, and Postwar Disposal* (Secaucus, N.J., 1982); Henry E. Simmons, *A Concise Encyclopedia of the Civil War* (New York, 1965); Patricia Faust, ed., *Historical Times Illustrated Encyclopedia of the Civil War* (New York, 1986); Chris Bishop and

Ian Drury, *1400 Days: The Civil War Day by Day* (New York, 1990); Mark Mayo Boatner III, *The Civil War Dictionary* (New York, 1959); Jon L. Wakelyn, *Biographical Dictionary of the Confederacy* (Westport, Conn., 1977); and J. W. Carnahan, *4000 Civil War Battles* (Fort Davis, Tex., 1971).

To identify those items in Clayton's letters that did not pertain to his experiences with the 19th Iowa, I used a wide variety of sources. The Eighth Census of the United States, 1860, allowed me to identify a number of individuals to whom Clayton refers in his letters. General information on the state of Iowa came from Robert R. Dykstra, *Bright Radical Star: Black Freedom and White Supremacy on the Hawkeye Frontier* (Cambridge, 1993); Edward H. Stiles, *Recollections and Sketches of Notable Lawyers and Public Men of Early Iowa* (Des Moines, 1916); T. D. Eagal and R. H. Sylvester, *The Iowa State Almanac and Statistical Register for 1860* (Davenport, 1859); Morton M. Rosenberg, *Iowa on the Eve of the Civil War: A Decade of Frontier Politics* (Norman, 1972); James I. Robertson, Jr., *Iowa in the Civil War: A Reference Guide* (Iowa City, 1961); Rick W. Sturdevant, "Girding for War: Conditions Underlying the Response of Iowa Counties to Troop Calls, 1861–1862" (Master's Thesis, University of Northern Iowa, 1974); Hubert H. Wubben, *Civil War Iowa and the Copperhead Movement* (Ames, 1980); S. W. M. Byers, *Iowa in War Times* (Des Moines, 1888); Leland L. Sage, *A History of Iowa* (Ames, 1974); Robert I. Vexler, *Chronology and Documentary History of the State of Iowa* (Dobbs Ferry, N.Y., 1978); Benjamin F. Gue, *History of Iowa*, 4 volumes (New York, 1903); Henry Sabin and Edwin Sabin, *The Making of Iowa* (Chicago, 1916). I also found valuable information in histories of Iowa communities. The best of these include: The Van Buren County American Revolution Bicentennial Commission, *The History of Van Buren County, Iowa* (Marcelline, Mo., 1976); *Portrait and Biographical Album of Jefferson and Van Buren Counties, Iowa: Containing Full Page Portraits and Biographical Sketches of Prominent and Representative Citizens of the Counties Together With Portraits and Biographies of all Governors of the State* (Chicago, 1890); Linda Lisle Greene, *Index of Pioneer History of Davis County, Iowa: Information Gathered by the Federated Women's Club of Davis County, 1924–27, Printed and Published by the Bloomfield Democrat, Bloomfield, Iowa* (Des Moines, 1996); *History of Davis County, Iowa: Containing a History of the County; its Citizens, Towns, etc.; a Biographical Directory of Many of its Leading Citizens* (Decorah, 1882); Davis County Genealogical Society, *1860 Census, Davis County, Iowa* (Bloomfield, 1988).

Finally, Iowa had a large number of newspapers in operation during the period covered in this book. The most useful ones for my purposes included the *Bloomfield Democrat, Keokuk Weekly Gate City, Burlington Hawk-Eye, Keosauqua Republican, Bloomfield Western Gazette, Fairfield Ledger,* and *Iowa City Republican.*

Brookville (Iowa), 191 n.

Brownsville (Tex.), 107, 109–111, 115, 155, 201 n.

Bruce, John, 45–46, 48, 117, 121, 141, 168, 175, 177, 192 n., 202 n.

Buckingham, Charles B., 191 n.

Buckles, Abner J., 7–8, 23, 28, 43, 46–48, 55, 62–65, 68, 72, 74, 89, 91, 93, 99, 109, 139, 183 n., 195 n.

Buckner, Simon Bolivar, 169, 213 n.

Bunner, Lafayette, 22, 188 n.

Burch, Oscar, 129

Burlington (Iowa), 208 n.

Burlington Hawk-eye, 208 n.

Burnside, Ambrose E., 42, 69, 192 n., 195 n., 206 n.

Business Corners (Iowa), 9, 32, 184 n., 189 n.

Butcher, William, 130

Butler, Benjamin F., 199–200 n., 204 n.

Byers, William, 109, 119, 153, 168, 201 n.

Cairo (Ill.), 69, 177

California, 65, 178, 181, 195 n.

Camp Benton, 185 n.

Camp Curtis, 30, 36, 43

Camp Elsworth, 183 n.

Camp Ford, 102, 112, 173, 201 n., 204 n., 209 n.

Camp Kinsman, 211 n.

Camp Lincoln, 6, 8–9, 183–184 n., 189 n.

Camp Parapet, 201 n.

Camp Pipestem, 197 n.

Camp Prairie Grove, 36

Camp Sigel, 13

Camp Sumter, 206 n.

Canada, 206 n.

Canby, Edward R. S., 121, 143, 151, 155, 205 n., 210 n., 213 n.

Cane Hill (Ark.), 33, 190 n.

Canton (Miss.), 86

Cape Girardeau (Mo.), 69, 195 n.

Carrollton (Ark.), 44, 46–47, 58

Carrollton (La.), 67, 91–92, 98–99, 102, 109–110, 114

Cassville (Mo.), 22, 24–25, 27–28, 36

Cedar Falls (Iowa), 211 n.

Centerville (Iowa), 208 n.

Chancellorsville, Battle of, 195 n.

Chattanooga (Tenn.), 113

Chequest River, 20, 26, 32, 35, 48–50, 77, 83, 86, 93, 109, 149, 154, 165, 168–169, 187 n.

Chickasaw Bluffs (Miss.), 196 n.

Choctahatchie Bay (Fla.), 125

Choctaw, U.S.S., 105

Cincinnati (Ohio), 2, 93, 171–172, 184 n., 193–194 n.

Clay, Henry, 92, 95

Clayton, Amos, 2–3, 6, 8–10, 13, 22, 24–25, 27, 30, 35–36, 47, 49, 51, 62, 68, 70, 73, 78, 82, 84, 89, 91, 100, 106, 109, 114, 123, 132, 136, 178, 186 n.

Clayton, Anna Grace, 178

Clayton, Ashford, 178

Clayton, Dorothy, 178

Clayton, George Washington, 4, 15, 23, 32, 43, 51, 55, 59, 64–65, 76, 82, 85, 87, 94, 98, 100–101, 109–110, 114, 117, 120, 123–125, 127–128, 132–133, 136, 138, 141, 144, 147, 149–151, 153–155, 157–158, 160, 162, 165, 167, 169, 171–172, 178

Clayton, Grace Smith, 6, 8–10, 13, 22, 24–25, 27, 30, 35–36, 47, 49, 51, 62, 68, 70, 73, 78, 82, 84, 89, 91, 100, 106, 109, 114, 123, 132, 136, 178, 183 n.

Clayton, John Quincy Adams, 4, 15, 43, 51, 55, 59, 64–65, 76, 85, 87, 94, 98, 100, 106, 109–110, 114, 120, 124–125, 132–133, 136, 138, 141, 144, 147, 149–151, 153–155,

23, 30, 35, 38–39, 68, 76, 144, 147, 149, 151, 155, 190–191 n., 210 n.

23rd Wisconsin Infantry, 173

United States of America: Sanitary Commission, 77, 138, 197 n.; State Department, 96; War Department, 1, 67, 97, 165, 183 n., 186 n., 198 n., 211 n.

University of Southern California, 178

Upton (Iowa), 22, 188 n., 207 n.

Utt, Norville, 8, 184 n.

Vallandigham, Clement L., 131, 206 n.

Van Buren (Ark.), 39, 41, 191 n.

Van Buren County (Iowa), 3–4, 22, 131, 134–135, 165, 179, 183–188 n., 192 n., 194 n., 205 n., 207–209 n., 211 n., 213 n.

Van Court, B. P., 207 n.

Van Valkenberg, John, 136, 208 n.

Veatch, James C., 155, 211 n.

Vicksburg (Miss.), 63, 66–68, 70, 72–74, 76–79, 81–85, 87, 89–92, 113, 119, 128, 195–199 n.

Virginia, 1, 10, 42, 192 n., 199 n.

Warren County (Iowa), 136, 208 n.

Warrenton (Miss.), 72–73, 87

Warrington (Fla.), 115, 117, 203 n.

Warrior, steamer, 177

Washburn, Cadwallader C., 95, 200 n.

Washington (Iowa), 184 n.

Waynesville (Mo.), 16

Weaver, James B., 207 n.

Weer, William, 60, 194–195 n.

Weitzel, Godfrey, 212 n.

Wells, James, 202 n.

Westcott, Alvin, 124, 205 n.

West Point Iron & Cannon Foundry, 212 n.

Westport, Battle of, 209 n.

White Cloud No. 2, steamer, 175, 177

White River, 24, 41, 44, 48, 55

Wilber, Charley, 123

Williams, Thomas, 196 n.

Wilson's Creek, Battle of, 12, 22, 32–33, 186–188 n.

Wittenmyer, Annie Turner, 77, 197 n., 211 n.

Woodruff, Josiah, 208 n.

Woods, Amos, 119, 138, 204 n.

Woods, Mehitabel "Auntie," 146, 210 n.

Wright, George G., 6, 20, 183 n.

Wright, James, 208 n.

Wright, Joshua, 191 n.

Yazoo City (Miss.), 67, 84–87, 89

Yazoo River, 70, 84, 196 n.

Yellville (Ark.), 53

Young, Mahlon M., 126, 206 n.

Young's Point (La.), 70, 73

Zephyr, steamer, 135

73161973R00153

Made in the USA
San Bernardino, CA
02 April 2018